ASSAULT WITH
A DEADLY WEAPON

ASSAULT WITH A DEADLY WEAPON

The Autobiography of a

Street Criminal

JOHN ALLEN

Edited by Dianne Hall Kelly
and Philip Heymann

With a Foreword by Hylan Lewis

PANTHEON BOOKS · NEW YORK

Library of Congress Cataloging in Publication Data

Allen, John, 1942–.
Assault with a Deadly Weapon.

1. Allen, John, 1942–   2. Crime and criminals—
Washington, D.C.—Biography.   I. Kelly, Dianne Hall,
1948–   II. Heymann, Philip B.   III. Title.
HV6248.A37A33   364.1'092'4 [B]   77-5297
ISBN 0-394-41510-8

Manufactured in the United States of America
First Edition

To my children, Cynthia, Darlene, and John, Jr.;
and to my sister Debra Robertson.
J.F.A.

To my father.
D.H.K.

To my children, Steve and Jody.
P.B.H.

In the interest of protecting the privacy of the people described in this book, all names have been changed with the exception of Jim Lyons; those identified as John's parents, siblings, wife, and children; and the authors.

Contents

ACKNOWLEDGMENTS

Janet Johnson's name doesn't appear on the cover of this book; but from the moment we began, she has worked with us, encouraged us, commented on our evolving product, and shared with us the ups and downs of the effort. It is a pleasure for each of us to acknowledge her crucial role.

FROM JOHN ALLEN'S POLICE RECORD

December 9, 1942	John Allen born, Washington, D.C.
1950 (date approximate)	Arrested for theft as juvenile. Committed to custody of Junior Village for fourteen months.
1954 (date approximate)	Arrested for possession of a deadly weapon as juvenile. Committed to custody of Junior Village for two years.
1958	Arrested for rape as juvenile. Charge reduced to carnal knowledge; placed on probation.
1960	Arrested for assault with a deadly weapon. Sentenced to six years under Youth Act. Served almost three years in Youth Center.
November 1963	Arrested for robbery, possession of a prohibited weapon (gun), destruction of movable property, two counts of simple assault. Convicted of misdemeanor (assault) and sentenced to four concurrent 900-day terms.
January 1964	Arrested for assault on a police officer. Found not guilty.
1964–66	Served terms at Youth Center and halfway house for 1963 conviction.
November 1966	Arrested for holdup, violation of National Firearms Act, robbery, assault with a deadly weapon (shotgun), and possession of a

	prohibited weapon (shotgun). Convicted in July 1967, and sentenced to one 5-15-year and four 3-9-year terms.
1967–69	Served terms in D. C. Jail and Lorton Penitentiary.
March 1969	1967 convictions overturned.
March 1970	Arrested and subsequently convicted for possession of implements of crime (narcotics paraphernalia) and possession of unregistered firearms. Sentenced to 1 year plus 10 days per weapon, plus fine. Sentence then reduced to 220 days.
Summer 1970	Escaped from Occoquan correctional facility.
November 1970	Arrested for homicide, assault with a deadly weapon, unauthorized use of a vehicle, carrying a dangerous weapon, assault with intent to kill, assault on a police officer, and escaping a federal institution. Convicted on last four charges. Served three years in D. C. General Hospital and D. C. Jail Hospital; then paroled.
July 1976	Arrested for violation of federal firearms laws (possession of sawed-off shotgun). Placed on probation.
March 1977	Arrested for armed robbery. Bound over for grand jury action; charges dismissed.

FOREWORD

Within Cell 80 I Sit Thinking, I Am Not Dumb Nor Am
I A Smart Man ... I Am Not A Good Nor Am I A Bad
Man, I Have Lived In Many Worlds, But Mostly In A
Poor One, The World Which I Am In Now Is A Dream
World, Dream, Dream, A Day Past, Dream, Dream ...
And Then Start All Over Again, Dream, Dream, Dream,
Dream.
                    —Written by John Allen while in prison

Assault with a Deadly Weapon is the autobiography of John
Allen, a small-time entrepreneur who worked the streets and
alleys of Washington, D. C., as boy apprentice and journeyman hustler over a period of more than twenty-five years.
Much as the legitimate businessman cultivates and uses
good-will as a part of his working capital, so did John Allen
cultivate fear and willingly use violence in the service of two
separable but common values—his material interest and his
sense of personal honor and respect.
    Through his story, John Allen can be seen from a variety
of perspectives: individually, as a forceful personality and a
family man with awareness, smarts, and dreams; occupation-
ally, as a money-oriented, urban street-hustler; racially or
ethnically, as a slum Negro and inner-city black; and tempo-
rally, as a child of post–World War II America.
    From John Allen's own perspective, the major impera-

tives of his life have to do with his occupation, hustling; his family, especially his children; and his sex, male. His awareness of race appears to be secondary and is expressed mainly in connection with his prison experiences or as one of the occupational hazards of contacts with the police.

John Allen—unlike Malcolm X, Eldridge Cleaver, and hundreds of others in prison at the same time—was not politicized racially during his penal experience. He was, however, politicized as a prisoner and was an active participant in the D. C. prison riots of the period. These two facts, as much as any, highlight him as an important yet little noted figure—the assertive nonconformist who nonetheless is not a rebel.

John Allen was born in Washington, D. C., one year after the formal entrance of the United States into World War II, during the third term of Franklin D. Roosevelt. After an apprenticeship of about ten years as venturesome youth and school dropout in the streets of Washington and two periods in residence in Junior Village, a juvenile detention center, his official record as journeyman career criminal began at eighteen, when he was convicted for the first time as an adult for assault with a deadly weapon—a gun. This was during the initial years of President Kennedy's New Frontier.

After about a dozen years of active hustling interspersed with prison terms during a period that spanned the rise and decline of the Civil Rights Movement, the advent of Black Power, the Great Society, the beginning and end of the War on Poverty, the Vietnam War, the campus riots, and Watergate, Allen involuntarily retired from an active career just prior to President Nixon's involuntary retirement due to the Watergate scandals. Allen was a victim of a prime occupational hazard—gunshot wounds that left him a paraplegic.

A number of John Allen's sentiments and acts can be read as counterpoints to some major national themes and particular economic and political developments of his time

—urban redevelopment; the call for "law and order" and the reform of the criminal code; the civil rights movement; black nationalism; and prison protest and reform. The comments that these evoke from him are characteristically wry, pragmatic, and apolitical.

On urban redevelopment in Southwest Washington:

> The reason we thought they was tearing down Southwest was that there was too many niggers close to the White House and the Capitol. Everbody has a reason for everything, and that was our reason.

On the "no-knock" rule:

> I'm glad I wasn't home when the police came that other night, 'cause during that time they was going wild over that "no-knock" thing, and there wouldn't have been no warning. The first thing I would have thought was somebody's attempting to rob me or do bodily harm to me or my family. I had plenty of guns and ammunition in the house. . . .

On race:

> The race thing runs deep with everybody. Black people don't like white people, white people don't like black people; Jews don't like Italians, Italians don't like Jews. It's a whole lot of nonsense, so I just try to avoid it as much as possible—even being a part of anything that's not fruitful to all people. The main thing I'd be thinking about is poor people and not if they're black, white, pink, or purple.

On the comparative risks of "my kind of crime" and white-collar crime:

> I don't feel that what they [big corporations and white-collar criminals] doing is wrong. To them, it's just making a buck—a group of people getting over. . . . There's conflict in there because my kind of crime is generally looked down upon, but the white-collar crime is an altogether different bag. Like Ehrlichman deciding when *he* wants to go to jail.

John Allen's story can be considered from the point of view of sociology, psychology, philosophy, law, and public policy, for it raises the classic questions about whether criminality and violence are qualities of the individual, whether the world of career criminals reflects the conventional culture of our society or is a counter-culture, and whether effective reform of the criminal justice system is possible. It asks what role violence plays in the "normal" suspension of morality in the service of personal interest in our society.

What then does John Allen, career criminal and parent, reveal and accomplish in this personal document? First of all, his narrative involves us vicariously in the factual details of his life, even as it did his collaborators in the writing and telling—the public defender, now law professor, who became a friend; and the law student. Many of the details of his growing up, going to school, raising a family, or starting out on a career are the bases for quick recognition and empathy. They may even have an ordinary quality about them. Other details may, for many, be less easily identified with and not so ordinary. These have to do with explicitly taking for granted fear and violence; viewing crime as a kind of job; and accepting violence, maiming, sudden death, and prison as occupational risks.

Although much of Allen's life is marked by uncertainty, poverty, the threat of disruption, and violence, his essential objectives and underlying sentiments do lie well within a framework easily recognizable by much of our society. "Everybody wants to have their own joint," he says, "own their own home, and have two cars. It's just that we are going about it in a different way. I think keeping up with the Joneses is important everywhere." There is even a certain rational orientation toward crime as work, a familiar if risk-filled enterprise that is not at all counter-cultural. Moreover, John Allen's life fits the ordinary experience of so many people in another way. He is not an unusual success, even in his own mind:

I've done a lot of things, and I've made quite a bit of money illegally. Way far more than I ever made legally. But still, if you look at it, it's all been on a real low level. . . . I recognize this, and I think most people recognize this, no matter how good their hustling thing is. They can hustle day and night, live comfortable, and do the things they want to, but they are still doing it on what other people would see as a small scale.

The question then arises, if he was not particularly successful, why did John Allen persist in his career of crime? Beyond just making (or taking) a living, an important feature of John Allen's life as a career criminal, a hustler, is the venture and the risk taking itself. Hustling and the possibility of a big or dangerous score can be fun and challenging. While paralyzed in his wheelchair and musing about the possibilities of resuming a criminal career, he says, "I still like the notoriety, the excitement, the danger—that's cool."

In his criminal career, the line between crime as work and crime as dangerous fun is not always clear; however, it is important to emphasize that in his personal code, the use of violence was not related to the fun and kicks. For Allen, violence is a serious matter, necessary both as an occupational technique and as a means of defending one's honor.

Robbing is an art, and the whole art of robbing is fear, and the main reason for robbing is to get what you come after —the money—and get away. You don't go there to hurt people. Sometimes you have to. . . .

Later he adds:

I *know* that I done a lot of cruel things, but it was something I had to do at that particular moment for one reason or another. I have never did something unnecessary, especially when it comes to violence. But sometimes, in order to get what you want, or prove a point . . . you had to be tough.

Violence has been an ever-present reality in John Allen's life. He was only twelve years old when he shot his gang mate with a gun he had stolen from his grandfather. He used this act of violence to stake his claim to gang leadership. Five years after, he shot another rival, Rock, in the cause of personal honor:

> When Rock tried to do what he did, this was outright disrespect.... You're not supposed to disrespect a man and his woman.

In fact, throughout his life he has used violence to punish any of his intimates who seemed to be withdrawing the respect he felt was his due. This was especially true with his women friends, including the mothers of his children.

Violence in the life and criminal career of John Allen, as in society at large, has many dimensions. Some violence is personal, some impersonal; some is premeditated, some seems accidental; some is essential to attain a goal, some incidental; some is physically maiming or lethal, some is verbally and psychologically intimidating.

John Allen's account points up the universal paradox of violence—that it involves both accentuation and cessation of feelings. How then does he deal with a life filled with explosive possibilities? Among the intriguing and all-too-human aspects of Allen's behavior and responses are the indications of a capacity for selection and compartmentalization—the ability to exhibit sensitivity and insensitivity, cruelty and tenderness, self-assurance and doubt at the same time, in ways that often appear inconsistent.

> Usually I didn't like to feel sorry for myself. I don't want nobody else feeling sorry for me either. But maybe this was a day when I did feel sorry for myself, and I said, "Look at all the beautiful things. Look at that bird's nest." ... I couldn't talk to anybody else about that because, of course, I always got to maintain my image of being "Big Al, the tough guy."

Perhaps it is the ability to compartmentalize his experiences, or perhaps his view of life as a drama, a matter of game and role playing, but John Allen does not appear to have an identity problem. He usually seems to know quite clearly who he is and to have a sense of his place as a street hustler who never made it big, and does not ever expect to do so. As a proud, self-proclaimed hustler, he fits that classic textbook definition: "an alert opportunist, concerned with personal as opposed to collective security." It's a mental framework within which he's always worked. "I always thought of myself as being a hustler. I come from a hustling family."

Yet there are numerous indications that John Allen also has quiet, painful expectations of recurring failure. Despite those, his confinement to a wheelchair, and a suicide attempt that he aborted himself, he is not merely a violence-scarred and violence-prone hustler-type Willy Loman. His choices, his style, his fate, appear to have been not so much imposed upon him by the world around him as chosen by him as a central reaction to that world. Allen is far from being a hero, nor is he an anti-hero exactly. He does have some kinship, however, with the men Dostoyevsky refers to in *Notes from the Underground* who "have rushed headlong on another path, to meet peril and danger, compelled to this course by nobody and by nothing, but, as it were, simply disliking the beaten track and have obstinately, willfully, struck out another difficult, absurd way.... This obstinancy and perversity were pleasanter to them than any advantage."

About a generation ago, in his book *Shadow and Act*, Ralph Ellison, in writing about Richard Wright and his autobiography, *Black Boy*, said that the blues is "the specific folk-art form which helped shape the writer's attitude toward his life and which embodied the impulse that contributed much to the quality and tone of [Wright's] autobiography." Calling the blues "an autobiographical chronicle of personal catastrophe expressed lyrically," Ellison added:

The blues is an impulse to keep the painful details and episodes of a brutal experience alive in one's aching consciousness, to finger its jagged grain, and to transcend it, not by the consolation of philosophy but by squeezing from it a near-tragic, near-comic lyricism.

Assault with a Deadly Weapon is essentially John Allen's blues—an oral history of a native son of the nation's capital —an "average (hustler) man," who tells what it was like for him in his underground U. S. A., almost incidentally during some of the best and some of the worst times in our nation's history, from World War II to Watergate.

Although not centrally intended to do so, this story of the life and career of a small-time criminal entrepreneur operating in the slums and from the ghetto, with interruptions for stays in correctional institutions, enriches the controversy concerning the rehabilitation and punishment goals and functions of prisons. It makes this and other issues having to do with crime and violence in contemporary life even more complex for the reader. Anyone who reads this account is likely to be left hauntingly aware not just of the differences and the gaps, but of the similarities and the links between the blues of John Allen, "average hustler," and the ups and downs of everyday life for the "average straight."

—Hylan Lewis

PREFACE

This book tells the story of a friend whose profession has been crime, a hustler who has played out his ambitions and hopes on a stage familiar to many of us only through newspaper accounts of violence in our inner cities. It is a story told by a man who has not escaped his environment, who is not looking back through the prism of attained respectability and affluence. His ambitions and hopes, even the neighborhood he has lived in, have remained fairly constant. Only his expectations have changed; a bullet in his spinal cord has taken care of them. Today he can no longer maintain a status and a way of earning a living that depend upon his being tougher, braver, and more ruthless than those around him. Yet John Allen lived most of his life as an agent of fear—the personal fear of those confronted by his gun and the general fear of a society that has called upon its police and prisons for protection against him.

When I first met John, he was in his mid-twenties. A powerfully built black man, he looked taller than his height of almost six feet. Everything about him said that he could handle himself in a fight and knew it. He seemed secure, even professional. Sitting in that small interview room in the cell block beneath the District of Columbia Federal Courthouse, he treated his new lawyer in a matter-of-fact manner. The atmosphere of such a meeting is usually a bit cynical, the client expecting and detecting skepticism as he tells a story intended as much to con the indifferent lawyer into caring as to convey the substance of a defense. John launched himself into this ritual, but not too deferentially. He would not sacrifice his pride in a potentially vain effort to win my wholehearted support.

The imposing courthouse and the barren cell block—those two enclosures represented the differing experiences in Washington which we brought to our first encounter. In seven years at the Supreme Court, the Department of Justice, and the Department of State, I had worked in a variety of impressive buildings and knew many of their occupants. John, on the other hand, had circulated in a city of rundown apartments, dangerous streets and alleys, neighborhood toughs—and a companion world of cell blocks, guards, and prisoners. He knew as little of "official" Washington as I of his world. Although he had grown up in a slum only minutes from the Capitol, he had never visited government buildings. The only white Washingtonians he knew were lawyers, policemen, guards, and fellow prisoners.

His life had been spent in the large black areas of Southeast and Southwest Washington, which he had left only on rare occasions. At the time we met, home was a three-room apartment in a development of box-shaped brick buildings across the Anacostia River from downtown Washington. The furniture was shabby, the apartment was crowded with people, the neighborhood lacked the trees and shrubs found in predominantly white Northwest Washington. If the visible difference between his neighborhood and the homes and shops of the residents of "official" Washington was vast, the social distance between the two areas, measured in the realities of personal contacts, was almost as great as between two countries.

After serving three years of their most recent sentences, John and his friend JoJo Hendricks had just had their convictions for the armed robbery of a liquor store overturned on appeal. For their new trial, they were assigned public defenders Jim Lyons and myself as counsel. Since I had only been working for the Public Defender for a few months, I wasn't anxious for John to learn that this was to be my first serious felony trial. Indeed, I was somewhat relieved by the implausability of the story John and JoJo told us. To have someone's freedom depend on my earliest efforts as a trial lawyer seemed like a great responsibility—one that I felt would be lessened if I thought that person was guilty. I asked John about his prior record. A recent conviction for assault with intent to maim and a charge of breaking a prison guard's jaw confirmed my early impression that this was a very rough man.

Jim and I began to investigate and file papers. The owner of the liquor store who had been robbed of about a hundred dollars at gunpoint laughed when we asked him if he could remember the men who had robbed him three years before. He had been robbed twenty times since, he told us. He could hardly remember a robber from three months ago.

We met frequently in the courthouse cell block with John and JoJo to discuss our activities on their behalf. The two defendants started to sense that we really were representing them—something they hadn't felt with previous lawyers. As I came to know John better, I realized he had little respect for the law and less for courts and lawyers. But the things he said and did indicated a commitment to the obligations of friendship and loyalty that seemed unlimited. He certainly would have accepted a life term before turning on JoJo. As it happened, though, JoJo decided to plead guilty to further John's chances of acquittal. John was found not guilty.

Through the course of preparation for the trial and the trial itself, something strange happened. The loyalty that the legal system expected me to show my client began to correspond to the loyalty John recognized as the fundamental quality of a friend. I, in turn, came to feel a friendship for him that was much more than the duty of a lawyer.

I wanted John to stay out of prison, but my moralizing did not help. "Some steal with a gun, others with a pen," he

would answer. We did discuss a few job possibilities, but
none was tempting to him. That left the threat of punishment. I still remember how he responded when I tried to
offer him some advice on the subject of crime soon after his
trial had ended. Noting that one of his younger brothers had
been in the courtroom throughout the trial, I said, "So much
of your life has been spent in prisons, so much of it has been
hard—what would you tell your brother if he asked you
whether he should hustle or be straight?" After a moment's
reflection, he replied, "I don't think I'd tell him what to do.
Telling him that would simply make him want to do something else, because he'd want to be his own man." The message—I want your friendship but not at the price of my
independence—was meant for me and set the tone for our
future relations. Then John went on, "I suppose I'd say to
him, 'If you want to hustle, hustle; if you want to be straight,
be straight. But whatever you do, do it well.' " Besides independence, he was saying, respect and admiration are what
count.

John and I came to spend days together walking, talking,
or just driving around. Slowly he began to tell me about his
family, his childhood, his friends, his way of life. I visited his
home. After I had gone to teach at Harvard, John returned
the visit and addressed my law students on the subject that
he knew best—street crime.

I talked to John about writing a book, but he was too
busy. He had gone back to hustling and turned to selling
dope. He became addicted himself, robbed other dope dealers, shot people, got arrested, and escaped. Only during the
time when he was in prison or in hiding did we lose contact
with each other. Finally, in a shootout with the police, he
took a bullet in his spinal cord that placed him in a wheelchair for the rest of his life. John was still in the hospital
when I again raised the idea of doing a book. He was ready.

I approached Dianne Kelly, then a Harvard law student,
about undertaking the massive job of interviewing, editing,

and organizing which such a book would require. She read-
ily agreed. Together we produced a list of about one hundred questions on the basis of my conversations with John
and the letters we had exchanged. Then I introduced Dianne
to John, who was being treated in the rehabilitation center
at Glenn Dale Hospital, in Maryland.

There, over part of a summer, they spent hours together
in daily interview sessions. Dianne and John established a
relationship of trust and friendship, which carried them
through heated as well as relaxed days of dialogue. What
emerged from the tape-recorded discussions was not the
"how-it's-done" account of crime we had foreseen, but the
far fuller story of a difficult life.

Dozens of tapes resulted from those summer interviews,
later transcribed into thousands of pages of dialogue. Over
the next year, Dianne inventoried the contents of those
pages, noted gaps and omissions, prepared more questions,
and sent them off to John. We had provided him with a tape
recorder; and lying in bed or sitting in his wheelchair, he
would tape his responses, adding other thoughts, memories,
and impressions as well. These answers were then integrated
into the evolving outline that Dianne was constructing as the
skeleton of the story. As letters and tapes continued to flow
back and forth, she undertook the task of editing a dialogue
into an autobiography, attempting to maintain chronologi-
cal accuracy without sacrificing the natural flow of recol-
lection and association experienced by John in his
storytelling. The words of the resulting book are all John's.
The stories are his, untouched in any significant way. The
organization and integration of those stories are the result of
Dianne's efforts. Everything that was written was sent back
to John, who read, commented upon, and approved the way
the story was put together.

What is left, then, is John's life and John's world as he
sees them. The crimes, the prisons, the relationship with the
police—these are all part of a well-organized world view

that includes much else: the meaning of family, the require-
ments of self-respect, the roles of love and jealousy, the
special place of friendship and loyalty, the role of women,
and, of course, the challenge and fear of death. John's story
is an invitation to understand the corner of reality that John
found and made his own.

What is so different about this corner of reality? John has
spent his life striving for independence, success, effective-
ness, and respect. In this regard, his dream is that of Horatio
Alger. For John, the "ladder of success" meant excelling in
toughness, shrewdness, courage, and ruthlessness toward op-
ponents. These characteristics, when mixed with absolute
and self-sacrificing loyalty and generosity to friends, as they
are in John, can be the prized attributes of a James Bond or,
for that matter, of an occasional White House aide. If we all
have secret heroes and role models, we could easily attribute
to John these particularly American models.

The rub, of course, is that daily life within an American
city is not supposed to be like spying, Watergate politics, or
a cold war. The permissible paths to success are supposed to
be limited by rules protecting the personal and property
rights of people we have never met or hardly know. For
most of us most of the time, the moral force of such rules
—even as applied to our relations with strangers—is such
that we hardly need the criminal law and its threat of con-
demnation and punishment, though these surely help define
and reinforce our notions of permissible actions. It is enough
to recognize that such strangers are, after all, very much like
ourselves and deserve to share the same chance to make their
way in life. In John's world, the moral force of obligation
to strangers was largely gone—in part because he let it go,
but also in large part because his corner of reality was so far
from theirs and his only path to respect so inconsistent with
theirs. All that was left of social obligation was its core:
loyalty and generosity to friends and family. All that was
left of the force of law was the threat of punishment by a

government that he did not really recognize as his own, by officials to whom he was obligated to deny cooperation.

What does a man driven to escape the shame of weakness, ineffectiveness, dependence, and failure do in such a world? John sought, and found, respect in his courage, his daring, and the fear he inspired. The criminal law—stripped of its moral authority—was to him the naked force of an almost foreign power. If the only obvious opportunity to flee failure is to excel in toughness and fearlessness; if obligations run only, though powerfully, to friends, then the fear of criminal punishment is just one more fear to be overcome. John overcame that fear.

—Philip Heymann

ASSAULT WITH
A DEADLY WEAPON

1

Family

It seems to me that the kind of neighborhood you come up in may make all the difference in which way you go and where you end up. There was a lot of people in my neighborhood that didn't do much work and there was a lot of people who did, but the majority didn't. Hustling was their thing: number running, bootlegging, selling narcotics, selling stolen goods, prostitution. There's so many things that go on—it's a whole system that operates inside itself. Say I was to take you by it. You want some junk, then I would take you to the dude that handles drugs. You want some clothes, I could take you somewhere that handles that. You want some liquor, I could take you someplace other than a liquor store. Of course, it's all outside the law.

That's how it was. Somebody was always doing something in each family. If it wasn't the adults, say the mother or father, then it was the son or daughter. I was sticking up; one of my brothers was stealing; one of my sisters was bootlegging; one of my uncles wrote numbers; one of my grandmothers occasionally wrote numbers; and my grandfather bootlegged.

My grandfather, though, worked on the same job for about thirty years, and I couldn't dig that at all. His main money came from bootlegging, but I think he had the job because he thought long-range. He knew they don't give you no pension for stickups, but I was too involved to see that. Like me, most people in our neighborhood lived in the present, turning that day. There was only a few who looked ahead and came out ahead, maybe got a little store and stopped everything. I even know a few people who got that store and haven't stopped. They're still doing things on the side. But the store or the laundromat, that was their goal.

In my early years, I was raised up in Southwest D.C. I think my mother was about sixteen when I was born, and most of my young life we lived with her parents, which are my grandparents. I remember them shuffling me around when I was about five because my grandfather's house would get raided, with all the gambling, bootlegging, and everything that used to go down. They'd wake me up with flashlights in my face. There was a lot of noise, a lot of flashlights being shined, people trying to run and hide. I would be shuffled through the window and told to go to my other grandmother's house, which was a few blocks away. The first time it happened was the first time that I had went from one house to the other in the dark. I was afraid and cold. I got over the back fence and I don't think I ever stopped running until I got there.

A few of the kids in my neighborhood had fathers at home, but most had broken families just like myself. The father was either in jail or just not there. Just deserted their mother or came every now and then. In my younger days I seldom saw my father. In fact, I remember one time that I hadn't seen him in so long that I didn't even recognize him, and that's the truth. That's the way it was with me, and so I would always stay with my grandfather. Perhaps that's why everybody say I'm like him.

My grandparents ran things like they supposed to be ran. My grandfather's about eighty now, real sick and very weak, but he used to run things with an iron hand, and I understood that. So I tried to stay on the good side of him. Some things I did that was wrong, he used to condone—like fighting. He used to love for me to be in a fight. But that's 'cause the whole environment was like that. The Southwest thing was pretty wild. The kids, we ran wild, and the adults were wild. It would be nothing for us to be on the front steps playing hide-and-seek and all of a sudden you hear bang, bang, bang, and people are shooting at each other in the street. And everybody ducking and hiding. This was normal. Eventually you'd be taking all this in. It's just a way of survival.

In Southwest everybody did the same thing, and it was a struggle just to get along. Some had a little bit more than others, some a little bit less. It was a close neighborhood, though—most people had been there for a long time. Everybody knew everybody's kid, everybody's dog. There was quite a few people who had come up from the South, but most had been born in Washington, like my parents and grandparents.

We lived the longest in Southwest on G Street. The houses were right on the sidewalk with no front yards but a lot of big old overgrown trees sitting right by the curb. We did have a large backyard, and behind it was a horse stable. Then there was a little frame house, which was almost like part of the stable only people lived there. There were three houses with airways between them next to that and then a big gray apartment building on the corner.

On the other side of the street was a place we used to call the barracks. Evidently it was an old army barracks that had been converted into a living area; people lived all through it. We used to walk up and down the wooden steps and look over the railings and play cowboy there. Then there was an alley. All our alleys had hip names—Brown's Court, Dixon's Court, Smoke Alley. But wouldn't nobody go through the alleys at night because of the rats. You could even see them in the daytime. They function just like people did, and I used to chase them, throwing rocks and then running away from them.

On the corner was a little Japanese store. You could take a book there—what you call a store book—get what you want, and the man would write it down in the book. Then at the end of the week he would get his money. Most people paid on time like they supposed to. I guess it was just a little pact they had formed among themselves in the neighborbood, 'cause at the end of the week everybody went there, bought the rest of their groceries, and paid their bill.

Now, I had a thing where I used to cop the store book and go over there and cop me some candy. Then my mother say, "Where did this extra twenty-five cents come from?" She always knew about her money all the way to the penny. Even though the man in the store knew what I'd be doing, he'd always ask, "Your mother know that you're getting this?" And I say, "Uh-hum." He knew, but it was an extra quarter for him.

In Southwest, when I was ten or eleven, there were stores on just about every corner—Jew stores, Chinese stores, Japanese stores, black stores. Most of the owners lived over their stores, so robbery didn't keep them from doing business. On Fridays and Saturdays everybody be paying their bills, and of course, the store owners were extra careful on those days. A lot of them had particular kinds of reputations —people used to recognize them just like they recognize my family for being the bootleggers of the block. The store owner was the man you could go to during the week when you didn't have any cash and get grub on the store book. People respected that. In the event that they was robbed or stuck up, most of the people in the neighborhood would be sympathetic to them. Very seldom anybody in the neighborhood would rob a store that was in the neighborhood, because store owners knew everybody and everybody's children.

The numbers writers, the bootleggers, the gamblers, the pimps, and the prostitutes—in that neighborhood, I knew them all and they knew me. I used to go to the store to pick up little things that the prostitutes wanted. There was a big numbers man named James, and for a long time I dug his cool. I dug his manner, his nonchalant way of dealing with people. I always felt like he was a real big shot. He was about the biggest because everybody respected him, he always had plenty of money, he always dressed nice, and everybody always done what he wanted them to do. I dug the respect that he gave and that he got, and the orders that he gave were immediately carried out.

Another dude, Sherman, was nice-looking—a typical pimp. Dark-skinned, well-groomed, well-dressed, tone sharp as a razor when it come to saying something to a woman. It impressed me the way all the women went for him, because Sherman was the type of pimp that didn't have to go solicit broads. They came to him, and this was an advantage he always had. James and Sherman, these were the people that got a lot of respect in the neighborhood.

As for white people, I never had much contact with them at all, except the insurance man. My grandfather was a great believer in insurance. No doubt he had life insurance on just about all of us. The white insurance man gave me fifty cents one day, when I was four or five, and that's when somebody first said something about black and white. And I didn't understand. As far as whites living in the neighborhood or coming in regular, that didn't happen. I seen white people sometimes when my mother took me downtown to buy shoes or clothes, but I saw very few white people otherwise. Not at school, not on the playground, nowhere.

When I was in kindergarten or first grade, I went to Smallwood School around the corner. On the next block was another school—S.J. Bourne. Originally S.J. Bourne was an all-white school, 'cause during that time, integration wasn't in. Must have been in '48 they moved all the white kids out and moved us in, and they condemned Smallwood. We used to play in it, though, even after they boarded it up.

There was a library several blocks away that would show little movies, cartoons, and always there used to be somebody reading stories. That person would always be white. So I thought that white people was real smart, 'cause everybody sitting down there listening and they reading. Can't nobody else read but them, and they was telling some hip stories. So I put them ahead of myself mentally because it seemed white people had accomplished more. They knew more. Occasionally when I ran into somebody white around my age, I always found that they could read better, spell better, and everything else, and I resented that. When I was seven or eight, I began to be more aware of words, and that's when prejudice started seeping in. Whites calling blacks "nigger" and blacks calling whites "redneck." That's how you begin to break people down into this category or that.

*   *

My family has always been close. I've got five sisters and three brothers, but I'm the oldest. So most of my younger days either they were real small or weren't even born. My sister Cookie comes next in age to me. Coming up together when we were kids, I really didn't like Cookie. Not at all. I used to do a lot of unkind things to her, but I'm glad that she growed up and didn't remember or didn't choose to hold it against me, because now I really love her.

My father never lived at home, but my mother, well, me and her were really tight. My whole family life was good to me as far as feeling for one another—like, I love my mother, I love my grandmother and grandfather, my sisters and brothers. I always felt that they felt the same way about me. They have shown me in many ways just how much they have cared, because I wasn't exactly what you'd call the best son on the block, you know.

My grandmother and my grandfather—my mother's parents—they were kind of brought up on the hustling life —they've been into all different things, but my mother was always kind of a square—she never really did anything. Still, I think she understood why I was kind of wild. I never disrespect her. That's one of the things that kind of bothers me now when sometimes one of my younger brothers or sisters will say something to my mother. I never did say nothing smart to her, out of respect and sometimes out of fear that she would get right on my case.

The main thing with my mother was worrying about me. Like, by the time I was ten, I used to stay away from home maybe two or three days—all night—and she not knowing what I was doing. Usually she just assumed that wherever I was or whatever I was doing, it was wrong, and so she worried quite a bit. But Moms never really got on me too much about any of the things I did. She always told me, "My son, whatever you do, you're my son." When I was younger, she used to threaten me with "Just keep on getting in trouble, boy. I'm not going down there to get you out." Then as soon as I got busted, here she come. I kind of knew it, and I think I used to take advantage of her a lot because I knew she would come.

Most of the time when I was coming up my mother had different little jobs. Exactly what she was doing, I knew it wasn't nothing professional. She'd do housecleaning or what they'd call day's work, going to different people's houses on different days—in another neighborhood, of course—and cleaning their house for them and getting paid. Similar to the old thing about black folk working in the kitchen. I remember her working in a restaurant as a waitress, and I remember her working at a college in the cafeteria. I guess I must have been around ten or eleven during that time, and I stayed on the streets so much that I never really had a whole lot of time for her. But she always was around if something happened. If I got picked up by the police or thrown out of school, she always would be on the scene.

Mostly I think my mother wanted me to have some hopes that I would be something other than what I ended up being. She was always thinking about us kids and doing without. I recall an occasion when I told her it would be all right if she didn't get me something for Christmas or Easter. I didn't present her with a lot of problems as far as buying things for me, because I usually got things for myself. On a lot of occasions, I got things not only for myself but for her and my younger sisters and brothers as well.

I never did talk to my family too much about what I was doing in school or on the streets. My mother would sometimes make mention of how was I doing in school and how I better stay out of trouble. So would my grandfather, but I wouldn't talk much because a lot of the time I hadn't been to school in a week or so. She never would know, and I'd make up some kind of lie.

I never really knew my father until I got older, but I think he kind of swept Moms off her feet at a young age, 'cause he was a flashy dude, a hustler, a musician. He played quite a few instruments, but his main instrument was bongos. He could also play the guitar, piano, and saxophone. From what my mother and them told me, he had the reputation at one time of being the best dancer in Washington, D.C.

I was like so many of my children—a love child. In later years, after I got a little older, him and I really grew kind of close. We got real tight. Just about the time he died, when I was twenty-three, we was really doing a lot of things together. I never disliked him even though he never really done anything for me as a child or later on, like helping me, buying clothes or shoes, stuff like that. It was Moms's job. He never did, at no time. He went his own way and Moms went hers, but I always respected him as my father.

My brother Leonard is probably the most like me in the family. His nickname is Nicey, but I calls him Nut. After a while he was beginning to do most of the things I had done. I would never try to discourage him, because I don't feel like preaching to what people feel they want to do. Knowing my brother and knowing how much he was like me, it wouldn't have done any good anyway. The few times I did try to discourage him, he would say, "Man, when you was such and such an age, you did such and such a thing." What could I say? Because I had.

Stickup—armed robbery—was my thing, and I could do that very well. After Nut got a certain age, he begin to start sticking up people. I said, "This is what you want to do, this is what you're gonna do, then you might as well know the right way." So he did a few things with me in later years, since around '69. I guess he's about seven years younger than me, a real quiet dude but very dangerous, and I knew it 'cause I used to be kind of quiet myself for a long time. One time if I had to set a dude straight, there wouldn't be no words. I'd just hit him in the mouth and set him straight. And that's the way Nut is—real quiet. Whatever I was telling him, he was listening, especially if it was something about sticking up somebody. He learned pretty well while he was in that particular bag. When I started getting into drugs, he was at the Youth Center. By the time he came out, I was rolling kind of big, so I made him one of my lieutenants immediately.

Now another relative, Henry, he was a different story from my brother Nut and me. Everybody who know us always said, "Johnny and Nicey, something wrong with them, they're crazy. But Henry, he's such a good boy." But people don't know that Henry was using heroin before me and Nicey ever was. But it lasted only a short while. Then he turned to the church, and it worked out pretty good. I haven't been to church lately, but they tell me he preach a pretty good sermon.

I asked him about going to the church, 'cause I was really curious. I said, "Man, like what happened? What made you get out of this bag?" This was before I found out that he actually used drugs. And he said, "Man, I couldn't afford it. You and Nicey been in jail enough for everybody in the family. So I know I didn't need to go. I just didn't have no income. You know I ain't gonna take no pistol and stick nobody up. I can't steal, so I turned to the Lord." So I say, "Solid."

Well, he got himself together, and I was glad of that. He

always in church. He just try to do everything within the system as much as possible. But he still a lot of fun to be around. When he's with me, we smoke and drink wine—he just a regular dude. But he knew that with a heroin habit, he'd eventually have to do the sticking up and robbing things, and he also knew he didn't know how to do them correctly. He knew that he would jeopardize himself as far as going to jail, and that was what he really didn't want to do—go to jail. So he just stopped. And I was kind of glad, kind of proud.

My youngest brother, Mo, during the time I was coming up was pretty young or even unborn—he's only sixteen now, so I'm twice as old. Out of all of us Mo is the tallest and also the darkest. He's pretty witty in his own way, even at the age of sixteen. Right now he helps me quite a bit around the house when I can catch up with him. They tell me that he's a pretty good athlete—football and basketball. I'm glad of that. One of his problems is he go to school, but he don't try hard enough. Another one of his problems is that he thinks being a tough guy really means something. Mo being my baby brother, I told him about the affection I have for him and the love that I have for him. But I also told him in a very nice way that if he ever got in any trouble or caused Moms as much trouble as Nicey or I caused her, then he would have to deal with me. He would find that even though I'm confined to a wheelchair, I am still the man that I've always been, and I plan to always be the man that I've always been. In simple words I told him, "Don't get into any trouble. I wouldn't like it at all. If you get into any trouble, then I will personally put my foot in your ass."

What I really want for Mo is for him to continue with sports and maybe get a scholarship and try to be something other than what his brother is: ex-convict criminal type confined to two jails—one the District jail and the other a wheelchair jail. I don't want any of my brothers or sisters or kids to go through what I went through.

2

First Conviction

The first time I got into really serious trouble was when I was seven or eight. When I was young I always liked to hang with an older crowd 'cause I figured that I could learn more from them. Kids my age, they didn't want to do the things I wanted. Nobody eight wanted to duck school: "I don't wanna duck no school." But the dude ten or eleven, he would go with me in a minute: "Let's go steal something." It wasn't that the younger kids wanted to go to school; they was just afraid of their parents. I should've been afraid myself because my mother caught me one time a block away from school and like to beat me to death about this school thing.

At that time, I had a friend named Freddie, an older dude about thirteen or fourteen who lived across the street from me. Freddie was a loner. His family treated him like dirt. His mother had remarried, and his stepfather dealt with him like a dog. I'm sure what made me like him was that Freddie was an underdog, and I have always been the guy that's for the underdog. Even at that early age. Maybe because I had always been an underdog myself. I used to hear the grown people talking about how his stepfather beat him, and I used to see Freddie a lot of times going to or from the store or sitting on his front porch, looking sad. So I just decided to make him my friend.

Freddie was average size for his age, but I believe he was

pretty tough. He could hold his own out there on the street. He wasn't too much like me because a lot of things I used to start. He never started much, but he sure could finish a lot of things. He was shy around girls because he didn't think girls liked him, and he'd be shy when he was over at my house.

I remember the time we met. Freddie was sitting on his step out front, and I'm comin' down the street with a big old bag of candy I'd stolen. I seen him sitting there looking all sad, so I ask him if he wants some candy. You know how older people be talking: "It's a damn shame the way people treat that kid." This what made me approach him in the first place. He always called me a funny little guy—I guess 'cause I was so small. Then he start things, like when I'd get in little fights he would take up for me, 'cause I never had a big brother—I was the big brother. By him being four or five years older, he knew much more than I did, and he would show me things that would really be amazing to me—easier ways to steal, better ways to operate.

I think the first big thing that we done together was a junk shop. There was one of them junk shop trucks that was loaded with them big bales of paper. There's a whole lot of bales on the truck, but this one particular bale was nothing but comic books. Him and I are messing around on the truck, walking around on the top of the bales, and we discovered the comic books. So what we do, we take those comic books, all we can carry. We go back around the corner where everybody at, let them know, and then everybody come back. Meanwhile me and Freddie we sitting there laughing at them, 'cause they falling off the truck, comic books sliding everywhere, but at the same time we were thinking the same thing: Gee, all these comic books outside, and the junkyard is closed. Wonder what's inside. Probably something a little better.

So we just laid and laid and wait. Finally the police came, and all the kids scattered, but me and Freddie end up back at the junk shop. We got in over this little jive fence. Now they have some dogs. Junkyard dogs is just like that dude Jim Croce sing about—that's exactly how the junkyard dogs are, *mean dogs*. But even though I get real scared, Freddie had a way with animals. I ask him, "What you carrying that bag for?" He says, "That's for the dogs." And I don't think it was no meat, but it might have been bread or something. So now the dogs are walking around with us real friendly. So we looking for what we gonna take, and we destroy a few things—naturally we *always* gotta *destroy* something. Just imagine two young dudes in a junk shop who can do *anything* they want. They can take anything that they are strong enough or able enough to carry away from there. They can break up what they want. I think I was kind of proud of myself for breaking into that junk shop—succeeding. I really had the feeling then that I was going to get away with what I was doing. So we destroyed things and took a lot of junk—flashlights, telephones. In fact, that's how we got a telephone—one that you plug in the wall, that you can dial out, but can't nobody dial in. A real old-style phone.

Freddie and I did quite a few things other than break into junk shops. One of the big deals with me when I was very young was the little prizes that started coming in cereal boxes. Little whistles or little men. You buy a box of cereal, and you get a deep-sea diver or something like that. I used to mess up *boxes* and *boxes* of different kinds of cereals in the Safeways or Giants or A & P's. Just go in the store, go round to the cereal counter and be careful that nobody could see me, then open up a box of cereal, stick my hand down there, and get the prize out. I might do that to three or four boxes every day.

During the summer we used to have a lot of street showers—open up the fire hydrants. We was really into that. One time Freddie had on some short pants and a little shirt. I seen his back. Looked like somebody'd put one of them bull whips on it. So I asked him what happened, and he told me his father had beat him with an ironing cord, a stripped-down ironing cord. Freddie said, "I ain't going for it no more." His mother had attempted to stop his father from beating him, and she got hurt too. Now, Freddie always had the idea of getting enough money or stealing something valuable enough so he and his mother could leave this dude. But it never came to pass. Finally Freddie told me he was going to run away. So I said, "You my friend. You're running away, I'm gonna run away." Of course, it didn't take much for me to want to run away. Whenever my mother threatened me with a whipping, I wanted to do it.

Now, at that time a dude we called Skeeter was also one of my good friends. Any time he felt like running away, I ran away with him, because any time *I* wanted to run away, he ran away. We talked about or planned to run to a different place each time, though we didn't always run away every time we said we were going to. New York—that always was the place. Why New York? I don't know. This was just one of the things you'd be saying. But running away as a kid, even though I did a lot of it, never got me very far. Run away for a couple hours, then get hungry, and run home faster than you ran away.

So Freddie and me decided we was gonna run away. We walking around up on 4th Street, and it's getting late and chilly, and I'm getting *scared*. We had no money, no nothing, so there was just this little coffee joint, a little restaurant called Eggs and R. I don't know what that meant, but I know there was a government building right across the street from it, and all the government workers coming to get coffee and donuts. The joint wasn't very high, even less than one story, so we decided that's where we wanted to be, inside Eggs and R.

We got a big oil drum and put it up against the wall, and Freddie climbed right off the can and up onto the roof. But I was much shorter, so when I could finally hustle up on the can, I really gotta scramble to get onto that roof and him pulling me up. Now, we used to play in this place called the chute-the-chute, which was just a big round thing where they send flour or sugar down. So when I see the big old ventilator thing up on the roof, that reminds me of the chute-the-chute. So I say to Freddie, "This is the best way you can go in—down through there." Freddie say, "Well, let me go first in case the fan might be on." So he slides down. And it's over top of an old grille, and he kicked it on in. So I slid on down. We got in there, and we had a natural ball.

I guess it was about one or two in the morning when we first got in. The police checked it two times while we was in there. Just come and try the door, shine the light over, then walk away. Get back in the scout car.

First place I headed for was the pie rack. Lemon meringue pie and coconut custard—that is my favorite. So I immediately goes there. Freddie all bent down over this big old thing of ice cream, with hands digging in it, but it's so hard, he can't dig in with his hands. So he's looking around for something to dig into it with. I got pie and I'm laughing and I'm eating and finally taking the pies and passing it in my face, and we having a ball. There's a few lunch meats in the boxes and we eating meat, grab a big handful of baloney, and we talking and finally we playing and we throwing stuff on each other, shaking up sodas—chhssssshhh! So we really wrecking this joint. We sat down at one point for a rest 'cause I was full and he was full, and he was saying, "Man, I ain't eat that much in all my *life.*"

We came across some cigarettes, and by then I was smoking anyway. I smoked Camels. So we bagged up all the cigarettes. We're gonna carry them with us. Then we run across the cigars. Say, "Now we're gonna try a cigar." Freddie's telling me how to smoke it, this big old ceegar. "You gotta keep on puffing." He puts a match to it, and I'm getting dizzier and dizzier. Hoo-hoo. I say, "Man, I don't like cigars." So finally I mash it out, and he got one hanging out his mouth, unlit.

And it's beginning to get a little light out. You can tell daybreak is about to start. The second time the police come by, they looked in, and I was really surprised, 'cause we had messed the joint up with ice cream and stuff all over the walls and windows, and they just shine the light, tried the door, made sure the two front windows wasn't broken, and that was it. So Freddie and I figured it was pretty safe—we had kind of clocked it the first time they came; this was the second time they came, and we figured they won't be back for such and such a time. What we didn't think was that the man was coming in. We didn't think that the place had to open up for business.

When we first see the man, he was talking to someone and getting ready to open the door. At the time I was directly under the spot where we had came in. We peeped over the counter and saw him as he was getting ready to put the key in the door. So then we was trying to get out. He put the key in the door, but he continued to talk. This gave me time to climb back up on the grille. The way we had it planned was Freddie would push me up there, then I'd reach back down and help him up, 'cause it's much harder going up—real slippery and you got to hold on to the sides—it's kind of narrow in spots and then widening up in other spots.

I finally make it. Then I hear the man holler, "Hey, what the hell you doing? Watcha doing?" And I can hear Freddie inside the chute kicking, phoom, phoom, phoom, trying to get up. I'm looking back down in there, and I can see shadows a few feet down, but I can't hardly see him. I'm saying, "Come on, Freddie. Come on, Freddie." You could hear him inside the thing, making a lot of noise, trying to get up there. Evidently the man ran in and grabbed him. And once he grabbed him, then Freddie trying to kick him, and at one point Freddie got to where he just touched my fingers. Touched, barely touched. I'm still reaching down, and Freddie say, "Run, Johnny Boy, run. Go home, go home," just like that, and sunk back down. And when his hand disappeared I jumped off the roof. I thought I had broke my leg. I didn't wait for the cans; I just jumped off the roof and went home.

Soon afterwards my mother asked me where I had been. Of course I lied and said I was here doing this and that, none of which she believed anyway. It must have been some time in the afternoon when it hit the neighborhood that Freddie was dead. I kept saying the man killed him. But they said Freddie was born with a heart condition. So I think the fear was just too much for him. Still, right to the end he was thinking about me, telling me to get away. That's what I remember most.

I don't think I accepted what happened—I didn't look at it like Freddie being dead. I looked at it like I would never see him again. I felt real bad. Freddie was the first friend I lost, and I was only friends with him for about a year before he died.

In the meantime my mother put two and two together. So I finally told her the truth. Anyway, everybody in the neighborhood knew it was me. My mother called one of my uncles and told him that she wanted him to take me down country, somewhere in North or South Carolina. And my uncle say, "Yeah, well, I'll take him down there after I get off work." But just like everybody in the neighborhood, the police figured it out too. Before my uncle got off of work, the police had got there. And that's how it all began.

I had to go to juvenile court in front of the judge, and I remember the judge talking mostly to my mother and not me, and I remember not understanding what was happening at all. Aside from the fact that they kept saying something must be done—"A kid at an early age involved with such things, and plus he been picked up this number of times before." So the next thing I know, I was in Junior Village.

*   *

We didn't have any fences or guards or stuff like that at Junior Village—it was just cottages. A certain number of kids stayed in one cottage, and each cottage had a counselor in the daytime, evening, and nighttime—round-the-clock counseling—who never did too much but sit around and make sure there wasn't nothing else happening. But anybody could have walked away any time they wanted to.

Even without the fences we didn't have a whole lot of freedom. We did everything on a time schedule. We ate by a time schedule. We did our little chores for that day by a time schedule. We had recreation by a time schedule. Most of them joints like Junior Village they run like jail—a lot of people think of it as jail and of the counselors as guards. I myself think of it as a stage of jail.

At Junior Village most of the day from about 9 to 2 or 3 was spent in school. The main subjects was reading, spelling, and math, because they ain't nobody know how to do that! There was a lot of people that could *draw,* but *nobody* could read. We had to go to that school, but to me it was only one teacher that really wanted to help. I think we kind of discouraged her—me and the little dudes that was there with me. You know how somebody's just too nice to work in a certain place? I wish I could remember her name, but I can't. She tried to help us a lot. But we really didn't accept the help that she was trying to give us.

My family didn't like the fact that I was in Junior Village at all. So my mother and my grandparents did their best to get me sent back home and not sent to reform school. My mother used to threaten me a lot about "farm schools." Instead of "reform school," it was the "farmer school." "Boy, you keep on acting up, and you going to the farmer school!"

My mother *always* came to see me on visiting days. But my grandmother never could stand to see me locked up. I remember when I was first at the District jail, my grandmother came to see me one time. All of them times I have been in jail, she came to see me just that one time; and it hurt her so bad to see me in the tank and talking on the phone; she couldn't touch or hold me, nor could I touch or hold her. She *never* did *ever* come back to that District jail to see me —not out of all the times I've been there. When I was at

Junior Village it was the same thing. My grandfather or my mother used to come and bring my sister Cookie, but never my grandmother.

I learned a lot of things at Junior Village—mostly more bad than good. Kids from all over town were sent to Junior Village. It was a tough little place; it was a place where you fought almost every day because everybody trying to be tougher than the next person. Before I got to the place, I knew all about it—what you supposed to do, how you supposed to act. That was the advantage I had hanging around with older kids. So the first thing I did upon getting there and getting assigned to a cottage was to see who had the biggest mouth, who was making the most noise, and I proceeded to hit him right in his mouth. Fortunately he wasn't very much bigger than me. He was kind of head of the cottage, and I was showing the others "I'm not gonna take no shit off none of y'all, and I'm not even gonna take none from him 'cause he all y'all's boss. And I'm gonna show him right now." So you just walk right in and fight, two or three times a day, and then you'd wake up the next morning and fight some more.

I also learned how to shoot crap pretty good. I'm not really much of a gambler, but I know how to cheat. I probably couldn't do it real well, but if I'm playing with an amateur, I could cheat on him. I learned the right way to go about housebreaking, the right way to get away from the truant officers, the right way to steal from the Safeway. And I learned about drop-pockets. You make a small tear in the lining of your coat, big enough for whatever you want to put in there; then you steal cigarettes. You take a couple of packs at a time and put it in there and shake it all down.

My fighting became much better because I did it more often. Lying. I used to lie, but before then I wasn't no expert at lying. I became an expert liar. I learned how to hot-wire cars right there in the place—on the superintendent's car. I learned to drive a little bit—I never got the opportunity actually to drive, people just described what was the brake, what was the clutch, what was the gear. So you take all of this in because this is knowledge that would be useful to you later on. And it was, now that I think about it. There was more older dudes that I hung around with, and naturally they had more to tell you. I really got into it my first time down.

Very few people that go into a juvenile joint come out with the feeling that "I'm not going back." They know they's going to end up back in a place like Junior Village, because they know the things that got them there in the first place, and they aren't going to stop doing them. Everybody know in the long run you are going to get caught again. If you continued to steal or hook school, then you're coming back. A lot of kids that did come back was kids of abandoned families—no father or mother. They came back more often than guys like myself that stole or hooked school. The people that didn't come back were people whose house had caught on fire or something like that, and they were just at Junior Village till their parents found another place. They hardly ever came back.

A lot of kids would come out and would tell about how much fun they had at Junior Village. They had a nice place to sleep, they was around people their age, and they ate good —what they considered good: it was better than what they was getting at home, and they was getting this three times a day! If they got a meal at home once a day, that was hip.

What *I* liked the best about Junior Village was scrapple and syrup and biscuits at breakfast time. But even though some of my friends really liked Junior Village and didn't ever want to leave, didn't ever want to grow up, I just viewed it as being locked up and being unable to do what *I* wanted to do. I didn't like getting paddled or switched or hit with a belt, but what I really couldn't stand was getting restricted—not being able to go to a movie or somewhere I wanted to go. That used to worry me more than a whupping did.

I never really thought I belonged at Junior Village because they didn't really what you call "catch me in the act." After talking to some of the older guys, I figured they needed more proof to send me there. And I think I was homesick. I don't care where you live or what you come from or what you do: if you be away from it long enough, you often get homesick.

That's one of the reasons I used to run away so much. It really wasn't no problem getting out of Junior Village. A lot of times we'd be lined up going to the dining room to eat and just break out running. There was a little pathway that led right up into the heart of Southeast, and that was our road to getting away. Most of the time anybody ran, that's where they'd run—straight up that hill. So they kind of watched that hill. It depends on who you was when you ran away. If I ran away by myself, some of the older kids would catch me and bring me back. But if I ran away with my friend Tony, who was older than myself and had a pretty tough reputation, then it was all right—ain't nobody try to catch us. So we just ran.

Tony always seemed to have some place to go. But this place to go really was nowhere. Hanging around, sleeping in apartment basements or old houses. Him and I ran away so much that I got tired of running away with him. Say you'd run away and you'd be walking the streets; the police would pick you up if they'd see you were not in school, and they'd ask you about school or where you live, and you take your time telling them or stutter or don't say nothing—then they take you in. Eventually they would find out that you were from Junior Village and return you. I went home a couple of times, but of course my mother took me back— doing the right thing. She never would let me stay at home. So even though I went home once or twice, afterwards I wouldn't go home no more.

The problem was there wasn't really anybody at Junior Village I could talk to. There would always be somebody saying, "You shouldn't do this" or "You shouldn't do that."

After a while you just don't want to hear it. But as far as getting into a person and setting a dude down and rapping to him, ain't nobody really do that. What most of us needed at that time was some individual attention to let us know that somebody did care. There was nobody sitting there trying to be your friend and trying to ask you what were your reasons for doing this. Then if you feel you have got a good reason for doing whatever you did, then try to understand it. They tell me things are much better today in them little juvenile joints, but that's really what is needed. A lot of counseling. Somebody to show some real concern and treat kids like human beings instead of just forcing their way on them whether they like it or not.

Actually, the counselors at Junior Village could be pretty rough. And I don't think too much that they did was in the rules of the institution. The thing was, whoever was in the cottage from 8 to 4, then we went by his rules and regulations—or hers, because there were also some dames that were counselors and some of them was pretty hot mamas too—they would tear up your ass! Some of the counselors had paddles, some of them used belts, and some just used their fists—depends on who they was hitting. If they was hitting one of the older or bigger guys, then they used their hands. Often the older and bigger guys would fight them back. If it was one of the younger or smaller guys, like myself, then we got paddled or hit with a switch—not what you'd call any real heavy punishment thing. Sometimes you got restricted from everything—not going out or not being able to play, and that was the worst.

I really don't think places like Junior Village are a good way to deal with kids that get into things at an early age. As a kid, you pay so much attention to how a dude's supposed to be a bad nigger, he really having his way around the joint with the counselors and with everybody. You start admiring people like that, you wanna be like them. You notice everybody respect him, and he ain't giving up too much respect to anybody 'cause he just a fuckup. So you wanna be like him, you wanna act like him and talk like him. I think down there I must of changed my voice about a hundred times 'cause I had a high-pitched voice and was bothered being small. And I changed my walk from supercool to ultracool. There was a big thing down there about talking. You had to express yourself, and you saying, "Damn, jive, listen man" and going through all the motions and the changes. What was happening in the institution was just a carry-over from what was happening in the street.

Instead of putting young kids in a institution, I think you could do other things with them. There's always a small portion that's not going to listen to anything regardless of what. I wouldn't care if God came down and said, "Boy, tighten up." It ain't gonna make no difference, they still be trying to steal his robe. But for the rest, I think there's got to be a lot of understanding about it, a lot of rapping.

"You. You. It's you. You got to do it. Can't nobody do this for you. You got to do it yourself. But all of us got the confidence in you, 'cause we know you got it in you to do it." This is what you have to do: you have to build their confidence. Let them know you got confidence in them to do such and such a thing, and when they doing it, they doing it purely on their own.

You don't want to be forced into anything at any time, because if you forced into something and it don't work the way you want it, then you blame other people. But if you do it because you want it, then you got nobody to blame but yourself.

Now, my grandfather wasn't no rapper. With him it was just koshk! Just grabbed you right off. And you tend to rebel against this even though it don't make no difference about the whupping—you don't care. One time I recall when I was about ten, my mother was beating me with a leather strap for something I done. I'm standing there and she beating me, and I just bit down on my lip so I wouldn't cry. I just took it. And I took it. And I took the beating. And the longer I wouldn't cry, the harder she beat me because she wanted me to cry. I don't think my mother beat me ever again with a belt like that. 'Cause I didn't cry. Not then, but as soon as I got out of sight and back up in the woods, I cried. I was up there licking my wounds.

My little brother was like this too—he did the same thing at a very early age. My grandmother was trying to train him to ask for the pot. So now he didn't ask for the pot, and he messed up his diaper. My grandmother cleaned him up, and then she got a switch. She whupped him, telling him over and over to say "pot." All he had to do was say "pot" and he would stop getting whupped. Nut wouldn't open his mouth. He would not open his mouth. He cried, but he would not say "pot." And I cared so much about him that at one point I was ready to run into my grandmother and say, "Please stop. Beat me." But my grandmother just kept whaling away, whaling away, and by him being much lighter complexion than I am, each time that switch came down on him it made a mark. Finally she stopped. She was convinced that she could not get him to say "pot." Then a coupla hours later after the beating had wore off, he walked up to her just as polite and said, "Mama, I'm gonna say 'pot' to you." And he did from then on. He was just determined not to say it then.

As far as hitting a kid, it's really up to the parents, but I don't think it's the best way to deal with a particular situation. Now, today the relationship that I have with my own kids is a beautiful relationship. Sometimes I *feel* like hitting them, but I control myself. A lot of times parents get things over a whole lot better to a kid when they don't be hitting on them all the times. It is really up to the parent and whether he'd want to bring his son or daughter up under that threat. That's what I see it as—under a threat. You know, I threaten my kids with bodily harm every time I see them. Just today I told my son on the phone, "When I see you, I'm gonna hit you in your chest." He said, "For what? I ain't did nothing." I told him, " 'Cause I feel like it." And I probably will. I will see him and I will hit him in the chest, but he know that this won't be no beating or no hitting on him. This is a part of him growing up and a part of me that's coming out and that I want him to inherit from me. You kind of want your kid to be tough. But I don't want my son to be like me. I don't want him to have to experience the things that I experienced when I was his age, because there's so many other things that are available. Just having a parent that's kind of been through the mill, I believe, helps a whole lot, because I try much harder to understand my kids. Harder than a square person would try, and I never give up on them.

3

Coming Up

I was in Junior Village for fourteen or fifteen months, and not too long after I got out we moved out of Southwest 'cause they was tearing it down and putting up hip new projects in Southeast. The reason we thought they was tearing down Southwest was that there was too many niggers close to the White House and the Capitol. Everybody has a reason for everything, and that was our reason. The Capitol wasn't very far from where I lived, and all around that area was nothing but slum. It wasn't a thing where, well, we're taking you out of this rat-infested area and putting you in a nice place. No, it was that the white folks don't want you niggers around by their Capitol, so that's why all of us is moving. Solid.

Getting into the project was a groove 'cause it was rough living in our house in Southwest. Going way back, there was seven of us lived there: my grandparents, my great-grandmother, my mother, myself, my sister Cookie, and my cousin Frog. We had three rooms, a kitchen, a bathroom outside, and another little room where my sister and I slept. We called that the dugout.

When we moved to Southeast, we had three bedrooms, a bathroom, front room, and kitchen; and there was grandmother, grandfather, mother, my sister Cookie, my brother Nicey, another brother, myself, and my cousin Frog. So that made eight of us until the other kids were born, but by then

I was moving out. Frog, myself, and Nut, we had a room, and my mother and the girls slept in another room. My grandparents had their bedroom, and then as we began to get older, Frog and I started staying in the front room on the let-out couch to make more space upstairs.

The biggest difference between our houses in Southwest and Southeast was something I couldn't figure out at first. In Southwest in the front room we had an oil burner. That wasn't too much hassle, 'cause you put some oil in it, light it, turn the little thing, and that was it. But when you got back to the other rooms, then it was coal stoves and wood stoves, and there's a difference between a cooking stove and a heating stove that you have to know about. And wow, what a hassle!

So when we moved to Southeast, the first thing I'm looking for is what kind of stove I got to be bothered with. When I get in the kitchen, I dig this little white stove. I'm wondering where you put the coal at. So the first thing I done was open up the oven. Look mighty clean in there, must don't go in there. One of my friends was with me; he didn't know no more than I knew, but he happened to turn a knob and the fire jumped up.

Everything I drew come to the conclusion that this is what you cook with. Now how do you heat this joint? So then my mother say, "Turn this dial on the wall, and it heat the house." I say, "Oh, no. I ain't believe that at all." "See these little things right here? The heat come out of them." So I said, "Well, who's fixing the fire?" I thought maybe somebody was in back of the house!

During that time, as far as money goes, my family usually got by, but things could get pretty tight. My grandfather worked for the D.C. Transit for thirty-some years; how he did that I don't know. Some money came in from that and from gambling and bootlegging. But when you're gambling, you ain't always winning, so my grandfather had some bad times as well as some good.

We dressed poorly, but we never went hungry. Still, I always had the sense that I shouldn't ask for things, that I shouldn't make too many demands on my mother even coming up. I recognized that I couldn't because I knew that our family wasn't in that position. If I was to ask her for a football uniform or something like that, she wasn't able to just go downtown and get a football uniform. So most of the things I asked her for was sensible things. She tried, on things that I really really needed. Sometimes I went without, but I always say, "Moms gave it a good try."

Sometimes we had trouble paying our bills. We always talking about getting put out. We never were, though. My grandfather was a hell of a dude. There's a couple of things he believed in, and that was having some place to sleep and having something to eat. Even though we was threatened a lot of times and a lot of bills went unpaid, we always had them two main things. As the oldest kid, I always felt that I was supposed to not only contribute to the family but look out for Moms too, and I'm glad that I did realize that at an early age. Ever since I can remember, I always tried to keep the family thing together and do a little something for Moms. I think most oldest kids in the ghetto or middle class or whatever feel some sense of responsibility to their family. I think we all did. All us heads of families, that is.

When I was small I was a great finder; I used to find everything. "Where did you get this, boy?" "Oh, I found that around the corner." Sometimes I'd break into a store and during this time I wasn't money-hungry—I wanted food and cigarettes and candy. Most of the stores had bars on the windows. Bigger dudes would bend the bars, and by me being small, I'd slide right through. I'd be wanting a bag of them canned goods, and they'd be saying, "The money's underneath the counter in the cigar box." I got beat out of a lot of money like that 'cause all the dudes would split the money up and just give me a couple of dollars. But I got some candy or cigarettes, and I was all right. My mother say,

"Where did that stuff come from?" "Well, I found it" or
"The nice lady gave it to me."

 You could always go about what they call the island up
by the wharf, and there was a classy joint up there called
Herzog's—a restaurant. People used to sit out on the bal-
cony and eat by candlelight. We'd be down below with
hambones—two sticks—playing and tap-dancing. And
they'd throw money down. If you could get away from
there without the dudes in the area catching you, you would
maybe have five or six dollars. That was a big deal, but a lot
of times you didn't get away. There wasn't no hiding no
money. You could put it anywhere. Them dudes would take
off your shoes, your socks, everything—and they'd find the
money.

 I'd contribute to the family in my own little way. I used
to give my mother money on the sly. I used to go in her
pocketbook or where I knew she keep her money and put
something in it, so she wouldn't ask questions. But then
seeing she had five or ten extra dollars, she'd check me out,
saying, "You buy plenty of ice cream for the young ladies
around here."

 In those days, summer months was more fun than winter
months 'cause you could do more things. You could stay out
a couple of days without coming home. You could sleep
right out on the playground, in abandoned cars, and you
wouldn't have to fear freezing to death. You could hang out
on the corner without having to find some place to stay
warm.

 When I did have to be in the house, like in winter, a lot
of times my mother or grandmother and myself, we'd be
sitting around the radio—one of those big, old-fashioned
set-up radios—listening to different things together. We
liked Jack Benny when he was coming on the radio. I used
to like the Shadow—"the Shadow knows"—and Superman
and the Lone Ranger.

 I went to the movies quite a bit too. On Saturdays they

used to show a lot of cartoons and a lot of these little chapters—Flash Gordon and Captain Marvel and Rocket Man—and I never would miss them. We used to get our money together—enough for one person to get in, which in those days was nine cents. Once this person was in the movies, he'd sit down for about five minutes, then he'd open the side door. Ten or fifteen of us would rush in there. The man might catch a few dudes, but he never got everybody out of the movie. This was a regular thing.

Otherwise, we used to play mostly outdoor games, like hide-and-seek, and we liked daring each other. If somebody dared me to walk across the railroad track, which went across the river, then I would do it. We had a lot of fun just taking a plain cardboard box and sliding down the side of a hill near the railroad track. It was part of a game, 'cause we'd always see who got to the bottom first.

I didn't have a whole lot of toys when I was a kid, but I did have some animals. At one time we had a rooster in our backyard, and the rooster was as bad as the average dog. Anybody couldn't just go into the yard. I was terrified of that rooster when I was five or six years old. Me and him didn't get along, and I used to throw rocks at him.

My grandfather used to breed rabbits, which was fun, but mainly I think of my dog. Blackie. That dog lived for twenty-some years, and they said that was really something for a dog—to live twenty years. When I was a baby, he was a puppy. We growed up together, the dog and I. I started walking when I was seven or eight months old, and my mother said it was largely due to the dog. I'd be crawling around on the floor, and I'd pull up on the side of the dog. He would hold me steady and walk real slow with me until eventually I learned to have my balance and walk by myself.

Most of the time in my younger years, I was in the street with friends, but I used to do a few things together with my family. I can remember my mother when she was still very young taking me sleigh riding. But things like cookouts and family picnics just wasn't done where we were. I wasn't even hip to it. If we went on a picnic, it was mostly through some kind of organization, like the church.

There's two days that I always enjoyed, even now, and that's my birthday and Christmas. I remember waking up after we fixed the tree—we always had a little pine tree—and I always felt good going into the little packages I had. Mainly when I was young, the big deal was getting a stocking full of candy and fruit. Most of the things we got for Christmas wasn't really what you call fun things—some clothes, some shoes, a coat.

When I was real young, I also used to go to church with my grandfather's mother. She was a very religious person because my great-grandfather was a preacher. So I went to church with her when I was five or six. I recall that we used to go to Daddy Grace and Father Divine and all that kind of stuff. My grandfather and mother made us go to church quite a bit in my younger days but didn't go too much themselves. A lot of times I would just fake out like I was going and didn't really go. I used to go sit in the woods, throw rocks at cars or something like that. As I grew older, I got less and less interested in it even though I do believe in God and the son of God, Jesus Christ, and all that.

For me and my friends coming up, school was only a place to be when it got too hot or cold out in the street. There was some things I liked about it, but it didn't have very much to do with education. I used to like to work in the woodwork shop and metal-craft shops—I was very interested in things like that. But at the time I was going to elementary school, unless you was a hard case, then you didn't get in the shop. I was a hard case, so automatically I made shop. You had the man teaching, and he was always rough and ready to fight; and as soon as you said something smart, he'd go right up side your head. Whap! So it was pretty rough.

*   *

There was an apartment area called Parklands not too far from my neighborhood on Stanton Road in Southeast. People that lived in Parklands, we felt that they was better off than us 'cause we came out of the project. So when we did things, we did it to them. We housebreak their property, or we beat somebody up and rob them. I recall myself saying when I was around twelve, "Man, we got to make some money. Let's go down to Parklands." The majority of Parklanders was black, very few white. But they was better off than us, and we resented that. Some of the things I did in Parklands I would never do in the project.

The project was my out for everything. We always felt that if we done something at Parklands and could just make it across Alabama Avenue to the project, we would be safe. You could go in almost anybody's house—right in the front door and right on out the back door. If something did happen in the project, then it would usually happen to a stranger. You never knew how they got to the project, but whatever happened, they was sorry they got there.

The little contact I had with blacks who was doing better than me turned me right off. I still remember going to a little party at Parklands. There was six or seven of us, and when they opened the door and let us in, they said, "Oh, Lord, here come the project niggers!"

I had an aunt who was in better shape than what we were, but I just didn't dig how she lived. I couldn't function in her environment. All she ever talked about was "That boy, he going to be bad." I recall thinking at one time that what people now call middle-class blacks was really rich black people. Man, they got cars, big color T.V.'s. I'd see them when I would be coming through somebody else's neighborhood, which wasn't often. I really disliked them people, 'cause it seemed like they thought they was better 'cause they had more. And I don't think that because some-body got a little more than the next person that he or she should think that he or she is better. Their luck's a little better maybe, but that's all. It was a fairly strong feeling we had of niggers against Negroes.

I never really thought of coming up any different than I did. I never thought how it would be if I was to come up in the suburbs or middle class. What I was aware of living at 2nd and G was that if I crossed 4th and G, then I was going to have to fight! In Southeast on Stanton Road we lived in a project called Garfield. If we went to another project, Berry Farm, then we could expect trouble. My world was limited to a matter of blocks, alleys, shortcuts getting through all the turfs. I didn't know what was hap-pening in Pakistan or even in Bladensburg, Maryland. I re-member riding out to the suburbs in my great-uncle's car once and seeing all these trees. It seemed like I was never going to stop seeing trees; no houses, nothing but trees. That was an experience for me, but it made me uncomfortable because I knew them alleys and back streets. I didn't know the trees. I would have been a babe in the woods, but in them alleys and little cutoffs, I was the king of kings.

The only way I ever knew about things that happened outside my neighborhood was through magazines. We had a T.V. for a while, and everybody on the block used to come and watch it, but it was Captain Video cartoons—it wasn't like sitting there looking at the six o'clock news. I didn't dig the television all that much, and I was busy doing other things. There'd be people coming in the house, sitting down looking at the T.V., all the lights out, and I'd be crawling around trying to check out the girls. There's no doubt I missed a lot of things.

I remember Adlai Stevenson running for President. There was a big car come into the neighborhood with a flashing sign saying, VOTE FOR ADLAI STEVENSON. I asked my grandfather, "What's that car all about?" And he said,

"Elections." I said, "Oh," like I was right on top of it, but it really didn't mean nothing to me. It didn't dawn on me to want to know anything about it, and nobody I knew ever talked about government or politics or nothing like that.

But I learned a lot from magazines. There was a group of people from one of those little community center things that come into the neighborhood and would give us old magazines—*Jet, Look, Life*. Then we'd always be hanging around the junkyard, and I come across a lot of books, but mostly magazines. Most of the time I really didn't know what was what because I was a very poor reader, but I was interested in the pictures.

Occasionally I used to go to upper Northwest and walk around and just dig how the whites live. I have been in a white neighborhood and was stopped by the police maybe three times—"What you doing around here, boy?" Being aware that I'm black in a white neighborhood and something could happen, I didn't do it much. But I feel like I know more about their world than they know about mine. I can tell some people that's maybe uptown in the well-to-do neighborhoods about my world, and they don't know nothing about what I'm telling them. But I have found out about them from curiosity and investigation.

Like a game I used to play a long time ago—magazine game. Me and somebody else be looking at a magazine, and everything on this page is mine and everything on that page is his. We turn the page and there might be a real pretty house on this page, and this is mine. And there might be a real pretty car on his page, and he say this is his. It was a mental game that I played with myself.

But I was more curious about the people than anything else. If you don't know a person unless you live in that neighborhood, it's not really easy to get to know that person. Because people are so suspicious of people, a lot of times rightfully so. My solution for that was to dress properly and go in some place, like a nice restaurant. I was inquisitive about things like that.

I also knew one or two Hell's Angels from the Virginia area, and they made me an honorary member. I used to hang around those spots sometimes, just to watch them. I found that most of them was from well-to-do or rich families, majority white. I dug the wildness. The whole gang was interesting to me. Here's a whole bunch of guys riding around on motorcycles looking rough. What is this all about? I used to go and watch them race other gangs, challenge each other.

Of course, I didn't do these things until I was in my twenties. When I was younger I wasn't really aware of things like that, and what I was aware of, I took for granted. Like living close as I did to the Capitol, I just took it for granted. To me it was an everyday thing. In my younger days, as far as knowing what be going on in the Capitol, I didn't. It was just the Capitol. I didn't relate the Capitol as being the capital of the United States, or I didn't relate D.C. as being the capital or the White House as being where the President live. It was just the White House. What went on there, I paid little or no attention to. It had to be something really outstanding for me to dig on it. Like the ambassador that got busted in the '50's bringing over narcotics. Or congressmen taking bribes, something that the papers and the media played up and you just heard about it. But it still didn't make any difference to me, because I always thought of it as instead of taking money with a pistol, they just taking it with a pen. Maybe not so much the government, but I think of the more well-formed organized crime now where it's mostly paperwork.

Sometimes I feel that from the President down—Congress, senators—they have things dictated to them to do certain things. How I arrive at this decision is I feel that if the president of the multimillion-dollar corporations, say G.M. or Du Pont, want something done, they get it done, and they get it done through these people. They the real ones that make a lot of big decisions. All the little class of corporations follow the big ones' lead.

I feel as though decisions that have been made by big corporations or big industry have affected me somewhere along the line, though I couldn't explain exactly how. I don't feel that what they doing is wrong. To them, it's just making a buck—a group of people getting over. Now, I'm gonna try to get over any way I can, and they getting over the best way they know how. There's conflict in there because my kind of crime is generally looked down upon, but the white-collar crime is an altogether different bag. Like Ehrlichman deciding when *he* wants to go to jail. Don't nobody tell me *I* can decide. If they wanted to come and get me today, they could do it. I don't like it, but then Ehrlichman has enough smarts to put himself in that position. If I had enough smarts to put myself in that position, then I'd take advantage of the opportunity and do it. So I can't fault him, but I can be mad with him. To think about it, say damn, here's a dude that can tell the judge, "Well, look, I'm ready to start doing my time now." It's strange. But mostly I just take a far-off attitude toward who's making the decisions. I don't ever think along them lines.

The decisions I've always been aware of are made by dudes who are up one day and down the next. There's a drug baron I know, a pretty big boy. He was supplying a lot of people with synthetic narcotics. When that first came out, he was one of the main controllers, and he put it in circulation and made a pretty big piece of money. Then he got into a couple of beefs, so he had to pay out for special lawyers. People talked about how good he was doing, how much money he was making, the diamonds on his fingers, the ride that he had. But two or three months later it was a totally different conversation—about how bad he was doing and how he lost some of his main connections.

It's really who you know and how much money you got that makes you a big shot. I seen a big drug dealer I worked for get as much as seventy-five thousand dollars' worth of narcotics without paying a dime. The same person that he got it from, I couldn't get a hundred dollars' worth from under no circumstances. You've got to keep in mind that drugs is a product, and it's a product that's high on the best-selling list, so that automatically makes it big business. Some of the same motions are being made that would be in legal business.

The only big shots I've been personally involved with have made it this way, through drugs or numbers or something like that. There's some other people I've heard of that are trusted and respected to a certain extent. Not trusted with information that might get somebody locked up, but trusted to go tell a problem to or to try to help you solve a problem. There's a congressman that people respect and other members of the Black Caucus in Congress that have got power and are legit all the way down the line. There's a member of the city council that I heard has done some good things. But when I think about who's got the power in my neighborhood, I mostly think about people who've got to the top in strictly illegal ways.

*   *

When I was ten or eleven, a day never passed without me stealing some things or getting into some fights. Sometimes I used to go to the playground, but most of the time me and my friends had our own little spots, little alleys and airways where we'd play or in abandoned trucks or cars. Beside the railroad track we'd play in the cardboard boxes. One of the main things we used to do was go to the Capitol, the monument, the museum, and play hambones and tap-dance like we did up at Herzog's. Around the Capitol by Union Station they got fountains that they used like wishing wells. People come from out of town visiting and they throw a quarter, a dime, in these wells. Our thing was to lay around and wait till a group come by and they throw some money in the fountain. Immediately we'd take off our clothes, get in the fountain, and get the money. Stealing watermelons and what have you off the wharf in the summertime was a lot of fun too. Then I used to love to go in Union Station. For one thing it was real easy to steal in there and for another thing, I liked to watch the people—going by, catching trains, getting off trains, just crowds of people going somewhere. Those were the only places I ever saw white people as a kid.

Remember, my world was small, and it had a lot of danger that you just had to deal with. If somebody lived two or three blocks away and came into our neighborhood, then they would have to deal with us. This was especially so after things got bad with street gangs, and it wasn't safe to go too far unless you went with a large group or had your own boys with you. Going by yourself a couple of blocks from your own block, you was in trouble. I lived at 2nd and G Streets, and every time I would go up to 4th Street, I'd have to deal with the dudes that lived in that area. If you go even further up to 7th Street, then you'd have to deal with the people in that neighborhood, and on up to 10th Street and the island. But I got a break up there 'cause my cousin Frog lived there when he wasn't living with me.

During this time, in my own neighborhood we weren't real organized, but we did have our own little system. My job was getting into places 'cause I was small. Maybe a dude that's heart wasn't too big, we'd leave him outside to chichi —to watch. We knew most of the time what we was going after when we went in these little places. Different guys would request different things. My main thing was carrying cigarettes and edible stuff. Most of the places we broke into at that time was just little corner stores that didn't have much that was really valuable aside from food. Once we got into a store we would break down in groups, just like I did in later years in stickups.

So say there's five of us. I go through a window and open up the door so everybody else can come in. The chichi man, he's outside watching. So that makes four of us in the store. Two guys would do nothing but look for money or what-

ever other things was of value—guns, watches, rings. Sometimes those little storekeepers will have a gun or shotgun up
under the counter somewhere where they could get to it in
case of an armed robbery. The other two guys would be
bagging things up that people wanted. A guy might have
wanted a certain kind of canned good and he'd say, "Get all
the sardines." Mainly we took cigarettes, candy, and food—
just childish stuff.

The splitting up of the things became valuable because
if you only stood on the corner and watch, then you didn't
get as much as the dude that went in. Of course, if you got
busted, you all got the same time, but ain't nobody look at
that. They look at all you're doing is watching, you got a
better chance of getting away than anybody else, so you
don't get as much. Later when I started sticking up, I
wouldn't do it like that. I would always give everybody an
even cut, even the drivers. I found that you get along a
whole lot better that way.

In those days, though, we never did no real skillful planning or taking down notes when we were checking out a
place we wanted to rob. Not like I learned to do later on
when I'd watch how many times a police routine check
went by. It was just like we see a place, and if it was easy
for us to get in by like climbing the drainpipe or going
through a window, then we'd decide to do just that. And
most of the times it *was* very easy.

The trouble come in if the people that owned the store
lived in the back of the store or over top of the store. When
you go into places like that, the people are always kind of
listening out for you. I have ran into that problem a couple
of times, but being fast on my feet got me out. It was strictly
amateur stuff that we did, and I think we got away with a
lot of it because it was so easy—it sure wasn't because we
was professional!

We always tried to get the dude that the neighbors didn't
like too much or the guy that was hard on the people who
lived in the neighborhood. Like, some storekeepers wouldn't

let people have credit till the end of the week. We used to call them just plain cheezy. Say you go in there for a loaf of bread and a loaf of bread cost seventeen cents and you didn't have but fifteen cents—he wouldn't let you out there! People like that—just plain scrooges. Now there was a lot of good storekeepers as well. Like, if we go out and found a store in another neighborhood where the people really like the storekeeper. Now, we don't really know him, but we do know that everybody all around there all right with him, so we naturally wouldn't go into his place for fear that somebody might see us and call the police or describe us for the people that own the store. We kind of stayed away from them type of places.

I like to think that all the places we robbed, that we broke into, was kind of like the bad guys. Now, there were all kinds of stores—black-owned stores, Japanese-owned stores, Chinese-owned stores, Jew-owned stores, and what have you. We didn't stick to no one particular pattern. Like, we wouldn't just rob all white people or all Chinese people or all black people. We kind of mixed it up. We wasn't prejudiced at all.

So by the time I was around twelve, I had got hooked up with some older fellows and we was really into it, hitting little joints. We be getting very much aware of the girls, too. We into quite a few things that kids like. Bicycles. I had numbers of bicycles—so many bicycles one time that I could of opened up a business in bicycles. I used to just give them away, sell them, sell parts.

Well, one day we went into a particular joint and got a nice piece of money out of it and some good foodstuff. Back in our little hideout, we start breaking the stuff down and splitting things up. Now, I'm noticing that the boss of the gang—the president we used to call him—is taking much more than what everybody else had. Naturally by me being the youngest member of the gang and the smallest, when I approach him about it he immediately had something to say to me that wasn't too hip. So I started an argument. It came to the point where we did a little struggling—he pushed me around and grabbed me. So now on top of his taking what I figure belongs to me and the rest of the guys and roughing me up a little bit, I figure something had to be done. Okay. So now I think about things like this: Because you the boss, you already up there. So don't take what yours and then take some of mine too. Especially when you're getting twice as much as what I'm getting in the beginning! I just wasn't going to let him get away with it.

Now, I had stole a gun from my grandfather some time before this. During this particular time, my grandfather was going strong in the bootlegging business and in gambling. Being a bootlegger and a gambler made him have a lot of weapons around the house. Dudes would come in and pawn their gun for a bottle or something like that. Lose their gun over the crap table. One particular day—you know how every now and then you just go through everything when you home by yourself—I find five pistols in my grandfather's mattress, and I take one of them.

Before I got that gun, I never had no regular experience with a pistol or rifle, even though I did have occasion to fire one once or twice before I stole that one. Nobody ever taught me how to use a gun; but during this time, the stables that was behind my house was just about ready to close down. A lot of times I would go through the alley or through the backyard and set up tin cans near the stable and fire away. Mainly it was this dude we always call Skeeter, who used to shoot with me. I remember on one occasion we found a gun after some people had moved. Of course, guns wasn't really that hard to get when I was younger. I seen plenty of guns that I could have stole or taken if you just was in the right place, and most of the time I was.

Skeeter and I kind of taught each other, and we learned from our mistakes. We used to shoot at a lot of different objects until we got to learn the pistol pretty well. That's one of the things that I learned later on in life: to know your weapon, especially when you're out there every day on the streets into this, into that. You into narcotics, you into prostitution, you into robbery and what have you. I had to know my weapon, especially like in '69, when ten to fifteen weapons a week used to go through my hands.

But then I didn't know exactly what kind of gun I had. Now, my grandfather used to keep a lot of bullets in the china closet, in the dresser drawers. What I would do, I would just get a couple of handful of bullets and they'd be all mixed up. All different kinds and sizes. I'd just try them out in the gun and see if they fit. If they fit, I'd try to find five more.

So this particular day after my argument with the boss of the gang, I go on home and find the gun. Sometimes I used to bury that pistol. I used to hide it in a lot of places—sometimes in the horse stables. I think this particular time I had it in the woodpile. I just got the gun and went back to our little hideout. I asked the boss, say, "You going to straighten it up or what?" And he said, "No." And I knew that I couldn't beat him straight up fighting. So I shot him.

He lost 'cause I shot him, and when I shot him, he acted like he was dying when it was only a shot in the leg. So automatically everybody else looked upon me as being the boss. A title that I didn't mind at all. I think that's kind of what I wanted all the time anyway, 'cause even though I had some say in a gang, I never would join any gang if I couldn't be one of the bosses or *the* boss. At that particular time, I was just one of the bosses 'cause I was an expert in climbing and getting in small places. Now after shooting him, it was like a complete takeover, so I was *the* boss. It was just part of the code. I had won, so now I was the number one boss. Simple as that. The other guys didn't feel one way or another as far as feeling sorry for him.

He wasn't badly hurt, so he still stayed in the gang for the day or two before I got busted, even though he wasn't boss any more. He was waiting for his chance to get back, but I had a little more heart than he did. I had the courage to do more things than he did when it really came down to it. Because I was much younger and smaller than most of the crowd that I hung with, I always felt that I had to do twice the job that anyone else did. It's like the old saying that black people have to try twice as hard. I had to do a better job for the simple reason of proving to them that I could do it, that I could hold my own. I was just as smart, just as rough, just as tough as they were. I let them know it. I let them know it every chance I got. Speaking up was just part of my nature. There have been a lot of times when other people could have spoken up, but I was the one that did it.

The thing is that all my life I always seem to make that first move. Sometimes I want to. A lot of times I don't. But I made it simply because I have to stay in tune with myself —always doing what is expected of me. That's why I felt I had to say something when that gang boss took more than he was due. I had to be the one. Back then the gang leaders had all the say, and it was like they was generals and we was privates. The gang leader had to live up to a lot of things, and if somebody else in the gang thought he could whip the gang leader—thought he could beat him fighting or in a knife battle—then he would simply challenge him. If the gang leader lost, then the guy that won would automatically take his place. Which is what happened with me.

But that time I didn't stay the boss too long 'cause I got busted for shooting him. Of course, he say he didn't tell, but I know he must have snitched on me. I've heard the police got him. I've heard that some of his people made him tell, but exactly why he told I don't know. He knew that snitching was against everything that we was brought up to do. That's the last thing in the world that I would do. I have my sneaking suspicion that he wanted to take the gang back. So he told on me and the police just come around to my house. They never did get the gun though. By the time they came,

I had put the gun in its final resting place, buried in my backyard. But they got me anyway.

I was about twelve years old and there wasn't a trial. In them days they just held you at the receiving home until your court date come up, and then the judge did his thing —either send you away or let you go home with your mother. My mother was there, but I never went home with her. It was Junior Village again for me, and I knew it. The judge wasn't that much harder on me, though he talked a whole lot harder. He said he should send me away until I was twenty-one, and man, I was scared 'cause I knew that old fool wasn't jiving. But I looked so sad that he didn't.

The second time at Junior Village was much easier. The first time I went there, even though I knew a lot of people, I had to learn my way around—who was the tough guys, who was the homosexuals, how this particular counselor was, what time to eat, what time to go to bed, and who to look out for. The second time I go, I'm already aware of all this. I knew what counselors was the roughest. I knew the top people—other inmates like myself that could move around a little more freely. The badder or the tougher that you acted, then that made you always have the easiest jobs. People tried to pacify you. The first time it took me a month or two just to feel my way around—learn things. The second time I just fit, like a hand into a glove.

4

War in the Streets

When I got out of Junior Village the second time I was almost fourteen, and the streets had really changed. Everyone had joined a gang, and the most important thing that was going on was gang fights. Now, a lot of these guys in the gangs were pretty big and pretty tough. I have been president or boss of several gangs, but only that once where I shot that guy was it through a takeover. Most of the crowds I hung with had a whole lot of experience, and until I had that experience I didn't make my move. When I did make my move, I made it through becoming a warlord—I just handled all the weapons. When the dudes called a meeting, they thought about me knowing how to do everything. I know the right place to hit somebody with a rock and a sock—that was one of the main gang-fight weapons—or I knew how to make a zip gun real well or I knew how to handle an ice pick and a straight razor or a stiletto or a switchblade. I even knew how to handle small rifles and pistols.

Gang fights involved just mobs of youngsters—maybe seventy-five or eighty youngsters to each gang. A lot of times gang fights took real finesse; a whole lot of planning went into them. If my gang challenge your gang to a fight, then my gang would have to fight in your territory if we didn't make arrangements to fight someplace else. We got quite a few challenges because the real numbers of my gang

wasn't known and a lot of people thought that it was much
smaller than the usual gangs. But it wasn't. In fact, I think
we had a little more fellows than some of the other gangs.
Then there was also the question of strength—how many
bad niggers live in that particular neighborhood?

We got a lot of challenges, which gave us some headway,
'cause that meant a lot of fights was on our own ground.
Now, a rival gang when they just outright challenged you
always wanted to use you as a stepping stone, just like boxers
do. They figure if they could chalk up a lot of wins in gang
fights, then they'd be in a better position to fight somebody
big. Now, the advantages of having a gang challenge your
gang and fighting in your territory is who knows your
territory better than you and your gang? We knew all the
little alleys and back alleys and the old houses to climb on
top or to go in or what bushes to hide behind, or what old
cars to hide behind, or how we would spring out and trap
them, how we would close them in in a particular block.

I recall one time in a gang fight we stole a car to block
off this other gang's car, which had their president and about
five other dudes in it. Usually cars like these would be stolen,
and when they came to a fight, they'd just drive in. Then
their mob come in behind them. Or sometimes they'll
drive through to see what they can see, how we set things
up. But we was always witty enough to never give ourselves away.

One of my main gang fight plans was this: to stay just
outside of the area we was about to fight in. When I lived
at 2nd and G, we had most of our fights on 2nd Street
between G and F. So now what we would do is stand some
people maybe on the other side of the street—about fifteen
or twenty guys—and give them some bats and other weapons. When the other gang come in, they count the dudes, see
how many there is, then report back and come to war.
Okay. When they come in, our fifteen or twenty guys see
fifty or sixty or as many as eighty guys coming, then natu-

rally they might throw a few bricks or pop off a couple of zip guns, but that would be it.

By our guys being outnumbered, the other gang would continue to come and our guys would continue to retreat. This retreat, it was beautiful. I used to love it, and I don't care who we was fighting. Every time they used to fall for it. If they'd fall on our territory, that was the best thing. The other gang would fall right into the trap we had laid for them. Then we would close off the street behind them. There would be members of our gang cutting them off. And we would just hit them from all sides. Both sides of the street, because most gang fights used to be right in the streets.

Every now and then we'd have guys on the rooftops with zip guns or guys up there with just a big pile of bricks. Maybe there was a guy in the gang who really couldn't handle a knife or ice pick or bat or chain very good, so we put him on the roof, let him climb up the drainpipe, give him a pile of bricks, and just let him whale away.

When my gang challenged another gang, then I would always try to find some kind of way of going into the other gang's section. We only had a one-to-two-to-three-block radius, that was our territory. I would ease onto their turf, especially if I knew where the fight was supposed to be held. I would always check it out and see if we could be ambushed, and what they could do or what I would do if I lived in that particular section of town. How I would fight it. Kind of like generals matching wits.

A lot of times I would send fifteen or twenty members of my gang into the other neighborhood. Okay. Now, a lot of guys was hip to this, so instead of attacking, they'll hold off. I knew this too 'cause I had the occasion where only part of a gang come into our territory, and then when we ambushed them, the rest of their gang came, so I learned from that experience. Okay. So now they didn't ambush those first guys, so you send in say ten or fifteen more. When you send in ten or fifteen more, then they are almost sure to get ambushed because the opposite gang is going to believe that's all you have. When they ambush them and they get to fighting, I'd bring in my reserves. I even figured out a way once or twice for some of my boys to get up on *their* rooftops and bombs away. It was a lot of fun. I kind of miss them days. I really do because I knew I was the best general there was. General John. Can't you see it now? If I only had my chance in the armed forces. . . .

I was in the Keystones in S.E. Then we changed our name from the Keystones to the Tagalongs. There were other gangs like the Southwest Stompers—we fought them —Peach and Honey, Tophat, the Mau-Maus. One of the most powerful gangs that ever came out of the district was the Mau-Maus, but *the* most powerful gang in Washington, D.C., in them gang-fighting days was Le Broit Park. Le Broit Park was said to have seven hundred members. They had branches everywhere—S.E., S.W., N.W.—but their main branch was in the N.W., up around the ball park. Because of their large numbers, they easily moved over quite a few gangs.

There was a time when I was up on their turf in N.W., visiting a girl I had met. At the time, I had on my Tagalong sweater and a little cap, letting them know that I was one of the Tagalongs. About six Le Broit Park members chased me clean out of N.W.

We also had occasion to get in a semi-big rumble with them. What it was all about I don't really remember. But when they came, they came. They must have stole every truck and car in seeing view. There was so many of them that it really wasn't even a fight. Seeing all the trucks and all them niggers piling off, then we knew we didn't have a chance. All them victories I had planned—there just wasn't no way. So we scattered. But we had to save face, 'cause when we scattered that didn't look too good. So we did a lot of picking, a lot of dummy attacks. We met on this playground field where we were supposed to fight. Twenty-five or thirty guys would rush the field, pop off some zip guns, throw some bricks and bottles, maybe get into a few tangles, and then back off. Hit them and run, hit them and run, until finally they just got tired of it. They didn't know where we was going to come from next, what we was going to do next, so finally they got off our turf. But when it go down in the books, they was the victors of that particular fight because of all of us scattering in the beginning.

Nobody ever interfered with the gangs while a fight was going on. As I remember it, the police always came when it was over or about over, just when everybody is either tired or hurt or shot or just plain scared. Then you could hear all these sirens and cars squealing, and of course everybody that could make it would run or be carried away. Both gangs would scatter.

The police didn't pose no real threat to us. We knew they had informers on the street even then, and if it was a big enough fight jumping off, they might come. But a lot of times they didn't even bother about it. I guess it was "Let all them niggers kill each other." When the larger gangs got together, with eighty or ninety dudes apiece, that ain't no little bit of niggers. That's a lot of hard heads. So when they knew about these bigger gangs getting into it, then sometimes they would kind of police the area. But 90 percent of the time the police never come until after, when there was maybe ten or twelve guys laying around on the ground or holding their faces or trying to limp away or drag theirself away to keep from getting caught.

There was usually a few guys that did get seriously hurt. When you get hit with a bat, then you seriously hurt. Or when you get hit with a chain or if somebody stab you with an ice pick or a straight razor or shoot you with a zip gun. I was just lucky, 'cause I was into this for about three years, from fourteen to seventeen, and none of them things ever happened to me. I mean, I've been beat up on—that kind of hurt—punched in the face, black eye. But real hurt like shot or stabbed or beat real bad with a bat, that never happened to me. A lot of my friends wasn't so fortunate. A lot of them still carry scars from old gang-fight days.

*   *

When I was around fourteen a couple of things happened that stopped me from doing little things and started me doing bigger things. I found out that people with little or nothing try harder to keep what they have. Like, I believe all ghetto kids start off yoke robbing or snatching pocketbooks or something like that. Now, I was yoke man of the year—I could grab somebody around the neck better than anybody in my neighborhood and hold them that way. So one day me and my friend Snap was in our hideout spot we called the hole in the wall when my cousin Frog came looking for us. He said there was an old man with a cane walking down Stanton Road who had a lot of money on him. So we decided to go after him. I would yoke the man, Snap would hit him, and Frog would be taking everything he could get—shoes, rings, money, and anything else.

Well, that old man fooled the hell out of us—he was like a bull. When I came up behind him and put my arm around his neck, he throw me on top of Snap and we both hit the ground. Then he takes his cane and come down with it on Frog's back, and Frog ran like hell. By the time I get myself together and ram into the old man again, he had hit me about three times with the cane, but I get him around the legs and pull him down. Snap was back in by then, but the old man was too much for us. We started to run, but the old bull was right behind us. He ran after us for five long blocks. After the Old Bull, as I call him, I never yoked anyone again.

The other thing that taught me not to take from poor people happened around the same time. I was just out walk-

ing the streets one day doing nothing, and all at once this
lady was in front of me holding her handbag in her hand.
And I decided to take it. Man, what did I do that for?

I walked beside her, and she looked down and said hello.
She look like she was about forty years old or so. I said hi.
I guess I looked like a little boy to her, but then that's
what I really was. I got that handbag from her before she
knew what had hit her, and I was off and running with it
under my arm. I went down through Camp Sims, which is
an army camp, and once I got behind the camp I stopped
to see how much money was in the bag. Then I heard
something. I looked up, and there was that woman coming right at me.

Off again I went down this long, long hill, and at the end
of the hill where the woods began, I stopped again and
began to go into the handbag. But there she was again, right
on top of me. So I took off into the woods, and when I got
to the stream, I run upstream and then crossed to the other
side. Man, I had to stop 'cause I had run myself out. I fell
in the woods and just stayed there, and soon I could hear the
woman coming upstream. I didn't move, hoping that she
would go right past me, but she didn't. When I looked up,
she was looking right in my face. She said, "Why did you
do that, young man? There's nothing in there but papers.
Ain't no money in it." So I said, "Then why the hell was you
running after me like that?" She say, " 'Cause I want my
papers back." I picked up a big rock and said, "Take your
damn papers and get out of the woods before I kill your
black ass up here." Then she got scared. I could hear her
making her way through the woods after she left me. Man,
was I glad! From then on I made up my mind that I would
never do anything to a poor person again.

We didn't lighten up on robbing the stores any, but it
was a whole lot of difference between yoke robbing and
breaking into a store. I think I felt that store owners could
take the loss when I broke in there. It wouldn't hurt them

that much, but it would help me and other members of my gang and their families and my family a whole lot when I did do it. Even though these people only owned very small stores, just by them having the store alone made me know that they was doing better than I was.

But like the old man and that woman, the people with very little fought so hard for the little they had. Say I felt like going out and robbing something, and there's a bank on one corner and there's a gas station on the other corner. Now you see the man pumping gas all day long, and he got a big old roll in his pocket. Which one would you rob? The bank, of course. Why? Less risk. The man been pumping gas all day long, he tired, he been working hard, and he's not going to give that money up as easy as a bank teller would. A bank teller in a bank behind the cage counting somebody else's money out to him or taking somebody else's money in, they not going to get hurt for their scratch. They going to give it up. But the gas station attendant, that's his money most of the time, and he'll take a loss if he's robbed. Sometimes he may even have to pay back what's been taken in a robbery. Most of the time, that's all he has. So I would rather walk into the bank any day with all their cameras and security officers and silent alarms and loud alarms and secret alarms and push-button flowers and all that stuff. I would rather go facing the cameras and the FBI than rob a gas station. Not only will the guy in the gas station buck on you, but he will pull a gun and shoot somebody.

Robbing is an art, and the whole art of robbing is fear, and the main reason for robbing is to get what you came after—the money—and get away. You don't go there to hurt people. Sometimes you have to. Sometimes you do it in self-defense or because a person is trying to protect their property, but most of the time that somebody gets hurt is when somebody bucks: "I'm not giving you nothing. If you want it from me, then you have to kill me." I heard that a lot of times, but you really don't have to do that. If you instill the fear the moment that the robbery started to take place, then you got more than half the battle won. When you succeed in getting away—find a good escape route— then that's the whole battle right there.

When I was a kid, before I really got into the stickup thing, my family kind of had other hopes for me and sometimes so did I. For a while I thought about going into the navy, see the world. My grandmother, she wanted me to be a doctor because I was good with my hands. And my mother, she wanted me to be a lawyer. Maybe it could have come to pass, but I really couldn't see it because that meant working real hard in school. I asked somebody about being a doctor, I think it was one of the playground dudes who ran little recreation things. And they was saying you got to go here for four years and do this for three years and do this for three more years. Before I could be a doctor, I'd be withered away!

I didn't become interested in law until my later years. By then, I thought I'd better find out a little something. Before that, it just wasn't in me. I had other ideas. I probably could have worked harder in school, but the one or two times I thought about college I always was thinking about what my mother going to have to pay. While I be laying back in college learning and being cool, they would have to be footing the bills! But nobody ever talked to me about getting a job, going to college part-time or in the daytime. I never knew.

People constantly saying, "Why don't you do better? Why don't you do this or why don't you do that?" I don't know how to do this; I don't know how to do that. This is all I know. I know how to steal. I know how to be hard on broads. I know how to stick somebody up better than anything. I know how to take a small amount of narcotics and eventually work it way up and make me some money. Fencing property or credit cards, I know how to do all that. But society says all that's wrong. I feel like it's survival, making the dollar. I don't have nothing against a guy that makes a dollar. Whatever his bag is, that's his bag.

No one ever taught me anything else. My old friends and I never saw the light—there was no one to show us the right things to do. But there was someone always ready to show us something slick or hip. We listening with all ears, but they never told us the part about jail. We had to find that out for ourselves. And there we learned more and couldn't wait to hit the streets again to try out something new. If it worked, good. If it didn't, then back in jail. By the time I got to a certain age, I just had forgotten all that stuff about jobs and college. I just omitted the whole thing. I was getting what I wanted out of street life, and I was doing far better than what I thought I would actually do.

You know, my grandmother would pat me on the head and say, "One day you going to be a good doctor like Dr. Snoobinoff or somebody." And I say, "Uh-hum." And all the time I'm saying to myself, Where the cash going to come from? Who am I going to operate on around here—some of these big rats? Now there's a few people from this neighborhood that have done something like that, become like businessmen, dentists. I know a couple of dentists that come up with me. I even know some robbers, dudes that used to steal with me, that became police. In my late teens there was a dude that was with me on a charge that is a detective now. He was one of the lucky ones. A few make it. Some got good jobs. Some wouldn't accept it like it was, and they wanted to change things. Of course, now everybody go about it a different way. Some dudes figure they'll work their way out. I say, well, I'll rob my way out.

Going to school didn't really teach me to do nothing besides the things I ended up doing. There was a few things I used to like, a couple of teachers I used to like, but it just wasn't enough.

In junior high, I was beginning to learn a little something 'cause I had a teacher named Mr. Samuels. And Mr. Samuels was a really, really rough dude. He drummed and he made you learn. It made it easier to learn 'cause Mr. Samuels was a big, black, bad nigger and was mean. He came out of the same type of neighborhood, same type of environment, and was out there before we were, so that automatically made him hipper than what we was or a little tougher. He not only would whip your ass if you did something wrong, but he also took the time to pull you aside when it was his lunch hour or after school, not so much to scold you but to really try to help you get into this learning thing. He was my homeroom teacher because he had all the supposedly bad dudes in his class.

But except for Mr. Samuels, most of the teachers weren't getting across to me. They couldn't think of things to keep me occupied, to keep me learning. I think that's one of the things I regret more than anything else. I really had no chance to learn 'cause classrooms were so filled. Always was filled. Never really had time to get to each individual, and I think in my earlier years that's what I needed. More individual attention as far as learning goes, 'cause after a time of being neglected, I just got uninterested.

When things got a little more interesting in school, it was because I was in a faster circle. I even learned a few little things in junior high school, things dealing with my profession. I think I stayed in junior high school about four years, but after a year I got tired of it all and started hanging in the poolroom and cutting up. We was doing everything. Go get some wine and get high. Come back and turn the school out.

As far as studying go, I had the most trouble with reading and spelling, and I didn't know why. I just never could read and never could spell. I really didn't like studying. This might sound kind of strange and you might not call this a study, but the only thing I can remember being interested in when I was young and I called it a study—my own little personal young-dude-out-of-the-ghetto study—was I used to kill things or hurt bugs and see which one of them would die first. Would the grasshopper die first or the cockroach die first? Two big old rats. You'd catch them in the kitchen. If the traps don't kill them, catch them. Hurt them and see which one dies first. That was a study. That's the only studying I did.

Most of my friends was pretty much like myself. They just didn't care one way or the other about school. But I don't care where you go or what you do—there's always somebody different from the majority. The loner. Maybe 90 percent of the people in my neighborhood did things my way, but there was always one or two guys or a couple of dames that played it straight. Went to school like they were supposed to and really got over later on in life. I ran across a couple of them at one time or another, and they was doing all right. But as for me I don't think I was better or worse at school than my friends. We came out of the same type of environments. We all had to do just about the same things, and our lives were very much the same.

One of the things that was real hip about school was we had a little protection racket going. Your position in that depended on your mob, what street you was off, what block you lived in, and just how tough you were—could you take it as well as you put it out? Normally I would walk up to another kid and say, "From this day on you have to bring me ten cents every day." And usually it would be a kid that I know could produce ten cents. A lot couldn't produce ten cents. You could say anything, but the ten cents just wasn't going to be there. As it went on, some was up even higher —fifty-cent dudes or dollar dudes.

So now some dudes will buck on you. They'll say, "What, ten cents? What you talking about?" You had to be able to show him why he had to pay you ten cents. So you immediately go up side his head. If somebody else approached him about protection, you understand, then he would automatically come to me. Now, if I was weak and couldn't straighten it up with whoever else was pressing

him, then I might end up having to pay to somebody else.
You had to be able to take it as well as dish it out. But if you
could fight, then nobody took advantage of you. I had a lot
of problems because I was small for my age. I had to fight
twice as hard. I got to be able to whip Joe Blow. And if I
can't whip Joe Blow, then everybody will get me. It's a way
of taking care of yourself, on your own, at a very young age.
If you're tougher than this guy and he got a peanut butter
and jelly sandwich and you ain't got no lunch, then half of
his—or all of it—going to be yours. The thing was there
wasn't never enough to go around. There wasn't a whole lot
that was doing better than most of the kids in the same boat
with me, but you always tend to look at the one who's doing
a little better, live in a different neighborhood. And them the
ones that always get pressed—beat up, money taken, lunch
taken.

Those dudes got hard times from everybody, so a lot of
them used to employ the fighters. They knew they couldn't
fight theirselves, so they immediately be your buddy, take
you to stores, buy you whatever you want, carry it for you.
They wanted you to be around, 'cause they knew if somebody else say something, you would immediately speak up.

It was really something, but it was a lot of fun. I know
one thing: out of all the things I've done—and I done more
bad than good—I done some cruel things, I done some unnecessary things, but I'm not really sorry for maybe three
things I done my whole life. 'Cause I like to have fun in my
life, and in school I had a lot of fun, just none of it had much
to do with education. I dropped out of school permanently
when I was about seventeen—I think it was '59. I had to get
a job 'cause my first kid was being born, Cynthia—Brown
Sugar.

5

Love and Other Troubles

My next beef with the law came when I was sixteen. Everything was on time from fourteen to sixteen years old. I had a few small beefs but nothing serious. At this time, I had a girl called Dee Dee. She was my girl for at least two years, so sex was nothing to us any more. In other words, I had her so many times that doing it was like a good fight, and there's no way I could count how many times I've had a good fight. So when I got busted in '58, the charge was, believe it or not, rape on Dee Dee!

This is how that came about. One day I heard that Dee Dee was seeing another dude. At first I didn't do anything 'cause I figured there was always someone to take her place. What I didn't know was my feeling for her was deeper than I thought, and I didn't dig another nigger messing with her. (In them days, it was all right if a black person called another black a nigger, but it was hell if a white person called a black a nigger. I guess it was like someone said: white people couldn't say "nigger" right.)

Anyway, I heard about Dee Dee and this other dude meeting after school, and I didn't like it, so I put my spies to work. One day my boy Snap and I was coming from the poolrooms when Reggie came up to us. Reggie used to go with Dee Dee before I did; in fact, I took her away from him, but he was one of my ace spies now. He told me that Dee Dee was at the school rec room with Shrimp, the dude that she was messing with. So my walk man—my partner—and I went up there, and when we walked in the door, I saw Dee Dee and a girlfriend of hers standing in the corner. I looked around for the dude, but I didn't see him anywhere.

Snap went in the bathroom and found there was a crap game going on. That's where Shrimp was, playing dice with some other dudes. I went in the bathroom and walked to where he was down on the floor with the dice. I stood over him and said, "What does Dee Dee mean to you?" He didn't answer until he had stood all the way up on both feet, and then I knew why they called him Shrimp. This nigger was two times bigger than me. He said, "She's my woman. What's it to you, nigger?" I couldn't cop out. I didn't say anything, just fired my right hand hard as I could up side his head. That made him back up. Then he yelled and run right to me with his head down, trying to get me around the legs, but I went to one side and got him with a foot in the face. That downed him, and Snap and I walked all over him with our feet.

I went out into the rec room and took Dee Dee by the arm. When we was out the door, I smacked her up side the head. I was giving her hell for messing around on me; she was crying and telling me she was sorry .

Then Dee Dee and I took the shortcut home through the woods. I was telling her she wasn't my woman no more, and she was still crying. About halfway in the woods we just stopped and looked at each other. She knew I didn't really want to put her down, and I don't think she wanted to cut me back neither. The next thing I know we were kissing, and of course the kissing led to sex—we were rolling in the grass, and I had forgiven her for everything. Night came fast and I had to get her home, but I didn't get her home fast enough. When she got there, her mother was waiting for her, and she couldn't explain why she was late or how she had got grass on her coat. So she told her mother what had happened. Then her mother called the man and changed the whole thing around.

I hadn't given it any thought after getting home—I just went up on the corner with the fellows when a dude came by and said the police was in the shopping center looking for me. The next thing I know there were two big white men standing behind me asking was my name John Allen. I said, "Yeah." They took me to the car while I was asking what I had done. They said, "Don't play with us, little nigger. You know what you done." I didn't say nothing else to them. They took me to the station, and my mother and grandmother came down and asked me what was up. I said I didn't know. Then all of a sudden Dee Dee and her mother came in. I couldn't believe my eyes. Her mother was talking, but the police dick told her to let Dee Dee tell what had happened.

Dee Dee wouldn't talk for a long time until finally the man said, "Put him in the back in a cell." I wasn't saying anything, but I was pleading with her with my eyes. She said, "No! Don't put him in no cell! He hasn't done anything I didn't let him do." Man, was I glad to hear that! She told the whole truth, so the rollers let me go home that night, but I had to go to court. I just knew that I was going to jail no matter what Dee Dee had told them, but it was the first time justice had smiled on me—I got probation. I thought that was really something.

My next beef with the law came when I was seventeen, and it was behind my woman Ann. Ann have three kids by me, but at this time she only had my first kid, Cynthia. Here's what went down. At the time, I had stopped going to school and was working at night. I was really trying hard to do right because I loved Ann and the baby. I was still hanging out with the fellows and drinking and smoking reefers, but not as much as before.

I was in love! Ann wasn't the only girl that had a kid by me, but she was the one that I loved. I had other girls even then. There was Sharon, who was pregnant at the time, and also this girl named Mary Lou. Mary Lou lived in Arlington on South Queen Street, come from a good family who owned their own home and all that. I really couldn't get over there much. I think Ann living next door to me played a large part in me caring for her and the kid so much. They was always around. Another thing. Whenever I got in trouble—and I must have been picked up one million times I know for one thing and another—Ann was always there. Even though at that particular time she was young and she really couldn't do anything, she would always be with my mother.

Even in them old days—gang-fight days and the smoking herb and drinking wine and fighting and stealing—through all that Ann stuck with me. She didn't always know why. So I just chalked it up to she cared something about me. Whenever I was in trouble, she came. None of the other girls that I had pregnant at that particular time came to my aid or wrote me a letter or anything, so it just automatically made me closer to Ann. Ann seemed to understand a lot of things about me—maybe she seen some good in me that nobody else seen. Exactly what I don't know.

Ann was real quiet, and even though we had a lot of fun together, I think she appreciated me more and I appreciated her more when we was by ourselves, not in the parties or the dances. Every now and then she'd have to fight to regain me or to let everybody else know that I was her man. Her friend Sharon had a kid by me, and she also had a friend named Judy Mitchell, who didn't have a kid by me but was my gal at that particular time. Anyhow, Sharon and Judy decided to jump on Ann. Ann whupped both of them. If you see Ann, then you know why. She never was a slouch, a sucker. She could rumble. She could take care of herself.

On the other hand, she was real passionate and affectionate. She gave me the affection that I felt I needed at that age and stage of life. She also was pretty smart in school. I remember she was in the seventh grade and I was in about the ninth. She used to do all my work all the time.

She always been able. She could cook when she was young; when she was ten or eleven years old, she could cook very well. She used to fix dinner for her family. Believe me, she had a big family. She's not no beauty queen, but in her young days she had a pretty old foxy shape that I used to like. I used to love to see her with her ponytail and with some white Bermuda shorts she used to wear all the time. They used to knock me right out. All I wanted to do was carry her in the bushes right away.

The vibes between us were really beautiful, and they still are, to a certain extent. I always been somewhat of a tomcat, but I never forget where home is, so we never really been completely erased from each other.

Anyway, back when I was seventeen, she was my main gal and had just had my oldest daughter, Cynthia. At this time there was a couple of bad niggers named Rock and B.K., who had a gang with some bad dudes in it. They were a little older than me and my gang, so that's why we never had a run-in before. What was happening was that Rock and B.K. had a lot of people scared of them, and they knew it. So they start telling the girls that if they didn't do what Rock and B.K. wanted them to, Rock and B.K. would whip them up or whip up their father or brother or boyfriend. Most of the girls were scared, if not for theirself, then for their family or boyfriend, so they did what Rock and B.K. wanted them to. Once they had a girl scared enough, they would make her meet them somewhere, then they would get her drunk, and then Rock and B.K. and all their boys would have sex with her. That's called a gang bang, or pulling a G.

One day I was down on the corner before going to work, and two of my boys came running up to me. They said, "Man, something got to be done about Rock and B.K." They was both mad as hell, 'cause Rock and B.K. and their gang had got to their girls. Then they told me they had got the wire that my woman was next. At first I didn't believe them. I thought they were just telling me this 'cause they were scared and they knew that I would do something. Then one of them said, "I ain't jiving, man. That is the wire I got from one of Rock's boys."

I was mad as hell. I said to myself, "This can't be happening to me, not me, and I'm not going to let it happen to my woman." I told my boys to get all the fellows together and let them know that we would more than likely be going to war with Rock and his gang some time that night. They said, "Solid."

I didn't know what to do, how to stop those two bad niggers. I wasn't scared. I knew I could whip Rock, though I wasn't sure about B.K. I went home and told Ann when I get on the bus to go to work, for her not to come out of the house for anything.

Now, the week before we had got in a fight with a roller, and we had took his gun. Snap had it, so I went to his house, told him what was up, got the gun, and told him to meet me on the playground at dark. Then I get on the bus just like I always do. My boys was on the corner, and when I looked out the other side there was Rock and B.K. and their gang on the other corner. I stayed on the bus till it got to the end of the line, then I got on the next bus coming back. I knew it would be dark by the time I got back. I didn't get off where I usually do. I got off at the stop before that and walked to the playground, where Snap was waiting for me. I asked him if anything had happened. He said, "No, man, not yet." From where we was we could see up and down the street both ways.

We were sitting and looking about an hour later, when I saw someone at Ann's back door. I told Snap, "Here it is. Let's walk." We went across the street and in her front door. Ann was standing at the back door, and I heard her say, "Tell Rock that I'm not coming nowhere." When I heard this, all I could see was red. I pulled her out of the door to see who she was talking to, and it was Rats, one of Rock's boys. I said, "What the hell do you want with my woman, nigger?" He said, "I don't want her. Rock want her." I said, "Oh yeah? Tell Rock I'll see him, and whatever he got to say to my woman, he can say it to me."

Rats left, and I walked down on the corner, and there was Rock and B.K. and about six or seven more dudes. I said, "Someone down here want to see Ann about something?" Rock said, "Yeah." I said, "What?" He said, "What do you think, punk nigger?" I smiled and said, "See me, nigger." Before he could answer I said, "I'll fight any one of you or all of you one at a time—just come on the playground." I meant it, and I think they knew it. What I didn't know was Rock and his boys heard that my gang was going to war with them that night, so they had come with bats, sticks, and everything.

As we was walking across the street, I see them coming out with the shanks, which was the knives we used to use. I don't think Rock and his boys had any idea what I had. Maybe they thought I had a knife or razor or something like that. They knew I was going to fight any one of them, but I knew I couldn't fight all of them at once. So we going across the playground and somebody threw a couple of bricks. When they threw those bricks, I turned and started firing, and everybody started splitting. I fired at Rock and hit him in the side. He turned round and round. B.K. said, "You didn't have to do that." I fired again and hit B.K. in the arm, and he turned and ran. The dudes with him went running all kinds of ways. Rock was still turning round and round, and then he took off. I fired at him again, and this time it got him in the leg and he hit the ground, crying, "Oh, why you had to shoot me, man?"

I was standing over on top of him, and if it don't be for Snap, I would have killed him. I was that mad. Snap grabbed my hand and the gun went off between us just as I pulled the trigger. I was afraid that I had shot Snap at first. Then I just let the gun go, and he took it and shot the rest of the bullets out and ran down the street. Snap saved me from a murder charge because I'm sure I was going to down Rock. I was going to take him all the way out.

As we went up the street, Snap was saying, "We got to get out of town." I walked to Ann's house and told her what had happened. Then I went up to our room to look out the window. I had some more guns, so I put them on the bed, 'cause I was planning to shoot it out with the rollers. But Ann's mother came up and said, "Son, please don't do that with your kid in here." The rollers were already running all around the back door and at the side and front of the house. Ann's mother was crying and crying, so I said, "Okay, okay," and I put all the guns away and walked next door to my house.

Now, even though I was seventeen at the time, I could have passed for thirteen 'cause I was so small for my age. The police all around the house didn't even suspect who I was. So when I come in my house, the police have my grandfather, 'cause him and I have the same name. My grandfather was saying, "Let me go, let me go. I haven't shot anyone in years." So I just went straight through to the kitchen, got a glass of water, drunk the water, went upstairs to the bathroom, come back down the steps, and told one of the white-shirts—one of the police—a lieutenant—that I was John Allen. And that was it.

Before Ann's mother talked to me, I had felt like shooting it out with the rollers was the thing to do, that I wasn't supposed to just give up. I knew that I was going to lose, but I figured, take as many with me as I could. If it wasn't for Ann's mother bringing up the fact about the child, I probably would have had Ann load and I would have been doing it. I think it was kind of expected of me that if they got me by killing me or capturing me or shooting me, it would have been a whole lot better.

The police knew who to look for 'cause Rock told them who shot him, but when we go to court, he wouldn't press no charge. But the government had to press charges because

I had pleaded guilty anyway. So it wasn't very hard. I had no case. They tried to make me sign some old thing. I said, "Man, I can't read or write." So the dude say, "Just sign right here. You can write your name, can't you?" I said, "No. I can't write, man." Because I knew I wasn't supposed to say nothing. I wasn't supposed to sign nothing. But I think that I was so mad and so confused that I just didn't care what I said. At that particular moment it didn't make no difference. It was just, "Yeah, I shot him. So what?"

So I was taken to the receiving home, where I stayed for three days. Then they waived jurisdiction on me, and I was sent to the D.C. Jail. When it came court time, I pleaded guilty to A.D.W. [assault with a deadly weapon] and was sentenced to six years under the Youth Act.

*   *

Out of the six years I got on the A.D.W. charge, I did almost three. I was sent to the Youth Center. On one side of the Youth Center is Lorton, where dudes go when they're convicted of serious charges, and on the other side is Occoquan, which is a rehabilitation center for alcoholics and for misdemeanor charges. Lorton is on kind of a hill, and the Youth Center is in a valley.

I learned quite a few things at the Youth Center that I didn't learn at Junior Village. One of the most important things I learned there was a trade. That was cooking. I had two or three certificates or diplomas to that effect at one time, though I've misplaced them since. When I was at the Youth Center, I worked my way up from plain kitchen helper to first cook and instructor. I taught other guys how to cook. That was one of the good things I learned there.

Of course, I learned a lot of other things, too, like how to stick for a guy while he took his thing—in other words, pickpocket. I learned that pretty good while I was at the Youth Center, but I never did put it into practice when I was in the street 'cause it just wasn't my game. I think one of the main things I learned at the Youth Center was unity—that you can get a lot more when you stick together. I realized it then behind a sort of riot that went down. We organized and stayed united, stayed together, and eventually we lost the battle, but our grievances was heard and publicized.

I was one of the few dudes that came to the Youth Center when it was just a couple of months old. It had opened up in September '60, and I must have gotten there around December. Before the Youth Center was built, whenever a dude from the District received a youth correctional act, then he was always sent to Ashland, Kentucky, which is a youth joint under federal control. At the time I got my youth act charge, you could get sent to any federal institution at all from Ashland, Kentucky, to Atlanta, Georgia, if they thought it was necessary. But by me getting into the new Youth Center close to home, I found that I knew most of the people who came in there.

The living arrangements at the Youth Center was really hip. You had your own room, not a cell. Each individual inmate had his own room. Each individual inmate was responsible for cleaning his room, having his room free of anything that the institution might consider as contraband. But he has his own room and not only that, but a key to the door of the room. Naturally the dormitory officer also had a key to all the doors, because they made a day-to-day inspection of the rooms.

At first, the educational program at the Youth Center was a thing like if you wanted to go to school, then you could go; and if you didn't want to go, then you didn't have to go. Everybody always got a job or some kind of work to do, so if you didn't go to school, then you just worked on your job. Then around the beginning of '62, it became mandatory to go to school a certain amount of days—in order to get educated, I guess. Anybody that refused, then he would have to work longer hours on whatever job he had.

That didn't last long because a lot of dudes that didn't want to go to school simply went because they didn't want to do the extra work. So the few dudes that wanted to go to school and get their education was being disturbed by the others. I even did it once or twice myself at that particular time. One of my favorite tricks to disturb the group therapy class was to tell everybody before the class would begin that once we got in, nobody should say anything.

So eventually the people running the joint said, "Well, there's some guys who want to learn and some guys who don't. So what we'll do, we'll give them their own choice, and we won't press that work thing." That's the way it ended up and guess what? I ended up going to school after work myself eventually three days out of a week. I even learned a few things. In fact, I ended up getting—they called the school Valley Central High—a diploma for my hard working efforts. Solid.

The Youth Center wasn't like most of the institutions that I've been in and out of, because at the Youth Center, there was always something going, not only illegal things but mostly good things, like sports. The Youth Center had a boxing team, which was the best boxing team in the Golden Gloves for about three or four years. They also had a pretty good football team and a good basketball team, 'cause most of the youths was very interested in sports. So after work in the evening, there was always plenty to do besides just sitting around watching T.V. I myself in the beginning did quite a bit of boxing, and I played football and things of this nature.

Now, one of the programs that they also offered was for guys that really wasn't good enough to make the varsity teams. They had this thing they called the intramural teams. When I came back to the Youth Center in '63 on another charge, I began to train other younger guys. By me being a repeater at that time gave me a little more status than the new guys coming in. I had twelve guys that I used to train for boxing. I was pretty proud of them because seven out of the twelve did receive trophies in their weight class as being champions in intramural boxing. Other than that boxing team and a softball team I had, which didn't do too well, I also had a basketball team, which actually won the intramural championship one year.

Now, they also had special days—in school I think we called it May Day—when we had track and field events. We would sometimes actually challenge some of the smaller college or high school runners to have track and field events. We had a lot of fun with the things we did, one of which was greasing up a pig and catching it. The first year that they tried it, it wasn't too hip. They greased up a pig and put him on the field, and there's about 150 guys out there, and they was told, "Whoever catch the pig get a carton of cigarettes." I felt sorry for the pig. Can you imagine 150 guys coming after a pig, and the pig so scared he just couldn't run? So bam! everybody was scrambling for him. That didn't end up too good for the pig, 'cause he was crushed and so was a couple of the guys. The next year they changed it around and made a little pen. Then they brought in six or seven pigs and greased up one at a time, and that was a lot of fun.

All in all, sports was time-consuming at the Youth Center. It took up a lot of free time that otherwise you'd spend sitting around thinking about devious things to do. It was something to keep your mind off of everything else.

*　　*

When I got out of the Youth Center in '62, I was wilder than ever. I felt that when I got the youth act charge for shooting Rock, I didn't deserve it. I felt that on the night I shot Rock, I was completely right and he was completely wrong, that the eight or nine guys with him was wrong, and if I hadn't have shot him, I probably would have ended up in the hospital. I felt that it was self-defense. Also, when Rock tried to do what he did, this was outright disrespect not only to Ann but more so to me, 'cause I was her man and you're not supposed to disrespect a man and his woman.

So when I came out of the Youth Center, I didn't try to control myself. I felt that during that time I spent there, I had really missed something, and at that time I wasn't aware of the fact that once time has passed, you never can get that time back. Like things will never be like they was in '62 or like they was five years ago or last month or yesterday. At that particular time, I felt that I had been missing out and I was just playing what you call "catch-up," trying to do everything. Not only on the streets and running with the dudes but also with the young ladies. I think that lasted about two weeks, and I was ready to quit them altogether. I was just trying to relive the time that I was away. My parole officer was pressing me for not working, but I didn't care.

It was about this time that I started to get tight with my father. He was just getting out of Lorton, and he was more like a very good friend than a father. When I was very young, my father still had some type of relationship with my mother, coming around every now and then. As I got older, once or twice when my mother and I was together, she would actually point my father out to me. Then getting even older, I approached my father and let him know who I was. I didn't see him too much after that, but I was aware that this was my father and he was aware that I was his son. Still, when I was a kid, sometimes I didn't see my father for years at a time.

My mother never did get into that bag about "Your father ain't no good" or "Your father left me." She never did down my father to me. I honestly believe that she cared a whole lot about him. I never told her this. It was just my own little personal opinion. The one that did down my father to me often was my grandmother. She didn't care for him one bit.

When I did finally get to know him, I found out he was a real good dude. He never treat me like his son; he never treat me like a kid. He always treated me like an adult and like a real good friend. He was flashy, cool, and he had a gift of gab—he could rap, he could really run it down to anybody. He also knew how to speak Spanish fluently and one other language, I forget what it was. He was just an all-around good Joe, a good dude. Me and him used to hang out, get a couple of broads together, and do our thing.

I think what really brought us together was an incident that happened with a dame of his a little while after I got out of the Youth Center in '62. He was going with this dame who was about twenty years old. I was older than her! That dame used to really make me mad 'cause she used to say things like, "You know, me and your father are going to get married." And I say, "Yeah? Solid. I don't see what he want to marry you for." Then several times the broad actually tried to seduce me. I told my father about it. I said, "Man, that dame ain't nothing." But he was kind of hopped up over her, maybe because he was around forty-something and, of course, she was so much younger.

On this particular occasion when the dame caused a lot of trouble, a friend of my father's showed up from Lorton, another musician that he know for quite some time. Well, he's showing the dude around and showing him a good time. Some way they end up back at his house, where the dude attempted to rape the broad.

Of course, my father wanted to get revenge on the dude, so naturally he came looking for me. It was one of them times when I had been out in the streets for two or three days on a gambling thing. I never been no hell of a gambler, but I used to do a lot of betting. I knew friends of mine that was really, really swift with dice, and I would bet on them 'cause I knew they was going to win. So this time I was coming home to bed, really tired, when I hear my father coming in. "Man, this nigger done raped my woman. We got to do this and we got to do that." His cousin Charles was locked up, and Charles had all his guns and things. So he asked me for something. I go upstairs and stack all the guns and stuff on the bed. What he picked was a shotgun, but the shotgun he picked is my favorite shotgun—a little sawed-off shotgun. So I tell him, I say, "I know you want to handle this by yourself, but wherever the shotgun go, I go."

So he picked up an old pistol and stuck it in his belt, and I break the shotgun down and put it in my belt. Me and him get the dude. We didn't down him, but we paid him back. But it only made me hate the broad even more, 'cause I figure she enticed the dude one way or the other. I don't think the dude would have done it on his own.

I never resented my father. In fact, I kind of admired him; I dug his style. My brother Rodney is just like him— he look like him, act like him, he even plays bongos. Rodney is my father's son, not my mother's. Knowing my father, he probably had more children than Rodney and me, but I never came in contact with them. I guess Rodney and I were just the cream of the crop for him. His main two.

Rodney lived with his aunt, and when we were kids, I knew much more than he did about street life, hustling life. All Rodney knew was go to school, try to be a good boy, and pay his protection regular to whoever he was paying protection to at that particular time. Of course, all that ceased once he found out that he was my brother.

There was a big difference between Rodney and me all the way up 'cause I was raised in the streets and he went to military school. The aunt that he lived with was not what you'd call rich, but she wasn't doing bad, and I guess she thought that this would be the best thing for him. Nobody in my neighborhood knew nothing about military schools, so Rodney had a pretty different life growing up.

The last time I saw Rodney was in '69, and it seemed to me he was into some pretty funny things. We rapped for a while, but then I never got to see him again. Once after I was hurt and transferred to the District jail, he did make an attempt to come see me, but he didn't know the proper identification, so they didn't let him in.

There was a young nurse on Lockward 44 North, where I stayed for a while after getting shot, who lived in the same neighborhood as Rodney. She used to tell me quite a few things about him, and the things that she was telling me wasn't too pleasant. Evidently he was having some pretty bad problems—money and all—and by him maybe not having the heart to pick up a pistol and get into stickup, he ended up in small-time hustling, living a kind of hippie-style life, from what I understand, which was a surprise to me, because the people that he lived with, they were well off. Aside from that news I got from the nurse, though, I haven't seen or heard from him in quite some time.

But we did have some good times together with my father back around '63. I remember one time when me and Ann and Rodney and his broad and my father and his old lady all got together and partied all day and all night. At one point, my father got his head back and he had a little thing he used to do just like Cagney. He would say, "You my big drink of water" to me and "You my little drink of water" to Rodney. We got to kidding around, so I told my brother, "Man, are you going to let that old dude talk to you like that? You had better straighten it up." I'm agitating him and getting them into it. They get to rassling and tussling, my old man kind of down rassling behind the couch.

So I'm laughing, I'm cracking up, it's getting to me. And then my old man say, "I'm ready for you, big drink of water." I immediately hit him with the coffee table. I came out on top, and I never let him forget it. I used to press him about it. I say, "Man, you're getting too old. You can't whup me now. I'm the youngest. I'm the strongest. You know you have to come and get me when somebody jumps on you." We used to have a lot of fun playing around that way. Nobody ever got seriously hurt—just bumps and bruises, swollen eyes, nose bleeding a little. After the rumble, we set down and kind of straightened up the mess, cleaned up the glass, then continued to party. I think it brought us a little closer together.

There was only one time that my father made me really mad, and that was when he called my mother a bitch. I didn't feel that he had the right to call her a bitch because she had did everything for me and he did nothing. Like he called for me and I wasn't at home, so my mother said, "Now why after all these years you want him? Why you didn't want to be around him before?" I don't know what his answer was, but I know he ended up cussing at her. She was pretty upset when I came home, and she told me about it. I got kind of mad, and went to see him. It's funny, he must have felt that I was gonna come; he must have known he was really wrong. Even in that short time he knew me well enough to know that I was going to do something about it, because I really love Moms.

I came down to my father's house with a shotgun ready to do him in, and he was waiting for *me* with a shotgun. When I came in, we kind of looked at each other for a while, and I said, "You ain't have to call her a bitch." So he says something like "Well, I'm your father." But I said, "Look at all them many years. Maybe you are my father, but you only had the title 'cause you never did anything else." So then he thought about it and we just looking at each other awhile. Finally he kind of laid his shotgun against the wall, and I relaxed a little. We didn't really say anything, and then he just ran to me. At first I was on the offensive, 'cause when he started to me, I jerked my shotgun up. But you know how you can tell on somebody's face what they're about the business of doing. Just a few steps before he got to me I knew it wasn't no violent move. He just threw his arms around me and started crying. That kind of got to me. Then I walked away a little bit with my head down, saying, "Now, man, just don't do it no more." That was a pretty serious thing, but it was the only real problem we ever had.

After we became friends, then I saw him regularly. I saw him as often as I could. I've always considered myself a man ever since I was about thirteen, but I was pretty much a man age-wise when him and I became really good friends. I used to stop by his joint, and him and I'd get smashed together. A lot of times we'd have dames together. I remember one time when I was around twenty-three he called me and told me a friend of his had come into town. The friend of his was an old girlfriend, and she had brought another friend with her. Why he didn't call one of his buddies I don't know. But I guess he just wanted to show his son off.

I knew that they came down for a good time, to go places and of course be with a man, so immediately the broad asked me how old I was. I told her, and she says something like, "Well, I'm ten years older than you." I said, "Yeah, like what difference does it make in the bedroom in the bed with the lights out and our clothes off?" It worked out all right.

A similar thing happened when I was fifteen or sixteen and my father lived on South Capitol Street S.W., which was right across the bridge that leaves from S.W. to S.E. We were seeing each other every now and then at that time. There was a carbaret-style place up at 14th and U, where my father was fixing to play one night. Being a musician, he got around to a lot of these type places. Now, there's a young girl there about eighteen, and her mother is the one who's sponsoring the affair. She's sitting around drinking a beer. I think I got a pop or something 'cause I don't like no beer. So the music playing, and the young girl and my father get to dancing. Then my old man say, "You want to dance with this dame?" So I say, "No, I don't do no dancing." Then they sat down at the table, and the broad says something like "Who is this?" So my father says, "That's my son. His name is John." Then she say, "Well, when your father come up here to play tonight with the band, who gonna babysit for you?" That blow my stack. So I say, "Why don't you come to babysit for me? Then I'll show you how much baby I really am." Then my father went on to explain to her: "Johnny, he small and he young, but he kind of fast, and he usually hang with a different crowd from other dudes his age." But the broad continued to laugh, and I continued to get mad.

The next afternoon he called and said, "Come down as soon as possible. I want to show you something." So I got there in the evening. He live above a little store. I walk in, and he just blasé and setting around the house in his underwear, being comfortable. Then he say, "Go look in the bedroom." And sure enough there's that dame, the same one. So I immediately begin to take off my clothes, 'cause I want her to see that I'm just as much man as anyone that she knows. When she sees me, she protests to my father. "What you doing? This little boy this and this little boy that." My father started laughing and closed the door, and I handled it from there. I really changed her mind, 'cause when she left there, she gave me her address and phone number and all that, but I wasn't really interested. I just had to prove to her that I was somebody.

I liked my father, and I respected him because he was my father, but I can't say I was proud of him. The man that I was proud of was my grandfather, my mother's father. He was my pride. My father's part of the family I had very very little contact with at all. For a time, my father lived with his mother, who was also my grandmother, but we didn't have what you'd call a close relationship. I knew that she was my father's mother simply because he told me, but right now if she came to see me, unless she told me who she was, I wouldn't know her. I don't even know her name.

It was through my mother's family that I first found out my father was on heroin. My grandmother would say to me, "Boy, if you keep on going the way you're going, you're going to be just like your father—a dirty dope fiend." So I begin to investigate, check out little things that he did to see if he really was using drugs. One time when I was fifteen or sixteen I actually seen him use drugs. He was tying himself up, and he was saying, "Boy, as long as you live, don't you ever do this right here." And he was shooting the heroin on in at the same time. "Remember what I say, boy." And his voice changed.

I kind of blame heroin for all the years he neglected me. I felt that he could have done much, much better as a musician or as anything that he wanted to be without the heroin, that he would have been a much better man, a much better father. I say he neglected me for all these years because he used dope, or he was in and out of jail because he used dope, or he lost his status as a good musician because he used dope. Everything that he did, instead of blaming him, I blamed on the dope.

My father died when I was twenty-three years of age. I was in the D.C. Jail at the time, and one evening when I was laying in my cell, I got word that I had a visitor. So I go down to the visiting hall. I see it's my mother through the glass, so I pick up the phone and she begin to tell me. She asked me had I heard about my father, and I said no. Well, the first thing come to my mind was that he had some kind of beef or a charge. When she told me he was dead, I don't think I really accepted it right off. I think it got to me more later, after I went back to my cell and I lay down on my bunk. I thought about all the years him and I never really had together, and I thought about them last few months that we were spending together and how much I really did dig the dude. I felt pretty bad about it. I often think of him now and wish that he was around.

I don't know exactly what he died from, but my suspicions are that he died from an overdose of heroin. The last few months him and I had been talking and being together quite a bit. He didn't show any signs of being back on heroin, because him and I used to do a lot of drinking, and a heroin user don't mess with a whole lot of alcohol. But when he died it was Christmas Eve, and I was told that an old friend of his had visited him, one of his old friends that was still about the business of selling narcotics. I think maybe that him and his old friend got together and got high, and by him being off of drugs for so long, it was just too much for him. But that's just my opinion. I don't really know. At the time he died, he was between forty-seven and forty-nine years old.

6

Cops and Robbers

In '64, I got involved in another beef, which was assault on a police. What went down was this. One night me and my boys was hanging around a little spot called Jiffy's Carry-Out. We was doing our usual thing—drinking wine and smoking a little herb—when three of the younger dudes decided to go to the all-night drugstore right around the corner on Alabama Avenue. From what I understand from them, they didn't go in there with the intent to rob or beat anybody up or anything. I think they only really wanted to buy some gum and cigarettes, but by being drunk, they was talking pretty tough, and so the lady behind the counter automatically get scared. Any lady probably would if three teenagers came in looking and talking tough, and smelling like wine. In getting scared, the lady immediately go to get the druggist, but it turned out for the worse, 'cause the druggist couldn't handle the dudes at all. Evidently he got a little pushy or ordered them out of the store, and by them being all fired up, naturally the next thing they did was jump on him.

So now what do you have? You've got a drugstore. You've got a scared lady in the corner somewhere with her hands over her face. You've got a beat-up druggist laying on the floor. You've got three dudes that came in for chewing gum and cigarettes, but now they got two cash registers. So what do they do? They takes the cash. Wasn't nothing to stop them, and it was there. Why would they leave it? They're thieves anyway and supposed to be hustlers, the kind I like to call rustlers. See, when you ain't a real hustler, you're a rustler. There wasn't nothing to stop them, so they just took the money. Afterwards they come to me and immediately started breaking down the money. None of them was even old enough to buy liquor or wine, so after giving me a quick run-down on what had happened, they tell me what they want me to get for them out of the liquor store. But I never get a chance to leave the carry-out. I'm still in Jiffy's when the police walk right in. There was a good fifteen or twenty of us in there, and the police picked them three right out. It's you, you, and you. Just like that. I guess somebody must have gave them a pretty accurate description. This was only about twenty minutes after the robbery, and we just didn't figure the police would come around the corner into Jiffy's looking for the dudes that did it. So after they pick them three, they take them right on out and put them in the scout car. So everybody kind of looking around, kind of wondering, except my friend Goofball and myself —we knowed what was happening.

I goes outside, and the scout car just getting ready to pull off, and I say, "Officer," and walk up to the car. So he say, "Yeah?" I say, "Man, what you locking them up for?" And he said, "Ain't none of your damn business—you want to go?" So I said, "No, I don't wanna go. I just wanna know so I can tell their parents, or if they got a fine, I could pay their fine and get them out."

At that point I had the feeling that I wanted to slow them up. I knew he was going to do exactly what he did. He started acting all wild, saying, "Well, you act like you want to go too!" I said, "No, sir, I don't wanna go, sir. I just wanna find out. One of them is my cousin." So I'm acting real humble and polite. Meanwhile, this little kid, about eight or nine years old, see that the man is rapping kind of hard on me, so he go in the carry-out and tell Goofball. He say, "I think Johnny is getting ready to jump on that police."

Goofball runs out the carry-out and hollers something—what, I don't exactly remember—but I know when he ran up to the car, the roller that I'm talking to swing the door open and grabbed him. When he did that, him and Goofball immediately started fighting. So now they rumble. Then the other police, he hesitate for a long while. Finally he gets out of the scout car and come around behind me; but by me paying attention to what Goofball and this first roller's doing, I don't pay him no mind.

Next thing I knowed, the dude was all over me, all on my back. I pushed him away or pushed him down, and when he came back up, he had his gun out and he's pointing it right in my face. I was scared. When somebody pointing a .38 at you at a short distance, the barrel of the gun looks like a cannon. In my imagination, I could feel bullets going through my body, tearing my body up. I knew one thing—that I had to get that gun. So this what I proceeded to do. I charge into him; and when I charge into him, instead of pulling the trigger, he drew the gun back and hit me across my eye, busted my eyebrow open. But when he hit me, I fell forwards instead of backwards, and I finally got his wrists and got the gun from him. I think he was as scared as I was, 'cause it seemed like he didn't know what to do.

Once I got the gun, I threw it under the scout car to get it out of the way. I didn't want to shoot him with it. I was so high on wine that I just charged into that gun and then started to beat up on him. So I'm over top of him, really working this dude over. I'm busting his jaws. Ronnie and the other two guys who robbed the drugstore get out of the scout car, and I tell them to run. So Bruce, Claude, and Ronnie run, but Ronnie come back and says to the police, "You dead now, sucker." And he started kicking him in the head with these thick Li'l Abner–type boots we used to wear, and I started stomping him too.

Then we start hearing more sirens, more police coming. So I looked at Goofball, and he got the other police where they half in and half out the car, with Goofball on top. So

I tell Goofball, "C'mon, Goof, c'mon. Let's move! Let's go!"
But he's got himself so wound up that he just continued to
beat the dude. As I turned to leave, this dude that I'd been
beating got up off the ground. He can't hardly see or nothing, but he's still trying to hold on to me. So Cub, a friend
of mine who was still a very young teenager at the time,
came up behind the man and yoked him. And when he
yoked him, the man just fell from it 'cause he was so weak.
Okay. Now by this time scout cars are pulling in from all
directions. I think the fear of getting shot in the back
stopped Goofball from running, but it ain't stopped me.
They fired at me about three times but they missed, and I
got away.

They did get Goofball, and he was locked up. So we
trying to find out exactly what they gonna charge him with.
First, we get this lady named Alice to call down there on the
pretense that she was his mother. And they tell her, well, he
just locked up for disorderly. But I knew better. So I say,
"It's some kind of a trick." They know that when one of us
be in any kind of trouble, we storms Number 11 [the station
house]. If there's a fine, then we pay the fine; if it's a bond,
we pay the bond. So what they trying to do is get someone
to come down there that was involved in this thing.

Meanwhile Claude and Ronnie still walking around the
street instead of going on home. So the police pick them up,
and Claude tells everything! I'm over at Ann's house when
the police come to get me. I say, "What's happening, man?
What's going on?" And Morgan, the roller, say, "Man, you
know what's happening." I say, "No, I don't, man." He say,
"What happened to your eye?" By this time my eye kinda
swelled, and I've got several cuts. So I said, "Me and my
woman was rumbling, that's what happened to it."

But they take me anyway and put me in one scout car,
Claude and Ronnie are setting in another. When we get
down the station, they bring Goofball from the hospital. His
head all wrapped up like he got a turban on 'cause they had

jumped on him so much. And he still arguing and fussing and cussing: "Lemme go. I fight any one of you motherfuckers. Come on with it." They got him handcuffed, and this big old Southern redneck just walked right up to Goofball, grabbed him in the collar, and hit him in the stomach. Boom! He knocked Goofball down. So when he knocked Goofball down, I'm not handcuffed or nothing—we's sitting in the office waiting to be questioned—I jumps up, and one of them says, "I wish I had you in Alabama."

So I start cussing and hollering and saying all kinds of things, and next thing I know two rollers hit me at the same time. One hit me in the face, and the other one hit me in my throat, which took my breath away. So I fell to one knee. Then Ronnie jumped up. He say, "Man, don't hit him, man. Don't hit him no more, he hurt." One of the rollers say, "Shut up. We'll kick your ass too." And Ronnie say, "But man, I'm a juvenile!" But before he could get "juvenile" all the way out of his mouth, one of them had smacked him clean across the desk.

Finally what they did was take Bruce, Ronnie, and myself over to Washington Hospital. But Goofball, he raise so much hell, they don't take him. Plus they don't really need to take him to be identified 'cause he was caught right on the spot. They carrying us over to the hospital, 'cause that's where the two police at that was in the fight. When we get over there, they take us onto the ward, and the two police lying right next to each other. The three of us stand in front of them, and one of the rollers that's with us say, "Any of these dudes look familiar?" So the one dude, his eye was swollen and he was trying to look, and then he say, "I think it was that one," and he points to Ronnie. The other one also picked Ronnie. Ronnie immediately go into his act. "Oh, Lord, no! It wasn't me, mister, please! It wasn't. Look at me good!" Get to opening up his coat and, "Look at me good, mister. It wasn't me!" So he carried on like that for about ten minutes, and he changed their mind. The dude wasn't really sure. He say, "Well, maybe it wasn't him." And then one of the detectives say, "It was him all right. It was him and this bastard here too," talking about me. He say, " 'Cause Claude Williams here already told us it was them." I looked at Claude. I couldn't *believe* it. He had told.

Then the police say, "Take him to the receiving home. Take the other to central cell block, and take good care of that witness." They put us in a wagon, took Ronnie on to the receiving home, and took me on to central cell block.

My trial happened in small court just a day or so later. I was only charged with a misdemeanor because the police just wouldn't admit that I knocked him down four times. He said he kept slipping on the ice. There was something the judge asked him that was very important. The judge said, "Officer, at the time this incident happened, what police equipment did you have?" This was the officer's answer: "We have a police car, a radio police car." "What equipment did you have on your person?" "I had a blackjack, I had a .38 service revolver, I had a night stick." "What did the defendant have?" "The defendant had his fists balled and started to me as if to assault me. Just as he approached me, I fell on the ice." The man was afraid to admit in court that I had knocked him down. The judge made a comment, something like "You was having quite a bit of problem keeping your footing, wasn't you?" His partner came in with an altogether different story, and my lawyer tore him to shreds on it.

If the police had told the truth about the matter, if the police had said, "The defendant approached the police car, inquired about the young men that we had arrested, then another youth appeared, and my partner and this youth got into a scuffle, and the first youth and I got into a scuffle, and he did assault me a number of times—also took my service revolver, threw it under a car, and knocked me down several times," then they would have got a conviction. But they lied. They didn't want the police to look bad. They wanted the police to be able to handle the youth on the street, but they couldn't handle us. I came from a pretty rough mob, so that was understandable.

I think the whole thing is this. A district attorney have a job to do, and his job consists of working closely with the police. In my particular case, I believe it was a breakdown of communication between the police and the D.A., because usually he will know just about what a witness is going to say, especially a government witness—not only know, but he would coach him or her in the government's favor in a lot of ways. Maybe the police in my case wasn't truthful with the D.A. I did assault the man, but I never got on the stand. I never opened my mouth. I just sat there and listened, 'cause that was my best defense. My best defense was none at all—just to be quiet and let them tell lie after lie. Most judges do know the important thing, which is that police and D.A.'s do tell lies as well as lawyers and defendants.

It's not a one-way street. When you get up there and you put your hand on that bible—"I swear to tell the truth, the whole truth, and nothing but the truth, so help me God"—the first thing come out of your mouth is "I didn't do it." But it weighs out. It weighs out because the police tell their equal amount of lies. The D.A.'s tell their equal amount of lies. All boils down to one thing. The police is a government witness, and he get up there, and his job is to try to help the D.A. to get a conviction, and the D.A. tells his lies or fabricate the truth or bends it out of proportion so he can get a conviction. On the other hand, the defense attorney also fabricates or bends the truth so he can get a better reputation for himself as well as get his client off.

I'm not saying that this happens all the time. I'm not saying that all D.A.'s are liars. I'm not saying that all police are. I have had occasions where police got on the stand and told it just as he had wrote it in his book. (They carry a little book and make their little notes in it of what happened when they made their arrests.)

But in my particular case, the judge didn't go for the police story at all, and I was found not guilty. They let me go. Ronnie gets sent to a training school, and Goofball got sixty days. I guess I was pretty lucky all the way around, 'cause that roller sure had a chance to shoot me when I went after him. But I experienced that more than once; I experienced that about three times. Much as I really hate the police and the system, knowing how dirty and nasty some of them can be, this still don't apply to everyone, and I think they be a little reluctant to hurt people at times. If I'd had a gun or a knife, it might have been different, but I guess he figured he could pretty much handle me without shooting me.

That assault on a police case took place while I was waiting to go to trial on a robbery charge I got picked up for in '63. In the end, that went back down to little court as assault, because the grand jury refused to indict me on robbery. This is what happened.

A few days after the robbery took place, I saw Officer Morgan sitting in the shopping center in an unmarked car with the dude that had been robbed. Okay. So when I walked by, naturally Morgan called me to the car. He asked me what's happening, and I gave him a whole lot of bullshit about I was straightening up. At the same time the dude that had been robbed was trying to see if he could make an identification of me. Evidently he couldn't make a positive identification right then, but a day or two later I was arrested and charged with the robbery.

Now, I'm over at the jail, and I've been laying there for maybe a couple of weeks waiting to go to court, when one of the old captains came and told me that there was an officer downstairs concerning the robbery I was charged with. He said they can do one of two things. They could take you downtown to put you on a line-up, or you can agree to have a line-up right here at the jail, and you can pick the people that you want to be on the line-up with you.

I was a little shaky about this. But after thinking, I decided the jail might be the best idea, because if I went downtown, I would have been on a line-up probably with nobody
other than myself that fit the description that the dude had
gave. When you're downtown, you're standing on a line-up
with eight people. It's all dark out there. You can't see what's
happening, but everybody can see you standing up there on
that little stage. The arena, I call it. The small arena. The big
arena is the courtroom, believe me. The lion's den.

I thought how if I went downtown, Morgan and the
witness probably would be sitting together, and when they
call me forward, I could just see Officer Morgan nudging
the witness, "That's him, that's him." So I figured that my
chances were better at the jail. The captain himself walked
around the cell block. I always know most of the dudes at
the jail, and when things like this come up, most dudes are
always willing to help, especially if they got a tight alibi or
if they had something heavy and it just don't make no difference.

Now, I'm walking around the block with the captain,
talking to some of my friends and asking them if they'd
appear on the line-up with me and getting guys that's about
my same size. I'm also thinking about the question of clothes.
I knew that if I stood in a line-up downtown, everybody
would have on regular street clothes, which would probably
all be different. At the jail they wasn't going to give us no
clothes, so we'd all have on them blue denim pants and blue
denim shirts, and look pretty much alike. So I got eight
dudes, most of which was my friends. For instance, there
was a dude on the other side of the block that looked a lot
like me only a little shorter. The inmate that worked on the
admitting desk said to me, "According to the time of your
robbery, this particular dude was already here, so if he's
picked, then he's still clear." I said, "Solid."

Now, the line-up was held in the rotunda of the jail. It's
the place where you see your lawyer, have visits, make calls,

and so on. Anyhow, it was in the middle of the day, so the rotunda was pretty clear. We lined up at the rotunda. The only thing we don't have on alike is shoes because you keep your shoes. They take your clothes, but you wear your own shoes. Everyone I picked was pretty much my size, pretty much my same complexion, and pretty much my same age.

Now, this captain that told me about the whole thing in the beginning was a hell of a dude 'cause he would not let Officer Morgan come up with the witness. I'm sorry that I can't remember his name. I only remember him as being an elderly white dude that had been at the jail for some time. Anyway, he made Morgan stay in the back of the rotunda. The witness came down the line, and he looked each and every one of us over one by one. In fact, he did it about three times. He walked up and down, looking and looking. Finally he picked a friend of mine who at the time of that robbery had already been in jail.

With that kind of evidence, they had to send it back to small court, which is where it should have been in the first place. When it was sent back to small court, a trial was held on assault charges, and this very same witness got on the stand and identified me. What had happened to me in that line-up before didn't even come up now, and I was convicted. So it was back to the Youth Center for another three years.

*   *

When I got out of the Youth Center again it was '66, and I was twenty-four years of age. About this time they were starting halfway houses. I was one of the first to go into this halfway house thing because I couldn't make straight up parole. At the Youth Center, a lot of dudes just go out on the street and report to their parole officer once a month; but if they felt a dude need more help to stay out of trouble, they'd send him to a halfway house instead. Evidently they knew that I was one of those dudes.

Now, at the halfway house they got no guards but counselors—counselors for everything. Personal counselors, group counselors, job counselors, counselors assistant to counselors. I think them joints are run too tight. I had to keep telling myself over and over, "This is pre-release." You've got a curfew, and if you're late you're punished. And you've got to have bedcheck, and a man can come and search your room any time he wants or search your person any time he wants. And no broads. I was fortunate because I had a room by myself, and every now and then I would sneak a broad in. You could go home on the weekend—Saturday or Sunday but not both, and only for that day and not overnight. We could stay up and watch television if we was upstairs. If we was downstairs outside, then we had to be right out in front till twelve, just like little kids. And then at twelve we promptly go in, and the man would take a head count.

The halfway house was on the third floor of the YMCA. Much as I disliked most of it, I kind of liked the challenge of dealing with this one particular white dude. I really dug him. He was the regular night counselor, had a big old jolly belly and a hell of a beard. He could play several instruments, and he used to play in some club. He was an alright dude. He used to try to catch us sneaking in and sneaking out, and that's where he got his thing from, trying to think what we would do next. And we got our thing from trying to get out on him all the time. If he caught you, there wasn't no reporting you to the man and getting no longer time. No. He'd just say, "I got you this time." I used to go up to the top floor, come down the fire escape, climb in the window, and he'd be waiting in my closet. He'd be sitting in the closet!

One night I wanted to go out bad, and I know he loves to eat. So I said, "Hey, chief, I'm getting ready to go up around Ben's Chile Bowl. Do you want something?" He said, "Yeah, bring me a chiliburger." I said, "Okay," and went on out. I ain't come back till about ten minutes to six in the morning, just before he got off and the other man come in. He said, "Hey, what happened to my chiliburger, man?" I said, "Man, I've been with my woman. I ain't been thinking about no chiliburger." And he and I laughed.

The other dudes that was inmates there with me was mostly friends of mine. There was one or two I didn't know, but most of us had been together in one jail or another somewhere. We were already pretty tight. But there was one or two counselors that I really didn't like. Now, I've had friends in a number of places like this, and overall the kind of people who run them—now, this is just my opinion—but a lot of them seem like homosexuals to me. They always nice to all the dudes, coming on with the suits and the ties and all that, but they really got all this girl in them. Whatever you are, then be that. If being a homosexual is your bag, then be a homosexual. If being a dyke is your bag, then be a dyke; or bisexual, then do that. If you're straight, then stay straight. Whatever. But don't be what I call a closet queen. An undercover punk. And that's what it seems like they was. They was undercover punks. They might be bigshots in the daytime, but from all I've heard, as soon as they get you in the office, they trying to zip the fly of your pants down and all that kind of stuff.

Of course, the halfway house did have some advantages if you really wanted to get involved and square up. For one thing, they were pretty good at helping you find a job. They got me one or two cooking jobs, but the only thing was that the people I worked for knew my background, and this becomes a drag because they never want to give you the top cooking spot no matter how good you are. I remember one time I went to that university up here in town—George Washington. They had some openings for a cook, and this dude Johnson and myself applied. I had taught Johnson how to cook. We went there through I think it was the Restaurant Association. So we sitting in the office, and the chef come in and we answered a few simple questions like "How long are you supposed to cook a roast of so and so many pounds?"

Well, I believe Johnson and myself could have handled that job pretty well because it was our style of cooking, what I call cafeteria-style cooking—cooking for large bodies of people. So the man tell me, "Yes, I think you ought to work out well, but right now we not hiring no cooks. What we really need is a man to keep this place cleaned up around here. We need some mop men, and we need a pot and pan man." So I said, "Oh, no. I didn't come here to mop floors. I came here to cook. There *was* a cook position open. Now, if you don't want to give me the cook position, say that. Or if you don't think I can cook well enough or that I answered the questions satisfactorily enough, tell me now. But don't tell me about no damn mop and no buckets, 'cause that ain't my style, and I ain't going to do it." Naturally we didn't get the jobs. So the record thing is kind of a problem.

In '66, when I was in the halfway house, I was working at this quaint little place called the Swiss Chalet. A lady owned the joint, but she stayed away a lot. She was from Switzerland somewhere. Every now and then she was coming around to the place, and I'd see her and talk to her. I think that she liked me, and I improved in my work because I ran into a lot of new things that I really didn't know about, like fondues and stuff like that.

The dude that ran it—the manager—had promised me, he said, "After you're here for a while and you learn the recipes, then we will talk about a raise." So I said, "Well, that's hip." Now, I had one main problem. I couldn't understand the waitresses 'cause most of them were Swiss or German. I wanted this job so bad, I wanted to do well so bad, that I ended up getting a friend of mine that could draw, that had some art techniques. I would describe to him what the dish would look like when I finished fixing it or show him a picture on the menu, and he would draw it. We had a couple of sheets of long cardboard, and he'd draw each dish on it and the name of it under it. And I had studied the recipes over and over and over—the whole thing took about a month. Finally I'm getting things in order, so when a waitress come in and I can't understand what she's ordering, I just have her point to it. She point to it, and I proceed to fix it.

After about six weeks of this, I approached the man about a raise. I said, "Well, man, I think I got it down pretty pat now." I had it so good where in the middle of the day, when business was real slow, they could leave and do whatever they had to do and come back in a couple of hours. I could run it, just myself and a couple of waitresses. But when I asked him about a raise, he didn't think I deserved it. So I took it for a couple of more days. So many things that the waitresses do—simple little things like building up little horseradishes in cups, slicing bread—no cook supposed to do. This is a waitress job. But when the waitresses don't feel like doing it or come in late, then I would have to do it. Then I asked the man was I a cook or a waitress? If I was a waitress, then give me a skirt. If I'm a cook, then let me keep my pants on. He got kind of angry, and so did I. So I left.

I had quite a few jobs—all kinds. I worked as everything from cook to running a junkyard, but they never lasted no long period of time. I worked two or three days, then quit. Most of the time it's my own fault. I can't say, "Well, I had a record, so everybody was down on me." No, this didn't happen all the time. Ninety percent of the time it was me. I really was the actual cause of losing a job, or I just quit or did something purposely to get fired or something like that. But the only reason I had the job in the beginning was to please my parole officer.

7

Hustlers and Squares

The whole time I was in the Youth Center, from '64 to '66, Ann stayed in my corner while I was down. By the time I was put in the halfway house, Ann and the kids—three wonderful, beautiful children—Cynthia, Darlene, and John Jr.—was living with my mother. They had been living together almost the whole time I was away. I had what I wanted.

The first day I was out was a Tuesday, and no one knew I was coming home. I had only a few hours before I had to go back to the halfway house. They were all glad I was out, and I stayed home with Ann, the kids, and the rest of the family for that few hours, 'cause I knew I couldn't come home again until that weekend.

After two days of looking for a job and hearing all that bullshit from the people at the halfway house, I was restless. So that night I went out down the fire escape, got a cab, and went to my grandparents' house. From there I walked to where Ann and my mother lived. I went into the apartment through the back way, but before I got to the hallway, I heard Ann talking to someone. She was saying, "Eddie, Johnny's home now, and what we've had is over." I understood then that she'd been messing with another nigger while I was away, and she was trying to drop him before I found out. But it was too late—I heard them.

As I stood there, I didn't know what to do. I was so damn

mad I wanted to die, but most of all I wanted to kill Ann and this dude Eddie. My mind and heart was full of hate. I couldn't get a hold on myself, and deep down I don't think I wanted to. I knew I was going to do something, but I kept asking myself over and over, What can I do? What? I couldn't even move. If only it had been someone else but Ann, anyone but Ann. She crossed me. Ann had crossed me. This couldn't be happening, but it was.

I got myself together and stepped into the light of the hallway. I said, "Bitch, you jive bitch. You crossed me." Ann looked up. I was standing there mad enough to do anything, and she knew it. She said, "Johnny, Johnny!" and the dude's eyes almost popped out. He was scared. He didn't know me, but he had heard of me. Ann could tell by the look on my face that I was going to hurt them.

The dude took off, ran into my mother's apartment and out the window. My mother's boyfriend was in the house too, and when he saw the look of death on my face, he went out the window too. But it was too late for Ann; I had my hands on her. She said, "Johnny, please, please. I was telling him that it was over 'cause you're home." I said, "I heard you, but it shouldn't have ever started, bitch." So I beat her and beat her, and all the while I was beating her I was calling her all kinds of names. She fell down, and still I beat her. I was out of my mind. My mother and sister was trying to stop me, but they couldn't. Then my mother hit me with something. I turned and was ready to hit her. It was the first time in my life I really was going to hit my mother. But I stopped. I looked down at Ann at my feet; then I looked at my mother. They all were crying—Ann, Moms, and my sister.

I ran out of the house 'cause I knew I was going to cry too. I couldn't hold back the tears, and I didn't want them to see me cry, because they never had seen me cry before aside from Moms when I was a baby. Man, did I cry! For two days I cried. I guess Ann was crying too, 'cause for the next three days she was in the hospital. I came home that weekend from the halfway house, and Ann was out of the hospital. It was a Sunday. I didn't say anything to her. I wanted to say, "Ann, please forgive me. I'm sorry. It won't ever happen again." But the words just wouldn't come out, so I said nothing. That night, when it was time for me to go back to the halfway house, I got in the cab, and Ann looked right into my eyes and said, "Johnny, I love you and always will." Again I wanted to say, "Forgive me," but nothing came out. That same night she left me.

I guess one of the reasons I got so mad was because messing around with other dudes wasn't something a woman was supposed to do. A dude can have a lot of women. In the old days or even now, growing up around the neighborhood you have this little girlfriend, that little girlfriend. The more girlfriends you have, the more girlfriends you going to get, 'cause the girls are constantly promoting you. "Wow, that Johnny, he's something else! I was with him the other night and wow!" So she telling her girlfriend. So now the girlfriend doing little things to make me notice her. So I might slide around her way. Then she got something to tell somebody else. And it just go on like this—the more you have, the more you get.

Now, a woman, a woman can be with two or three dudes. Say, she have a dude tonight, have another one tomorrow, and another one the next day. Automatically she becomes a canine, a dog. That bitch ain't nothing—she'll fuck anybody, any way, any time. It just don't seem right for a dame to be messing with a whole bunch of dudes at one time. Now, I have known dames that did it in a way where they made it right to onlooking people. A lot of people wouldn't say it was exactly *wrong*. I always say everybody should do what they feel like they want to do. But it's just a sticker, the label that other people have put on you. They would automatically mark her as being a dog.

Most dudes give their women a lot of respect. I demand a lot of respect from any woman, especially a woman that

I'm involved with. But in order to get the respect that I demand, I give a lot of respect. Very seldom would one woman that I know or be with be aware of another woman. I remember a time when it didn't make no difference whether she knew or didn't. And I had a little thing I used to say: "I don't need you, bitch. Just like I made you a star, I can make somebody else a star." I thought I was God's greatest gift to women. That's what I thought, but after heroin cleared out my brain, I found out what it really was. Everybody just wanted dope or money.

In the thing with Ann, my reputation played a big part, because this wasn't supposed to happen to me. Maybe to other dudes, but not to me. And then I cared about Ann; I really did. Maybe it was wrong, maybe it was the way I think, the way I act, but I just couldn't accept that happening to me. If she's my woman, then she's my woman—that's it.

I guess my feelings were really hurt, 'cause I was kind of involved. That's another thing about me that I try to conceal, especially since I became older. In other words, I could really care for you, but I would always keep it with me. I would try very hard not to show it on the outside or inside for fear that I just get kind of wrapped up in people, especially when somebody's real nice to me.

I done had quite a few women, all types—square, whores, married—the whole lot. There's been times when there's been no feelings—I just liked her, or dug the way she looked or the way she dressed or the way she acted. But there's been several times when I've been deeply involved with this person. Then it really hurts when they cross me. And when I'm hurt, I strike out. Always. There's no other way for me to get relief but to strike out. Then, when I do strike out, I am relieved if I feel like I hurt them as much as they hurt me. There's been a couple of dames that I really had it bad for, including Ann. But I kept telling myself that she is a woman. I'm saying, "Like Johnny, you can't stop her from being a woman. And this is the normal function of a woman—to have a man." But I forgot all that when I saw she had crossed me.

When Ann left me, the kids stayed with my mother—they were about nine, six, and five at the time. After I got out of the halfway house, I used to see them every day 'cause I lived not too far from my mother's house in S.E. They would come down to my apartment on weekends, and I would go to my mother's house every day. Ann used to go to my mother's house regular to see them, though not every day like me.

It was more usual for the mother and not the father to keep the kids in a situation like that, but it was real important to me that I have them near me. I had been in positions with different broads with younger kids not as old as my kids were at that particular time, kids that wasn't mine. Eventually these kids would begin to call me "Daddy." I didn't think it was fair, and I would always discourage that. My main reason for not wanting my kids to be around Ann and another man was that real deep fear within me that they would accept this other man. Even though they knew that I was their father, they might begin to call him "Daddy." Or maybe it was even deeper than that. Maybe I thought that I would lose their love in some way or other. Because my kids are everything to me.

I've always been real close to the kids I've had with Ann. I always was around Cynthia, Darlene, and John Jr.—I call them Sugar, Bruce, and Wank. After all, Ann lived next door to me, and even though I went to jail when Sugar was small, before that, when she was just born, I used to keep her with me all the time. As for Bruce and Wank, even though most of the time they were young I was away from them in jail, my family and I still had a lot of contact with them.

Now, I've got some kids that I've never seen in the flesh. I've only seen pictures of two kids. I've got kids that I haven't seen since they were two or three years old that's just as old as Sugar now, and Sugar's fifteen. I have a daughter named Carolyn that's fifteen years old, and I haven't seen her since she was six or seven. But them three, they was always around me, always close-by. And I guess I did care more.

There is nothing I would like better than to get all my kids together—all at one time—just to get to know each and every last one of them myself. Just get into each and every last one of them like I am with Brown Sugar, Bruce, and Wank. All of my sons are named John Allen, but they had nicknames. I would like them to really get into each other, not like me and Rodney so late in the years. But it seems like that is the way it's going to be if they ever meet at all.

*   *

When I came home from the Youth Center in '66, a lot of people had got more aggressive—even myself. A few of the guys had gone into the service. Some that wouldn't stick up when I left in '64, by the time I came home in '66, they were sticking up. A few had went into narcotics. There was a few that had got older and got smarter, because they got out of it: but for me and most of my close friends, all we did was get more aggressive in crime.

After Ann left me and while I was still at the halfway house in August of '66, I was coming back from a home visit one day when some of the dudes I knew told me two dames was looking for me. No one knew who they were, but they were coming back later. I went up to my room, and about an hour later, somebody yelled up, "Hey, Big Al. Them two dames are back." I went down to see who it was and found an old girlfriend of mine—Princess.

I had first met Princess in '62, when I was just coming out of the Youth Center. She was fourteen or fifteen years old then, and she was one of the neighborhood girls that I was checking out. I dug the way she looked, I dug the way she dressed, but I knew she was kind of young, so I was a little bit afraid of her. At first, I used to keep away from her, but it seemed like everywhere I went, she was there. She was just there. Anyhow, I end up knocking her up, and right after I knocked her up I went to jail. This was in '63. She didn't do a lot of sticking by me in jail. She came to see me once or twice and sent me a few pictures, but that was about it.

After I'd been in jail awhile I started to hear stories through the grapevine about Princess. She had the baby and didn't go back to school. Then I heard that she had started working in the red-light district. So then I knew that she was a prostitute, a big mama, and that she was getting money. I heard that she was really getting over in that world, doing pretty good.

So when she showed up at the halfway house that day I was glad to see her. She was looking even better than before. We went into a room to be by ourselves, and she started telling me why and how she became a whore. After I went to jail, she got a job in a carry-out uptown. Every night she and her friend, Lollipop, would watch the whores and the pimps with big cars and lots of money come in there. Lollipop and Princess felt like they looked as good as any of the whores around there, so why should they be making forty dollars a week when they could be making that and more every night? So they started tricking on their own as outlaw whores, which is what a whore is when she's got no pimp. They eventually dug that being without a pimp was dangerous, so they got pimps to front for them, and pretty soon the pimps was taking all their money.

Then the question came up about what should she do now that I was back? Should she continue to prostitute, or should she go back and try to find a job? Was we going to try to make it together again? I told her to give me a little time to think about it. In the meanwhile there wasn't no sense in her stopping her profession, since it was paying off so well, and at that particular time I was just coming home and kind of dragging my feet, looking around for a hip partner so I could do a few things as far as stickup went.

So Princess started giving me some of the money she was making, and for the rest of the time I was at the halfway house, I was what you'd call semi-pimping. She was out hustling and was giving me a lot of money, but she didn't cut back the pimp she already had till I got out in September of '66 and moved into a place in S.E.

Now, I really hadn't had nothing to do with prostitutes before, so I learned a lot about it in the time I was pimping —from September till November of that year. A whore needs a pimp to protect her from a lot of things—from Johns that don't want to pay, from other rip-off artists and hustlers on the street. Take 14th and T Streets—quite a few prostitutes all up and down that area. So now, of course, everybody can't do good. Somebody got to do bad. There's a few outlaw whores on the street. When a dude or maybe some other dame know that a broad is a outlaw and she don't have a pimp, if she making good money, they'll rob her every night. They'll wait just as pleasant till she trick with every trick she going to trick with, and then they'll take all the money. And there's nothing the outlaw whore can do 'cause very seldom would she carry a weapon.

Princess taught me a lot of things, like if she gave me two hundred dollars, then she'll always be holding back a hundred unless I was witty enough to outsmart her out of it. I was supposed to get all the money 'cause I was the pimp, I was the protection. Whoring is a business. So a whore got to keep control of herself at all times. There's no time for pleasure—this is a money thing. You saving yourself for your main dude, which usually is your pimp. When she come home and get into bed with her pimp, now is fun time. Then she can let herself go completely; she can whoop and holler and do whatever she pleases.

I had a small stable of girls—I think the most I ever had

was five at one time. The thing with me was I enjoy sex quite a bit. If in the event they made a nice piece of money the night before, I would often say, "Well, you all just stay home tonight." They knew what that meant—that I was going to try to run through all five of them. Now, during this time my brother Nut was about fifteen or sixteen, and this was a real, real kick to him. I used to let him pick out a dame. I'd say, "Which one you want? Take two for tonight." At the time we had a pretty good joint to live in on Mississippi Avenue, three apartments attached but setting by themselves. (Every time I go past there now I have to laugh—they've turned it into a police station!) Our living conditions was good because we could afford it. At that particular time, we had the money. It wasn't a long-time thing, but it was good while it lasted. Like the good angel said to the bad angel, "I told you to be good or you'd lose your wings." And the bad angel told him, "Yeah, I lost my wings. But I was hell while I had them." I wasn't no real down-to-earth pimp—one stomp-down pimp—but when I was pimping, I really was raising hell.

My whores were giving all their money to me. This was part of their lifestyle, what they accepted. A pimp, he would provide her a place to stay that was usually real hip. Clothes, all the necessary things that she would need, occasionally a little money for spending change. But other than that, it was strictly her giving him. Like I heard a broad say, "That nigger used to be my pimp. I bought him a Cadillac." They proud of the fact. It's a status thing—how good their pimp is doing.

There was also a lot of things that went on as far as trying to get the best girls. If I feel like one of my girls is not doing up to par or that maybe another pimp could handle her better, then that would bring on a trade. You could trade whores. You could even give one away to another pimp as a gift or to pay a debt, or you could lose her in a card game.

A whore had to be tough, because if she start off at sixteen out there on the block, by the time she's twenty-four or twenty-five, she's done for. None of the good pimps want her, and she has to figure out what to do. A lot of them broads will go on then and be madams and end up with their own girls and their own joints, and that's hip; but a lot of them just fall to the wayside. Like, I talked to Princess about a month ago, and now she's an alcoholic, stumbling out of her mind. Others find a dude and actually fall in love and get married. I have heard it said by many dudes—especially old pimps—that whores make the best wives. I've heard that said many times.

Even though my whores were making a lot of money, I just didn't like pimping that much. It ain't my style, even though a lot of dudes said I had the coldness for it as far as heart went. I missed stickup quite a bit. I always kept my eyes open for different things—casing joints. I would watch places and watch different people. Watch dudes going to night deposit boxes. It was a habit that I couldn't break. In fact, I do it even now. What I really missed was the excitement of sticking up and the planning and the getting away with it—whether it come out to a car chase or just a plain old-fashioned foot race outrunning the police—knowing all the little alleys and shortcuts to go through. I think that's why I was only in the pimping bag for a few months.

Another thing I didn't like about pimping was that it was really hard work. Pimping is a twenty-four-hour job. Ain't no rest. You constantly plotting and planning and scheming and playing on the broads. Your conversation always have to be up to par. You always have to tell them the things that they want to hear in order to keep your stable together. There's all kinds of pimps. A gorilla pimp just whup a broad all the time, and they fear him. Then there's the supercool dudes that raps everything off, and I kind of put myself in that thing. I was a rapper. You had to constantly think and plot—like, say you didn't want a particular whore any more.

You couldn't just fire her: you had to think of a good reason, plus make some money off her by maybe selling her to somebody. Pimping is a day-by-day all-the-time thing, and I always had to maintain my image. And then, that sex thing was taking a terrible toll on me. By me being the type of dude that I am, I was really deep into that thing, and it was many a time when they really should've been out working when they was home with me. I was just about killing myself. So pimping took a lot of energy and a lot of thinking. Constantly rapping, telling the broad something, then contradicting yourself and getting confused as to what broad you told what. You got to keep all this straight, can't have your shit raggly no time.

I really didn't have no lot of trouble with my whores 'cause Princess helped run my stable, and they all got along together beautifully. There's a kind of sisterhood thing with whores. Most of the time they're a good bunch of dames as far as sticking together, sticking with one another, helping each other out. I even found through experience that a lot of them stick together much better than some so-called good girls or broads that are straight and are supposed to be good girlfriends. A lot of them are just good broads that got bad breaks, like they got turned out or was runaways. So they didn't give me no hassle. I guess my main problem was that I let sex make a bum out of me, just like I did with drugs later on.

*   *

I would say that the majority of broads that messed around with drugs were into the prostitution bag too. A lot of them, that's all they knew. I have also known a lot of broads that deal drugs themselves to support their habit, or they steal— they're boosters, shoplifters. They'd work in teams. There'd be anywhere from four to eight of them that every morning have a driver take them from store to store, Maryland to Washington to Virginia. Then they come back in the afternoon and lay all their merchandise out for display in the high hustling area. The crime-ridden areas, they call it. Normally the people around there can afford to buy it, especially the drug dealers, who might not even give up money. They might deal for drugs: "Well, that'll be a spoon of dope for that particular shirt or that jacket."

Very, very few broads go into individual stickup by theirself. I do know a broad named Ocean and a little broad named Carol, and they done very well together. Carol bought a car, a Cadillac, of course, and somebody went to the point of cutting up the top of her car—a convertible—and the tires. I assumed that it had to be a dude that's jealous of her for being so good at stickup.

Of course, broads always got the advantage, especially when it come to sticking up drug dealers. A dude will let a broad in his house any time, 'cause he's not expecting no dangerous move from her. Now, I've worked with quite a few dames. I had some dames that did nothing but look good, stand up, and knock on the door. When the dude peeked through there and see this fine dame, he immediately opened up. The next thing he knew, he on the floor and I'm stomping all over him.

But I'd say that most of the girls that growed up with me ended up on the welfare roll, with an armful of babies or married to some no-good sucker. A whole lot of them didn't participate in illegal things other than to steal on a small scale. There was only one or two that really got over, 'cause most of them started having babies at a very early age and seemed to be just too tied down with that to get into anything illegal.

For a man, pimping is a good way of making money, but the fastest way is narcotics, and the safest and best way of all is numbers. The numbers business is the greatest business of all. In my opinion, it's one of the biggest, biggest businesses that's in the United States today. Poor people and rich people alike, they all play numbers. You play numbers on so many things. A broad with six kids and fifty cents to buy a loaf of bread for their breakfast can have a dream that some number or other will come about; and she would take half of that fifty cents and play a number. Most people, all they know is for a nickel they can get twenty-five dollars if they hit. If you hit big, ten or fifteen dollars bring a couple thousand dollars. That's your money. You don't pay no taxes; you don't have to pay nobody. But what they don't know is that the odds of hitting the number in the first place is 999 to 1.

Everybody play numbers. People got pet numbers, numbers they play every day. Playing numbers can be a real important part of living for a lot of people. Whenever there's a hit, it's publicized, and that make everybody else more anxious to play. When Sonny Liston and Floyd Patterson had their big fight, Sonny Liston weighed, I think, two hundred twelve pounds, and everybody got on that number. The number came up.

People play numbers for different reasons. You might dream about a dog biting somebody or somebody falling into some water or catching some fish. They got dream books where you has to look all this up. Like, around my grandmother's house, it's nothing unusual to find a dream book anywhere. "You know, I dreamt about so and so the other night." "Look it up here in the dream book. That's 102. Better play that for about a week." See, for every kind of dream, a number goes with it, and that's the number you bet.

The people who run the numbers business don't like to mess with a good thing, so they usually run it very fair. Say John Q, Average American, played 000 every day. So he going to put a dollar on that every day, and that's a dollar that man don't have every day. So now, after the man had played the number for five or ten years and it ain't never come up, it come up, and they don't want to pay him. But they think of all the money they done made off him and say, "Well, give the man his money, and he'll continue to play the numbers."

The highest people I know in the numbers business was the backers. I robbed one or two backers. The numbers backer, the boss, he take the money from all over the city from all the runners, all the other little dudes in between. Then that boss got to turn in a certain amount to his boss, one of a few top men in Washington that eventually end up with all the numbers money. But they in turn only take a certain percentage and pass it on to the mob. Nobody really know where it all end up—all anybody knows is that it's the mob.

That's been one of my little ambitions—to get into the numbers business. But I've been too busy doing other things and never take the time, 'cause in the beginning it's kind of a slow grind. If I wanted to go into numbers right now, the first thing I do is get my own book, which means that I would have to have some kind of stake in case someone betting with me got a hit. So you have to have a bankroll. The only other way to start is at the bottom being a numbers runner, the pickup man, picking up and writing numbers for somebody else and then turning in. Maybe five or six years later you end up being a backer, and then on and on. It was too slow for me even though it was safer, a whole lot safer —the fines was low, the sentences was low, and with so many police and high officials playing numbers, there wasn't much danger in it. Maybe that was the reason I didn't really go into it, just like I didn't like pimping—there wasn't enough excitement to it.

Even though I was usually involved in all kinds of these illegal things, there were a couple of times in my life when I tried being square. For instance, around '58 or '59 I got a job and was taking night courses. I was pretty much staying around the house and not hanging out. For a while I was really hoping it would work out. See, you get tired. You get tired trying to be a tough guy all the time. People always expecting this and that. But something always seemed to happen to mess it up.

I kept on getting arrested unnecessarily. Two famous police in my life—Officer Morgan and one other officer—they are the cause of 50 percent of my arrests. Single-handed. These two guys used to press me no matter what happened. If somebody got their pocketbook snatched, they know that I wouldn't do it, this wasn't even my thing. Still, they'll come and get me. If somebody got killed up the street, they'll come and get me. Don't matter what—if a store got broke into, they'd come and get me. I got tired. I trying to tell my parole officer. I say, "Man, these guys pressing me. There's no way I'm doing all of this. I'm trying to get it together." My parole officer say, "Well, if you wasn't doing something, they wouldn't keep bothering you." So I just got right on back to the bag I was in. And after that I never slowed down no more, just kept right on going from one thing to another.

8

Stickup

I'd been pimping only a couple of months in the early fall of '66 when one of my oldest and closest friends, JoJo, showed up. We knew each other as kids. Even though he wasn't from my part of town, we used to visit each other. I would come to N.W. every now and then, and he used to come to S.E. sometimes. I began to introduce him to some of my S.E. friends. Then we got even tighter on juvenile range in the D.C. Jail, which is where they put juveniles when the government waives jurisdiction on them and treats them as adults. When I got indicted for shooting Rock, and the government waived jurisdiction and sent me to the District jail, JoJo was already there. I'm a few years older than him, and around that time I was seventeen, so he had to be about fifteen years old. If I remember correctly, he was in for stealing cars. I didn't stay on juvenile range very long before I made bond and went out, but I never forgot that JoJo was still there. After pleading to the A.D.W. charge that I had, I got the Youth Act; and when I get to the Youth Center, who's there? JoJo.

We got a brother-type relationship. I kind of adopted him, and he kind of adopted me. In doing so he adopted my family too. My sisters and brothers, he always regarding them as his sisters and brothers, and he always regarding my children as being his nieces and nephews.

Now, JoJo don't do a whole lot of talking. He more of

a listener, observer, a stone-face type of dude. He was different, but I dug these differences, and I dug that he was the kind of dude that I wouldn't mind being with—real quiet but double dangerous. He the kind of guy that can sit down and can stare at you for an hour and look clear through you. Never blink. Never move.

So by him and me being such good friends, I was really glad to see him when he visited me while I was pimping. He had just been involved in a robbery and assaulting a policeman—shot a policeman and killed a police dog. He went to court, got out on bond on Friday, and came to see me. We partied for a few days and had a good time. That Monday he was notified to come to court. So he come, and they told him they was ready to start trial right away. This was something he hadn't expected, 'cause he'd only been out on bond a couple of days. So naturally he tried to get it postponed, but they started picking a jury, and before the day was over they had jive started on the trial.

His lawyer was a flakey dude—I don't think he really wanted to represent JoJo. His heart wasn't in it. Because of the charges, I guess. The next day, Tuesday, the police that JoJo was supposed to have shot was there at the court. And the police and the D.A. was constantly trying to offer JoJo a deal. But JoJo didn't want to cop out; he figured he had a better chance fighting it.

The D.A. really bearing down. He telling JoJo, "I'm really going to make it hard for you," which he did. So the police told JoJo, "I don't know who shot me"—it was too dark and he couldn't see—"but when I get on the stand, I'm going to say *you* did." Then the D.A. said, "It couldn't have been nobody but him." So the man repeated, "I'm going to say that you shot me."

The court adjourned for lunch, and JoJo never did come back. He came to me and told me what was happening. I said, "Well, man, what you going to do?" "I'm not going back." I said, "Solid, that's all right with me." So he say, "You got any pistols?" I go to my room, where I got them stashed in a wall, and I took out some guns and let him take his pick. I said, "What you gonna do now?" And he said, "Well, man, what *you* gonna do?" I told him, "Well, I really don't dig what I'm doing now."

So we both decided that what we wanted to do was hook back up like we had in the past. We began to check out different things, little joints, and we done a few little robbery-type things. We was just getting by.

But there was a constant search for JoJo. The FBI was after him, trying to make a deal with him. One particular day my mother was down at my place so I could give her money for my sister or brother, and I was in my room with a broad. So my mother answered the door, and it was the feds. They asked my mother if I had any company, and she said, "Yeah." They automatically assumed that it may have been JoJo—my mother don't *say* it's a dame! So they kicked my bedroom door in and fell in there, one down on his knee, the other up by the door, holding these pistols! And there I am with the dame!

Finally they get to rapping with me. They asking did I know JoJo and all this kind of stuff, which I know they already know. The feds are the only real police. They really do their thing, and they're the onliest ones that I really, really respect. Like the District police or the state police, I have often gotten out on them. But we always try to limit what we do to stay away from the feds so they won't get involved, because once they get involved, a bust is sure to come. So they asking me did I know JoJo and did I know his whereabouts and had I seen him. And I was saying, yes, I know him; no, I don't know his whereabouts; no, I haven't seen him in quite a while. So one of them said, "Well, we want your friend pretty bad. He jumped bond, he wanted for this and he wanted for that. We would be willing to give you some help in the event that you ever get a beef. You scratch our back, and we'll scratch yours." So I said, "I really appreciate that. And if I should happen to see him, I would be glad to give you a call." The man dug that as being so much shit, so he say, "Be honest. Would you really call us?" I said, "Man, you want me to be honest? No, I wouldn't call you or anything like that." And then, all of a sudden, he tried threatening me: "You know you on parole, don't you? If you get a beef, you're going to jail." So him and I arguing for a few minutes, and finally he left his number with me. I said, "I'm going to tell you this. If I see him, I'll try to talk him into turning himself in. If he go for it, good. If he don't, then that's that." So they leave. Ten minutes later, here come JoJo bouncing through the door!

That kind of thing happened a couple of times. He usually wouldn't come directly to the house. He'd drive by, beep the horn two or three times, just slow down enough so I know it's him, and keep on going up to the parking lot in the next block. One time we was having a little get-together. We really outdid it that night, and everybody fell all over the floor and the chairs and the couches. What made us really aware of the danger was one of my sinks was stopped up, and the maintenance man come and fixed the sink while everybody's still laid out and everything. Man, just as he leaving somebody dig it and say, "Damn, if he can do it, the feds can do it too!" And about twenty minutes later the feds did come! They must have had some kind of tip or something, but just before they came in, JoJo went out the window, and they missed him.

Meanwhile, JoJo and I was getting kind of restless, so we decided to plan something really, really big, something that should've paid thirty or forty thousand dollars. This kind of big money we had never been into before. It represented a lot of power in our position. So we planned something nice for a big old store, like a five-and-ten, way, way uptown amongst the embassies. JoJo used to work at this particular joint and knew its ins and outs. So we planned and planned for two or three weeks. We looking at the joint dinner time, in the afternoon, checking it out, checking it out.

What we had planned to do was get the office early in

the morning before they had a chance to send any money out to the cash registers—about fifty or sixty cash registers all over the place. So we put our little workmen's outfits together and plenty of tape, so we can tape everybody up. We really was kind of set on this, but what we didn't antici-pate was morning traffic—we had to be there at a certain time. Okay. We got it all planned and scheduled for this particular day, and we get up early in the morning, get everything together, and we on our way. Then we run into all this traffic! There's some *long* lines, everybody trying to get to work! So when we finally get there, it's too late. There's nothing we can do. Both of us is mad and disap-pointed because the way we had it planned, it surely would have been successful.

We was pretty angry, so instead of coming back to S.E., we messing around uptown a little bit, and we run into a dude that's a friend of JoJo's. This dude is telling JoJo about a liquor store that cashes checks on Friday. Ordinarily we wouldn't rob no liquor store even though they pay good. Liquor stores are pretty dangerous. There's always guns, and you're more apt to get hurt or hurt someone and not get a substantial amount of money. Oftentimes the police be in the back, or there's more than three or four people in the store, and maybe out of four, two can use their guns pretty good.

So this dude telling JoJo, "Yeah, man, they cash checks every Friday, and they have a large amount of money there, anywhere from three to four grand, maybe five." All he wanted for this information was a hundred dollars. JoJo tell me the dude pretty reliable, but *I* didn't like the idea. Now, during this time I didn't use no drugs and this particular dude was a drug addict, he was a junkie. So I'm saying, "That junkie don't know what he's talking about." But JoJo kind of believed in him.

So we go to look at the joint, and it's a cheesy little joint. It really was! So I say, "Man, they don't got no five thousand

dollars at *no* time." JoJo say, "Maybe that's the throw-off."
So we check the joint out a couple of times. Now, the owner
of the joint, he standing right in the window. He see us come
by there twice, so he get suspicious. He send the clerk in the
back to get a gun, but before he can get back with a gun,
we're coming in. That owner was really nervous. It took
him about five minutes to get the cash register open. Meanwhile, I'm thinking that big money can't be in this cash
register. So I'm asking the man, "Where is the cash? Where
is the check money?" And the man kept saying, "There ain't
no check money. There ain't no check money." Meanwhile,
the man that he had sent for the gun, he coming out the
back, and he see us standing there. He see the shotgun and
the pistol and everything, and he say, "Hey, boss, I don't see
the gun, boss." So I said something like "Nigger, come on
out here!"

The joint was dingy, a dim little place. I had on a stocking mask and was carrying the shotgun. JoJo had sunglasses
and Band-aids across his face, and he had the pistol. I make
the clerk lay on the floor while we going through the cash
register, checking underneath the counter for this big
money. In the cash register was, I think, one hundred and
six dollars. I am very, very mad. This right here ain't nothing. So I said, "Man, by the time we buy gas and get something to eat, it won't be worth it!" Anyhow, we been in there
too long now, 'cause usually—and I don't care how big the
establishment is—if I stay in a joint over three minutes,
there's got to be a good reason. My thing was to get the
money and roll on out of there. Anyway, I put the owner
and his helper in the refrigerator room, but I don't lock them
in there. I should have, as it turned out. I remember looking
around for something to stick in the door so they couldn't
push it open from inside, but I also remember thinking, We
got to go. We got to go.

So we walk up the corner and around another corner to
where the car parked. Meanwhile, the owner and his helper

done got outside the box and outside the store to where a truck driver's making a delivery. The black dude see us bending this corner, and he get the truck driver to drive up that way. Somehow the guy got our tag number. But we didn't know nothing about that at the time.

We get in the car and pull out, and we talking about it: "Damn, man, we gonna have to get up early next Friday morning so we can take that big money!" At that point, we wasn't worried at all about getting caught for the job we just pulled. We stopped at a light, and we can see traffic ahead backed up, and we way back in that traffic. Suddenly JoJo says, "Man, there's a wagon behind us. It's a police wagon!" Their light was going round and round about two or three cars behind us. So I say, "Just be cool, Jack. Maybe it ain't us that they looking for, so don't panic." Meanwhile, a couple of scout cars come in almost directly behind us. Now I *know* they looking for us. So I tell JoJo to *get it*, and when I say, "Get it!" JoJo immediately pulls out of the traffic onto the sidewalk. Vroom, vroom. He goes down the sidewalk the whole block. There's a lady with a little kid standing on the corner, waiting for the light to change. She turns around and sees the car coming, and the police had also come up on the sidewalk in pursuit, with all their sirens going; and when she see all these cars coming along the sidewalk, she kind of dumbfounded. I'm trying to look at her and looking back at the police, and when we do get to the corner, beeping the horn, beeping the horn, we just drove right past the lady and the little kid. And when I look back, I see the little kid's hat fly off from the wind of the car —that's how close we came!

So we moving; we doing it, something like ninety, a hundred miles an hour, weaving in and out of traffic. And I'm telling JoJo, "Keep beeping the horn! Keep beeping the horn!" Of course, the sirens are doing a job for us as far as getting the cars out of the way. Everybody just pulling over. But this one dude, we get right up on him before he decides to pull over. We rolling close to the parked cars, and he riding in the outer lane, and when he cut in it's almost blocking us. Just as he cut in, JoJo hit it that much harder, and we went right into his front end. Crash! That pushed us into the parked cars and messed up the door on my side. So I'm trying to hold on to the door. Sparks coming from it, and I'm almost falling out when JoJo pull me back, still holding the steering wheel. Finally we get it together, and we rolling again.

All this time I was trying to figure out how we was going to get away. I was thinking that once we got up around Florida Avenue, there was a lot of big trucks up there. The main thing was, during the chase, the longer you stay in the car, the more chance you're going to get busted. The police going to block you up. The best thing to do is to try to get ahead of the police enough so you can abandon the car. So we going pretty fast, and we see a police on motorcycle come down off of New York Avenue and just park right in the middle of Florida Avenue. He gets off his motorcycle, pulls out his gun, and just stands there! I guess he really thought that we would stop. We ride that old Ford up on its back wheels and keep going. When we get to him, he dig that we not going to stop, so he proceeds to dive out of the street. I think we hit the motorcycle and turn it over. He never did get off a shot at us, and in fact there wasn't no shooting going on at all. I guess everybody was too busy driving.

At 6th and Florida we turned and went through a gas station. We were doing all kinds of things, going around curves, running into things. Then, when we get to 4th and Florida, we decide to make another turn, but the axle's bent on the car, so by the time we turn up 4th Street, the car had slowed down to about forty. And I'm telling JoJo, "It's time to get out of here!" So when the car slows down a little bit, I come out—bam—I rolls on the grass right by Gallaudet College, which is a deaf and dumb school. JoJo never left the car for maybe another hundred feet before it came to a dead stop. Later on, the dude down at the precinct that put the little pins in the map came up to robbery squad and said, "I just wanted to see you all, 'cause you must have had rockets in that car. Every time we tried to block you off, you'd go through it!"

Anyhow, the police are so close on that by the time I stand up (I think I hurt my ankle on the curb), they got me. There's police everywhere, but they not concentrating so much on JoJo for some reason. They got their guns on me, and I don't move. I'm just standing there with my hands up, making sure they ain't going to kill me. I just kind of gave up. They apprehended me, and in doing so, they neglected JoJo. A couple of minutes later I think they realized that there was somebody else with this dude! But by the time they realized it JoJo is coming out the car. He got a big, long .38, and he climbing up on the chain-link fence at Gallaudet. That's when all the shots fired. Just as he get to almost the very top, all of them started shooting. JoJo grabbed hisself like he shot. He holding on to the fence with one hand. First he gonna fall back this way, but then he fall over on the other side. He did it so convincingly that *I* thought he was hit. And I say, "Damn!" By this time they got me down on the ground, handcuffed up, my clothes all pulled around, they searching me. After the shooting, they was so sure that one of them had hit JoJo—there was about four rollers shooting—that they didn't rush right over there. They just keeping the crowd back and taking care of me. I'm laying on the ground, my face in the dirt, and I'm thinking, Damn! JoJo's shot all up and maybe dead. And I happen to glance over, and I see JoJo kind of peep up off the ground to see if anyone was looking at him and then jump up and start running! I was really glad.

So they kept saying, "We got one suspect apprehended and are in pursuit of the other." And I kept saying, "Damn. JoJo gonna get away." I found out later that what JoJo did

was run into Gallaudet College, and believe it or not, a deaf
and dumb dude told where JoJo was. What happened was,
the detectives and police was everywhere, and JoJo had
slipped in behind some bushes around this dormitory. There
was one motorcycle cop come real close to him—JoJo told
me this later on—and JoJo was going to pull him in there
and get his gun, 'cause he had dropped his own pistol. But
before he could do that, a detective walked up to a deaf and
dumb dude, showed him his badge, showed him his gun, and
the deaf and dumb dude point to the bushes.

So they got JoJo, but I'm still unaware of the fact. By
the time I get to robbery squad, I'm limping 'cause my leg
hurt, I'm kind of disgusted, but I figure I'm gonna be out on
bond, so I ain't too worried. I'm just trying to figure out
what the hell I'm gonna say. They caught us with everything in the car—the shotgun, the masks, and the money—
the hundred and six dollars. All that chase and shooting,
somebody could have been killed, and it wouldn't have been
worth it.

When they finally brought JoJo in, I say, "Damn, Jack,
I thought you got away." And he, in turn, had thought I had
got away because he kept hearing them say over the radio
that "one suspect was apprehended." He assumed that it was
him, and vice versa. So they get us in robbery squad. They
handcuff me to a chair on the other side of the room. The
captain of robbery squad, after checking both of our
records, told one of the rollers walking around, "Don't get
near either one of them. If they make any type of move,
outburst, or anything, *shoot,* and I'll straighten it out." Now
why he said all this I don't know, but after he said it I wasn't
planning on doing nothing. I might have talked a little tough
at first, but I thought, This dude sounds pretty convincing.
If he didn't convince the guy he was talking to, he did
convince me.

So this is where they begin to make a lot of mistakes.
First of all, they went back to the store to get the owner.

They say to him, "We got the dudes that robbed you. Come and look at them; come identify them." An officer had found some extra coats in the car. Neither one of us during the course of the robbery had on these coats, but once they got the witness there, they told us to put on the coats for some reason. They also told us to stand up against the wall. I immediately refused: "I'm not putting on no coat. I'm not putting on nothing. This ain't no line-up; I ain't standing up in no line."

Another thing was that when they first brought the witness in, both of us still had handcuffs on. Everybody else was walking around, pistols at their sides, wearing white shirts and ties. Here I am with a black turtleneck, and JoJo got on a plaid shirt, plus we were black and everybody else was white. So when they say, "Do you see the guys that robbed you?" there wasn't no choice! Then they made us get up and told us again to put on the coats. We refused, and then they said, "Put on the coats or else!" So we put on the coats and stood against the wall.

The witness, he looking at us and looking at us. Once he got right up on us, and us with those coats on that didn't have nothing to do with it. He's saying, "I don't know. I'm not sure." And the police saying, "That's them, man. We caught them with your money and in the same car that the dude had followed." They tell us to turn around and face the wall, but I could still hear the man saying, "No, I'm not sure." One thing about that particular witness, later on they must have evidently convinced him real strongly, but at that time he just wouldn't say yes or no. So he leaves, and they bring in the next witness, his assistant, the little black dude. And he say immediately, "Yeah, that's them."

They took JoJo out to get fingerprinted and mug shots. Meanwhile, they taking a statement from this second witness. Now, they also taking me right by the witness. He says something smart, I forget what, and I say, "Man, you making a mistake, man." And he says something smart again, and I

spit on him. That was kind of a bad move. One police yoked
me, and another one hit me in my gut, and I'm handcuffed.
Then they take me across to a little room just before you
get to the fingerprint area. The police who is taking me is
a regular street roller, but the dudes what's jumping on me
are detectives. Now, this roller that first handcuffed me and
carry me to get fingerprinted, you know, kind of a young
white dude, he don't have nothing to do with it. He just
stood back. The detectives was above him or represented
more authority than he had, but he probably could have
gotten in on the beating up and nothing would have been
said. But he just didn't get involved.

Well, in this little room, they done their thing. They
really just beat me, not unconscious but they gave me a good
whupping over there. One of them yoked me and was trying to choke me, and the other one started hitting me all in
the stomach. I can't use my hands, which are cuffed behind
me, and I can't let them just keep beating and beating me.
Finally I fell to the floor. I think, If I stay down here, they'll
start to kick me; if I stay down here, they might *kill* me. So
I get up, and I kind of run into one of them with my
shoulder. Just as I did, he kicked me right in the groin and
I folded up again. The pain's so sharp I can hardly move, but
I'm so mad that I got to do something. So I'm trying to run
into them, and as I come to them they ram me into the wall.

So my face is swelled up, I'm beat up, bruises everywhere, and then they give me back to the little officer, who
all the time stood there quietly, politely, and watched. He
half carried me to the fingerprint place. When we get there,
he gotta take the handcuffs off. 'Cause he's seen what they've
done to me and the way I was reacting to it, he's a little
afraid to. I guess he figured with my hands loose I might
have took care of myself a whole lot better. Then he says
something like "Man, I didn't have anything to do with them
beating you up, and I really don't like it. Now, I'm not
saying this just to be saying it so that you can be cool. But

if I take these handcuffs off and you start something, man . . ." So I said, "Yeah, I understand, I'm not going to do nothing, I'm too tired. Just take the handcuffs off, get me fingerprinted, and tell them I want to go to the hospital."

A couple of hours later they carry me over to D.C. General and say I was hurt in the process of banging into cars. So there really wasn't anything I could do or say to make them think anything different. I didn't even try. There wasn't even nothing said about what really happened in court. It was just one of them things that police do often and get away with.

I got out on bond after a short while, and it didn't come to trial till July, so I was on bond from November till July. During that time I went back into pimping, but I didn't get involved in nothing big. Meanwhile, JoJo went to trial on his original beef, and he end up getting twelve to thirty-six years for the robbery, shooting a policeman, and killing a police dog.

The D.A. offered me a cop to a robbery charge, but I wasn't accepting nothing. I had worked things out, and I thought I could beat it. But once we get to trial, things kind of change. My story was that I didn't participate in the crime at all. I was there after the crime was committed. Just in the wrong place at the wrong time. Whoever participated in the crime, they left, and then some kind of way JoJo and me met up. I had witnesses to this effect.

JoJo's story was that his car had been stolen and that he saw two dudes with it and scared them away. Then he got in the car without noticing any of the stuff in it and was just driving downtown when he saw me at a bus stop. He stop and we talk, since we good friends. I get in the car. When the police begin to chase us, I just assumed that JoJo driving a stolen car, but I know that whatever we do, if we stop right there or run, I'm not going to be involved, 'cause I didn't steal nobody's car and I don't know nothing about it.

I had three witnesses who testified that they was with me at the time the robbery happened. I had a friend named Pete, and his grandmother was one of my witnesses. Her story was that I knocked on her door around such and such a time asking for Pete. Of course, the D.A. went into how did she know exactly what day it was, and she recalled reading in the paper the next day about the bust. "How did you know exactly what time it was that he knocked on the door?" She said, "Well, it was time for me to take my medicine, and I glanced at the clock. Then I answered the door, and it was Johnny." Her story was kind of strong by her being a grandmother, an elderly lady, and pretty well together mind-wise. The D.A. couldn't trip her up, so he asked this question. He said, "Are you any kin to either one of these defendants?" She's no relation to me or to JoJo, but it was just something that he said to stick in the jury's mind—maybe this old lady is some kin to them and that's why she's saying this. My other two witnesses told that they met me on Georgia Avenue coming from Pete's house and that they walked me to the bus stop, where JoJo picked me up.

That was our story, but it wasn't good enough the first time around. We was convicted. I got three to nine years four times running concurrently with a five-to-fifteen year sentence. JoJo got the same thing for five three-to-nine's running concurrently with five to fifteen, but consecutive to the twelve to thirty-six he got on the previous charge. It looked like he was never going to get out.

9

Prison Life

During the final day or so of the trial, which lasted five days, my lawyer told me that things didn't look too good. Well, I could see for myself that things didn't look too good. The other side was winning. They had made us out the bad guys, in other words. Later, after the conviction, my lawyer told me there was some pretty good grounds to appeal on, so we immediately began our fight for the appeal.

It turned out to be a long fight, and I spent the next two years, from '67 to '69, in the D.C. Jail and down at Lorton. As usual, a lot of dudes I knew were already there, and I just kind of fit right in. Myself and quite a few of my friends, we been in and out so much that we automatically the dudes that run things. We'd have jobs in the dining room or as tiermen working on the tier. See, in the jail, each cell block is divided into levels called tiers. The first cell, that's where the tiermen live—or probably two tiermen. You got that whole row of cells down there. Your cell stays open, and you be responsible for making sure everybody have what they need. You responsible for taking up the sheets on Thursday morning for the laundry. You responsible for having the tier all swept down and mopped down, keeping the shower clean, and stuff like that. A tierman is a good thing to be because you kind of got the run of the block. Ordinarily everybody locked up. But the tierman can go from tier to tier, in and out of the cell. Maybe somebody got a buddy on the tier downstairs, so he just go down there, set in front of the cell, talk to him, then come back up.

The block sergeant chooses the tiermen. The officers always like to have all the so-called tough guys working for them. That way they think that nothing will ever go down that they don't really know about. In the event something flares up, then they got all the tough guys on their side, 'cause they treat them good. They let them have the run of the block and do what they want to. I have even seen officers turn their back while some young dudes have been seduced or raped because certain dudes was doing it. If it was somebody else that did it, they would automatically be busted and charged.

Now, most of the time when a dude is very quiet in jail, he be left alone, 'cause you don't never know where a quiet dude coming from unless he show a lot of feelings within his face. See, when you first come in the D.C. Jail—the Iron Queen we call it—you don't usually raise no lot of hell. You kind of hope that you would see somebody you know. A lot of guys, if they don't see nobody, they hope they can make friends with somebody, 'cause they can't take care of theirself. They have to have a crutch; they have to have another guy to take care of them. Otherwise, somebody will turn them out, make them out homosexuals. Oftentimes, this type of dudes get advantage taken of them.

Now, dudes like myself, like I say, are well known. If I went into jail right now, it would be, "Big Al this or Big Al that. Hey, Big Al, what's happening? What kinda beef you got now? Where you at? I'll send you some cigarettes; I got some candy." Dudes in my caliber, we get first choice on all homosexuals. We get our pick.

Most homosexuals are easy to pick out 'cause they come in with drags on. At the jail there is a special tier for them, a special range because they can't be mixed with the population. They have to separate them to prevent chaos and for their protection. Sometimes though, one or two slip through

who aren't so obvious. There's a lot of them we call undercover fuck boys. But the drag queens, they is just what they
are made up to be, drag queens. They'd have on their little
rings, and they talk like broads and they act like broads and
they just do it all. They have on their little tight pants and
fix their clothes like broads. A lot of them look like broads;
a lot look like apes; some of them look like Charles Atlas.
They's old ones, young ones, in-between ones. Everything.
They all there. I recall one time when we had a disturbance
at the jail the homosexuals complained that they could gov-
ern theirself in the population as well as anybody else. Before then, after the evening meal and after the dining area
was cleaned up, all three tiers was opened up and they'd let
everybody—except the homosexuals—come downstairs and
watch T.V. They'd only open their cell and let them out on
the range. And you'd see dudes standing there and looking
up and talking, just like you talking to a woman—"Yeah
baby, Mama this and that." After this little disturbance happened, they let them out with us. And that was really something for about a week!

I went to jail at a very early age. If I had been weak and
somebody would have took advantage of me then, it would
have carried all the way over into now. I would have had
trouble every time I went in. Dudes that come in that maybe
never been to jail before and not strong enough, once it
happen, long as one of them jailbird niggers see him, then
he'll always be a faggot. Simple as that. It wouldn't make no
difference where he went, it would always follow him.

Now, people don't always jump on him and make him
out a homosexual. Some dudes just talk and seduce him, and
that's the kind that I hate the most—a man that let a man talk
him into playing the role of a woman. I can't stand them. A
lot of homosexuals are outright homosexuals. Fine. But
there's this kind of dude that you talk to, and he will try to
play the role of a man during the day, then at nighttime have
two or three guys around his bed. I guess a lot of homosexu-

als was probably born homosexual or became homosexuals early in their childhood, and they can be a lot of fun, because they really don't care. They know what they are, and it's what they wanna be. I have a lot of homosexual friends like that.

Most homosexuals will try to form some kind of steady relationship, and they always try to pick a dude with a reputation. That way, they protected. They can walk around without the fear of being grabbed and molested without giving their consent. "Be cool, Jack. That's Big Al's woman." Now, *some* homosexuals can take care of themselves pretty well, and they don't need no man. They just free-lance with anybody. And there's some that can take care of themselves that always seem to get a weaker dude, and they look out for them. So sometimes it works in reverse. It's a hell of a thing.

But once you get involved, you really get hung up on it. At first, I was dead against a man saying, "This right here is my woman" and be talking about another man. I said, "What the hell's going on? Freaks, all of them freaks!" But you locked up two or three years, you want to get one of them freaks. Like Dale. Dale was a friend of mine. He was a dude that at some point when he was really young changed. He was trying to tell me about it a couple of times, but I never really listened. By the time he was seventeen, he was all-out homosexual. And the very first time that he put on drags, he got busted. He went to this joint where a lot of homosexuals hang, and he got accused of breaking out a window there. So the next day after he got arrested, he setting there in the bull pen ready to go to court with drags on. And the dudes are checking him out. He look pretty good, got a wig all fixed, and looking hip. So they make their move. Something like sixty-some dudes have sex with him. All types of ways. He had a mouthful, an assful, and two handsful, and was still rolling. The marshals of the court come in and see it, then go away. They evidently thought that this was what he wanted. Finally he just passed out. They brought him around; he passed out. He kept continuously passing out till they finally let him go.

He's around seventeen at this time, never been in any jail, any institution. He had to put his age up in order not to go to the juvenile receiving home, and so he came through the jail and fell into all that hell. I didn't go to court or nothing, that day, but I heard about what happened to him. So when I seen him, seen how pitiful he looked, I felt sorry for him. And through me feeling sorry for him, I started kind of looking out for him. Now, the dudes knowed what had happened to him up the court. So when they catch him, it was like the same thing over again. So when he started going on the yard, he started walking with me. Nobody bothered him. He begin to dig that. It made him want to be closer and closer to me, and we ended up being pretty tight.

I remember another time when I really got into it. This was up at Lorton, and my friend Bobby Brown was in the cell next to mine. My cell partner was a tall dude named Peewee Roberts. Near us there was a homosexual that was not locked up where homosexuals usually be, and he was on our tier. Dudes was giving the homosexual a lot of play, a lot of attention, but Bobby Brown saw that I wasn't and asked me, "Man, everybody else cracking on the whore. Why don't you?" I said, "Man, I ain't thinking about it." But I had other plans. I knew eventually I was going to get it anyhow. I can do a lot of different faces, and I would never do anything but look at that homosexual in a strange kind of way, always wondering what he's like.

So finally the homosexual come past my cell and say, "Hey, Big Al." I looked crazy, and I could hear Bobby Brown panting like a hound dog in the cell next to mine. He was dead serious—he wanted that homosexual. This went on for a week or two, and finally the homosexual asked me, "Why don't you never say nothing to me when everybody else do?" Then I turned to him and said, "I knew eventually that you were going to say something to me."

That night I had Peewee come out of my cell and go into the homosexual's cell with this other dude named Hotcakes. Then the homosexual come into my cell and stayed the night. I tapped on the wall and told Bobby Brown, "Guess who's over here, Bobby?" He say, "Who?" I tell him it's Terry, the homosexual, and he say, "Man, you lying." I made the homosexual say something or stick his hand out so Bobby could see it, and finally Bobby took his little cup out. (At the jail we used to do a lot of things with our iron cups. We used to take that sand soap and shine the bottom of them, then look up and down the tier like a mirror.) Anyway, Bobby took his little cup, looked over and saw the homosexual, and he was really excited, like the homo was in his cell. I went through a lot of changes that night, laughing and bullshitting with Bobby. He sat up all night with his ear glued to the wall. I used to really get on him about that.

Sometimes there is a lot of racial tension in some joints. It depends on what joint you're in, what particular jail it is, where it's located. The majority of prisoners at the D.C. Jail are black. The jail is mostly black ran but fortunately by dudes that have got enough on the ball not to try to press white people. Some other joints are majority white and are white ran.

Some of the places have a lot of conflict with their racial thing. I've seen dudes come from other joints saying, "Wow, I'm glad to get away from all them whiteys. Whiteys was everywhere. I was scared to death. I thought they was going to kill me. I see we have the upper hand down here." Then you have to tell them, "No, it ain't like that. Here we are all people, all prisoners. If a hack do something to you, a whitey might be the first one to jump on a hack to save you." You change people's minds, and they change their opinion about all the people. It's a hell of a thing.

Actually, the usual feeling at the jail and at Lorton was kind of a prisoners-against-guards thing. The prisoners didn't have too much trouble among themselves, though some of the young, militant-type black dudes didn't get along so good with some of the white dudes. But I know some white dudes in that penitentiary that will escape and be with you no matter what. Also a white dude will often prefer to be in a dormitory with Black Muslims because Muslims are real clean and they hardly ever say anything. I know quite a few white dudes down at Lorton that even asked to be in the dormitory where the majority of Muslims are.

I think those movement people are beautiful. Of course, I don't agree with a lot of the things they have to do as far as religion goes. My personal opinion is that they worship the Honorable Elijah Mohammed more so than Allah. It supposed to have been God that gave the Honorable Elijah Mohammed certain pointers on life support and so on. Like, you're not supposed to eat pork. I was born and raised on pork. You aren't supposed to drink and smoke—this is a hard religion. You're not supposed to be with this woman or that—I love all women. I'm going to be with every one I get the chance to be with—black, white, or polka dot. But these people are beautiful if they can do all that and get by —they can do more than I can do.

I went to some movement meetings and it would be the "white devil this" and "the white devil that." It got to be a drag for me. I went because I like to know everything that's going on, but I couldn't stay with it. Some of them would tell me, "You the fruit of Islam—you gonna be here when the mother ship come." And I'd be saying, "Yeah, the mother ship, hmmm. Pass the pork chop." That was me. I couldn't change. But I admire them because they did. If it was me every day, I would die. And they're very much into that separation business. I wouldn't go personally. If that's what they want and they succeeded in getting it, I might come down to the boat and shake a few of them hands, but I'm not getting on, and they can call me and say what they want to say.

A lot of dudes come into jail and get into the movement for protection. Say a soft dude or maybe a potential homosexual come in jail, so first thing he do is join the movement. I know of a dude named George who was down at Lorton, and he was in my dormitory. At that time, drugs was coming in really heavy on weekends. By Tuesday or Wednesday, things had died down, so everybody wait for the next weekend. All week long this boy would be walking around acting like a real Muslim. "May Allah bless you and all your trials and tribulations." Then, when the weekend come, he'd want to shoot dope. "Hey, what's happening, poppa? Can I get two or three of them eggs?" So what happen? After a while he couldn't pay. He was a fair-looking boy, so they propositioned him. First thing he do is run to the Muslims. "They trying to take advantage of me! They trying to take my manhood!" They promptly told him, "Well, you been shooting that dope. Now you straighten it up. You're no longer part of the body." They push him right on back. They usually know when a dude is sincere and when he's not, and they was a very strong group in jail.

Another thing about the Muslims—that race thing don't press them at all. Most of the old jailers like myself don't have no problems neither. But I know some white boys that you just can't say anything to or do anything to. No matter what color you are or how bad a nigger you are, it don't make no difference. They not going to take it. They are going to hit you in your mouth or maybe take your life.

Sometimes it would really be silly dudes that do silly things that start bad feeling. I remember one time we had a riot up the jail, and we demanded to see Mr. Kemper on the yard—no police, nobody but Mr. Kemper and two reporters. Kemper agreed to this if we stop tearing it up and just drop all weapons. But there's about five or six young boys who want to tear up. So they are out there jumping on the white dudes. One old man couldn't understand. He was one of them type of white dudes who didn't belong in jail in the first place. He had never said a racial slur to anyone. He shared all his properties with everybody or anybody that asked. If one asked for a cigarette, he gave it to them, and he didn't look down his nose at people. So when they hit him I got mad, and I wasn't the first to speak up. But I was glad that they did speak up, because eventually I would have said something myself. So we pulled those young dudes to the side and told them real polite to stop fucking up. Leave him alone. The man is holding his nose that's bleeding, and I really felt bad. Do you know that bunch of crazy niggers just kept right on? So finally some of the old timers got together and took them all away in the corner and politely spanked them real nice. I enjoyed that, and I was doing the most spanking. Now, at one point, I believe I hated too, but that was before I began to check things out—I just didn't know. All I knew was what somebody had told me. "This right here is because of whitey. Whitey the cause of that." You grow up with them constantly saying this, and you believe it without checking or knowing. Then I found myself getting really tight with some white dudes, and I'm saying to myself, "I'm supposed to hate so much, and these dudes ain't supposed to be my friends. They supposed to be trying to do things to me and conspire against me, but they not. They my friends." Fortunately it was at an early age that I did begin to check things out, and I discovered that most people just don't know. They be talking hate and at the same time they be Christian folk talking about the church, about love. I was confused, really confused.

The race thing runs deep with everybody. Black people don't like white people, white people don't like black people; Jews don't like Italians, Italians don't like Jews. It's a whole lot of nonsense, so I just try to avoid it as much as possible —even being a part of anything that's not fruitful to all people. The main thing I'd be thinking about is poor people and not if they're black, white, pink, or purple.

I been in quite a few jail and prison riots in my time. Some of them didn't amount to nothing, just a lot of hollering and screaming. And some of them was really something. It don't take too much to start one. There may be only five or six dudes that really want to get their point over. Everybody else just want to tear up something and raise hell. So they glad when these dudes speak up, when somebody's strong enough to stand up, so immediately everybody stand up behind them. It's kind of a rebellion thing. You got me in jail, but you ain't gonna break me. I said that to myself many, many times, especially after I was hurt. I'd say, "Yeah, you got me in jail, and you also got my body confined to a penitentiary"—meaning my wheelchair—"but you never have my mind." It's the same thing in a riot. You'd be saying, "Yeah, you got me in jail, but what the hell? You ain't did nothing. We still doing what we want to do."

Medical conditions, food, and recreation—them are the three main things that riots always jump out about. Also, not having time to talk to your lawyer or not knowing who your lawyer is, or your lawyer not responding to your correspondence and not coming to see you; your visitors being semi-harassed by the things that they have to go through to get in the jail; and not being able to touch your visitors.

At the D.C. Jail, they call the place you see your visitors the tank. At one time there was a telephone on each side, and it was just a little spot that you could see through. Like the man tell you: "You Booth 12." Then you go in the tank, go past the other inmates, and you'd look through this little thing shaped like a diamond. There was your visitor, and that's all you could see of him. You tap on there, and they look and pick up the phone, then you rap. Later on, in the early '60's, they changed it. They took all that iron away and made some type of protective glass, where you could see your whole visitor at least. Whoever thought of that, it was a very, very good idea.

A lot of times there are no particular reasons why a riot begins. Two guys will just start up fighting, and the officer come in and try to break it up, and immediately a riot will start. Everybody want to let their frustrations loose, so this is the time to do it.

I don't remember exactly what the riot in '67 was all about, but it was a pretty good one. What went down was this. I was in Cell Block 2 at the jail; me and JoJo was in the same cell. We was the east side, and the majority of the dudes that had bucked was on the west side. I think the whole block, everybody participated in it, and they just sat down. It was an orderly thing. They didn't holler; they didn't make noise; they didn't do anything. They just set there. They had prepared themselves for it. Everybody had a little money and went to the canteen a couple of days previous to that and bought a lot of stuff.

Now, being on the opposite side, we really didn't know what it was all about. Evidently they had set down in the dining room, and at the end of rec time, at eleven o'clock, when the man say, "Go on back," nobody move. Now, the first day it happened, we had gone back to our cells on our side. We heard about it that night, that there was a riot going on on the other cell block. We's tapping—ting, ting, ting, ting—and that's one thing I never could learn, how to read that. I could read some of it, but some of it I couldn't. Tapping on the walls and reading lips, I really wanted to get into that, but I never did.

Anyhow, they said this was a peaceful demonstration, that they just wanted to talk to the man. But what they didn't know at the time was that Kemper was out of the country. And Mr. Schmidt was assistant director. Mr. Schmidt was a pretty fair man, a pretty good joe. But the next day, after we got all the details as to what happened, we decided that we gonna set down and sympathize with the other side. There's two separate dining rooms, so thirty or forty of us set down in ours, while the hundred or so dudes on the other side are still setting in theirs. This go on for about three days, and nobody try to force their way in.

During those three days everything was cool: there

wasn't no tearing up nothing. So what they did, Schmidt came on television. He announced that Kemper was out of the country and that he would not give the order for the officers to come in there and put us back in our cells. He said something like "As long as they are nonviolent, we won't be violent." We had managed to hook our T.V.'s back up, so we saw this on the morning news.

When he said that, everybody was kind of relaxed, 'cause we knew we wasn't doing anything violent. Then we heard all this noise. I thought the whole jail was being bombed or something. They came in like storm troopers. It *had* to be two hundred and fifty police, all of them with their helmets and gas masks, everything on. Immediately they storm the side where the hundred guys at, whupping dudes with sticks, whupping them up the steps, down the steps.

Okay. That gave us a little time. But there was a smaller number of us, and we knew we was gonna have to fight much harder in order not to get hurt. So we take these benches, the benches that we set on to eat, put one on one side, one on the other side against the walls, tie a sheet to the end of them so we can pull them in, fall on somebody, and set one right up in front of us.

Meanwhile, we hear the gas guns going off on the other side. We can smell the gas. So everybody's taking their T shirts, wetting them, putting them around their face and across their eyes. Okay. The first wave of officers, before they got exactly to us, for some reason changed their minds. They turned around and went back. I suppose they probably said, "Well, there's too many them niggers. We gonna get reinforcements." I think they went to get some kind of game plan.

It took them about two hours to get them guys over on the other side together. Meanwhile, they're just watching us, watching us, but never coming close enough. And we had said that we was not going past the points of these tables, 'cause that thing might fall in on us, break one of us up. But this white boy named Roach, for some reason or another, he went *past* the tables, halfway into the dining room. Just then the main force came in, and they beat that boy so bad. I'm standing there with a big iron water pitcher because we had no weapons. And I'm saying, "Damn, if they beat that white boy like that, they gonna *kill* one of us niggers!"

By the time they get to us, we already pulled the things on the sheets, and we don't get none of them. All it do was make a lot of noise. A friend of mine named Ralph, he constantly saying, "Don't be scared! Don't be scared! They got wives and children just like us! They don't want to be hurt!" And I'm saying, "Ralph, they got sticks and helmets and things on," and he saying, "Don't be scared! Don't be scared!"

Now, our ranks break a little bit and a few dudes run up the steps. This was bad, 'cause the police catch them up there by theirselves and like to beat them to death. Finally the superintendent of the jail, he say, "Put down any weapons you may have, and go back to your cells. Everybody go back to their cells." This old boy named Teddy—he used to be there down the Youth Center with me too—he hollers up, "Fuck you. We ain't doing nothing," and when he said that, all the hacks in the world came down on us. And everybody—like I wasn't the first, but I certainly wasn't last —trying to get up those steps. I was hit twice in the back with a stick. I turned around, and I kicked one of them in the groin. A few dudes had decided, "What the hell. I'm gonna fight it out if they kill me." But really it wasn't no contest, 'cause the hacks won.

We eventually ended up back in our cells. When JoJo and I got to our cell, there was three dudes already there. All of them was buck naked, and one of them was underneath JoJo's bottom bunk. So me and JoJo trying to figure out what the hell's going on. What's happening is, they're taking everything from everybody. They's taking all the clothes. So we said, "You all in there, come on out of there.

This is our cell." So the hack saying, "You better get in that cell." I said, "I'm not going in with all them niggers in there, man. They gotta come out and find their own cell." So finally they come out and we go in.

They don't try to rough us up or nothing too much after the day we go on back, but they take all our clothes and feed us sandwiches for about a week. The complete jail was on dead lock, which means nobody allowed out their cells for nothing. And as soon as it get dark, they cut out all the lights. But in a way, this was a lot of fun, 'cause everybody slept all day and we whooped and hollered all over the cell all night.

One thing I never figured out though, was why all those hacks come in there after Schmidt went on T.V. and said they was going to be nonviolent. I think maybe somebody was putting pressure on him from above, 'cause Ed Schmidt really was a pretty square shooting dude.

*   *

After I moved from the D.C. Jail down to Lorton, I remember we had a big riot there in October of '68. What started it all was John Wayne—*The Sons of Katie Everett.* Everybody had been watching the flick since it came on at nine o'clock, and it went on maybe ten or fifteen minutes after eleven. Everybody jive want to see the outcome of it. You watch something for two hours, you want to see the last ten or fifteen minutes. Okay. Cool Sam—this is a hack about seven foot something; a big, tall, mean dude—he came into the dormitory. I was on the little walk during this time, in 3 Dorm. So they telling everybody on the little walk to cut the T.V.'s off. But they never went around the big walk to tell anybody anything, so most of the guys on the big walk never knew what happened until the next day. Anyhow, Cool Sam came in and started cutting the televisions. When he went out, the televisions came on out behind him. And this happened all the way around the walk, from 2 Dormitory all the way to 13 Dormitory. We threw the T.V.'s out the windows, out the doors, as long as they got out on the walk and was broke up. So that's what started things.

At the three thirty count the next afternoon, when everybody usually get off their job and go back to their dorm, wasn't nobody to count. Wasn't no police nowhere on the hill. Everybody wondered what's going on. But taking advantage of the situation, they breaks into the canteen, the commissary, getting all kinds of stuff. Setting a little jive fire here or there.

A couple of hours after that, somebody say, "Man, it look like a million people outside the gate." What they was doing, they had organized all the hacks. A riot squad. Soldiers. Everybody was there. That was their game plan: a show of force. And that's exactly what they did. They came in and they whupped many heads. We supposed to lay on our bunk with our face in our pillow. Each bed got a little iron name tag. The dude come out and look at it and say, "I don't like this motherfucker here. I don't like this bastard." Then he proceed to crack your skull while your face is buried in that pillow. And one particular dude kept looking back, looking back, and I seen the police walk up to him, grab a handful of his hair, and take his head and bust it on the edge of the bed. Bam! He almost blind him, that what he did.

During that riot, I went all off and hit a hack. For that, I stayed in the sweat box for about four days. It's one cell, and it got a big steel door that they lock. So it blocked away from all the rest of the cells, and there's two giant radiators back there. They call that "punitive segregation." They took all my clothes, everything but my boots (I wouldn't give up my boots). They had me there for a while, then they moved me around the other side, and that was "administrative segregation." That way you got some grub, where on the other side, all you had was that weight-losing stuff, three cans a day. That was it. On the administrative side, you ate meals.

For hitting the hack, I got a charge of assaulting a federal officer. But I ended up getting a hung jury, and that was that. Still, while I was waiting for that trial, I got put into the wall—that's Cell Block 2, maximum security—and some of my friends were already there. Most everybody had assaults on the police. So we on dead lock. Everybody else on the block is not. They can watch T.V., out of their cells for the day, can go out for rec and come back; but we couldn't have no rec or nothing.

All told, I was isolated on dead lock for about eight months, and I was in a cell by myself even longer than that. For eight months they let us out only once a week to take a shower. That's the only thing. They fed us in that cell. We did everything in the cell. No recreation, no nothing.

The first time you go to jail, they say, is the hardest. Any time you go after that it's like you know where to go to get things, how to do this and that. A friend of mine used to tease me, "Damn, Allen come back and fit just like a hand in a glove." But after a while of constant repeats—coming back and coming back—and I was repeating—it gets hard again. So when I was in dead lock, I started writing, 'cause there was something inside me that felt like I wanted to put it down. I didn't show what I wrote to anybody. I don't think anybody really understood how I was feeling. But I knew, and I had to put it down.

In jail you have to maintain a certain amount of respect, you have to maintain your reputation. But there were times late at night when everybody asleep, when I thought about the past and about the future, how I would like it to be, and I would actually cry. But I would never do this openly or in front of anybody. When I wrote down what I felt, I was really saying something that in a way I wanted people to know and in another way I didn't. I wanted other dudes like myself to know that I understood late at night how their thoughts was and that we all sometimes have to let out a little cry. But it was meant for other convicts, not the dudes I was living with. I thought that if I felt this way, with my reputation, then there had to be a lot of other tough guys feeling the same way.

We all playing our roles. "You're a tough dude." Everybody did, there's no doubt; but you got inner feelings, and these feelings have to come out. How they come out depends on you. They come out sometimes in a hostile way. I been accused of that quite often. But at the same time, being by yourself, being alone late at night, then it come out in another way.

> There Are Two Things That Can Make A Man Cry, Love, And A Jail Cell, It Matters Not How Strong, Rough, Tough, Or Even How Weak You Are.

> Strong, Rough, Tough, And Weak Man Cry In A Cell If He Is In There Long Enough, Cells Kills You Slow, Little By Little You Die Away Inside, At Night When All Is Asleep You Think Of How It Use To Be And How You Want It To Be In The Future, Then With Your Face Deep In The Pillow Comes The Tears From Your Eyes.

> Cell, Cell, Cell, Oh Cell, You Have And Hold My Body, But I Promise You, You Won't Get My Mind.

> Lord: Help Your Most Humble Slave. I Can See, Touch, Smell, But Can't Hold What I Want, Freedom, Freedom.

> Tention, Tention, Sorrow, Sorrow, Hard, Hard, Hard, No One Knows The Hell I Am In, And No One Cares, Hurt, Hurt, Cry, Cry, No One Knows What Or How I Feel, And No One Gives A Damn, But I Will Be Strong, Strong, Strong, To The Bitter End.

> Within Cell 80 I Sit Thinking, I Am Not Dumb Nor Am I A Smart Man, I Want To Be Loved And Cared For, I

Give Respect, And I Got Respect, I Am Not A Good Nor Am I A Bad Man, I Have Lived In Many Worlds, But Mostly In A Poor One, The World Which I Am In Now Is A Dream World, Dream, Dream, A Day Past, Dream, Dream, A Night Past, Dream, Dream, A Week Past, Dream, Dream, A Month Past, Dream, Dream, A Year Past, And Then Start All Over Again, Dream, Dream, Dream, Dream.

Another Sleepless Night In This Cell, Thoughts Of How I Want It To Be In The Future, Some Good, Some Bad, But Mostly Beautiful Thoughts, Dream World Please Fall Upon Me And Take Me From This Madness For A Few Hours.

I Have My Eyes To See You With, You And All Your Lovelyness, I Have My Nose To Smell You With, The Sweet Smell Of Youth At Its Best, I Have My Lips To Kiss You With, A Sweet Kiss Of Love I Will Place Upon Your Lips, In Hopes Of Tasting The Sweetness Of Your Tongue, Deep Within, I Have My Ears To Hear You With, The Tenderness Of Your Words, I Have My Hands To Touch And Hold You With, The Beauty Of Your Youthful Body, I Have My Mind To Think Of You With, Sweet Lovely, Tender, Beautiful, Sexy, Wonderful, Nice, Good, Happy, Gay, Thoughts, But Most Important Positive Thoughts Of Love, For Eternity.

There Are Two Kinds Of Freedom For Me, Freedom From The Cell Which Holds Me, And Freedom From The Cells And Walls Within Me.

My People: The Black People, My People Have For Many Years Cryed For Freedom, For Many Years Died For Freedom, I Have Heard The Crys Of The Liveing And Of The Dead Black People, And I Must Cry Harder, For Our World Is A World Of Blackness.

Black Women Are The Most Beautiful And Strong Women On Earth, There Beauty Lies Within, There

Strength Is What Gives Us, The Black Man The Power
And Will To Go On, And When We Can Step Know
Longer They Carry Us, Respect Them For They, Black
Women Are The True Mothers Of Life, And Liveing
Proof That Black Is Beautiful And Strong.

The Black Man Has Gone Thru And Is Going Thru Hell,
"My God" Where Do It End, Is There Another Answer
Other Than Death "If So" Please Show Us.

Damn The Tyrents, If Death Is What Await Me, I Will
Die Fighting, It Matter Not What Way I Die At The
Hands Of The Tyrents, As Long As I Fight Back, "My
Death" Will Be A Beautiful One.

Children Are Beautiful In Every Big And Little Way,
They Ask All Things Of You, But What They Want And
Need Is Love, Oh, My God, How I Miss Loveing, Careing
And Holding My Children, Damn This Cell, Damn Me
For Being In It.

Make No Mistake About It, This Is Hell In Its Lowest
Form, A Cell, A Cage, It Holds Me. But Not My Dreams,
For I Am A Dreamer, And One Day My Dreams Will
Become Real Or Death Will Take My Dreams And I.

My Days In This Cell Is Growing Short, The Hurt, The
Suffering, The Lonelyness, The Hell I've Been Though Is
Almost At An End, Soon There Will Be No Bars In My
Way, But Yet There Will Be.

Looking back on all the things that I'd done, all the chances
I'd took, all the times I spent in jail, it was crazy. I knew it
then, when I wrote that stuff down. I felt that if you in a cell,
just day after day and it don't bother you at all, then you
off, your mind ain't right.

Life's too short to spend any of it in jail; but if you there,
then step and be a man. Somebody's always gonna take
advantage of you some type of way if you not a man, if you
don't stand up for yourself. I felt at the time it was madness,
a maddening place. I felt that before I would come back to

it I would die—and I almost did. Sometimes I enjoy solitude, but too much solitude can be hazardous to you. A lot of times I was fighting the loneliness. The cell may have held my body, but I promised it wouldn't get my mind. I was physically locked up; it wasn't nothing I could do about that. But I wasn't going to let them break me.

I feel that the administration spend more time trying to break a man than they do trying to rehabilitate him. You go to the institution, they give you an opportunity to get a little education, and you take it. But other than the reading and writing education, they don't train you for something you can do on the outside. Ain't no place around here you can make license plates. What *I* mean by rehabilitation is that you come out and you function like everybody else function. They should train you for something you want to do and could do on the outside that would fit into society.

Now, freedom is a very important thing. You would put your life on the line for freedom. On visiting days, you see people coming in and going out. You got a visit from your sister, your mother, your wife. They was there to visit, but then they left. So you could see freedom. You could look up in the sky and see a bird flying within the walls and then fly over the walls. You could see freedom all around. You could see the sun and moon at night, shining on the wall. The grass and flowers, and the trees and rain. I could see it, I could touch it, I could smell it, but I couldn't have it.

When you on the inside, one of the worst things you can do to make your time harder is think about the outside. But the one thing you do the most of *is* think about the outside. There were days when I'd be just sitting around thinking and maybe feeling a little sorry for myself, especially when I didn't get no visitors or mail. I felt like somebody should love me enough to write me a letter or come and see me. It wasn't happening often enough. So this what made me sneak away in my own world in my cell, getting lost in my thoughts.

When I was in solitary confinement, I had different

moods and reactions all the time. It was beginning to get to me because I had been locked up for almost three years, and two years of it I had spent in solitary. Sometimes I prayed to get some type of relief from the trials and tribulations I was facing. And there were a lot of times when I really wanted to be close to a woman. I missed sex and just being with a woman. In jail you get to the point where just seeing a woman is a relief.

Being in solitary, your feelings are so mixed, your whole attitude, your whole outlook on something, could change in minutes or seconds. You could be completely pleasant and easygoing this hour and the next hour you can be furious and ready to hurt somebody, or do something destructive, or even hurt yourself—I seen that happen a lot of times. Just thinking about it brings back a lot of bad feelings.

*   *

I didn't fear punishment because I knew I could handle it, but I'm more than sure that most of us that are dealing with the system as people going in and out of jail have some really deep feelings about these things. Like, I can't stand to hear sirens. They really bug me. One of my brothers, when he was small, every time he'd hear a siren, regardless of what it was—firemen or police or ambulance—he'd actually hold his ears and scream and holler 'cause he couldn't stand it. I didn't go that far, but I really can't stand it, just like I can't stand to hear the cell closing behind me. The cells in Lorton in the block and the cells at the jail are pretty much the same. There's a hand-controlled box that the officer had the key to. If he wanted to open a particular cell on the gallery, then he would open up the box—the number of each cell is on there—and he'd just flip that number and throw the cell open. At chow time, he'd flip them all, and everybody would step out and go to eat. When that was over, everybody would step in their cell, and he'd flip them switches back and then that hmmmmm clang! That just do something to me.

I guess that's maybe why some dudes will keep escaping over and over, even though they usually get caught. Like Mark Miller. When we met at the jail in '66 or '67, I think he had something like ninety-three years. They said it was fifty-four years in the paper at the time he escaped from Lorton, but I think it was altogether a total of ninety-three years that he had. He didn't make it no secret that he was going to escape. In fact, when he was at the jail, he tell me, "As soon as I get to Lorton, I'm leaving." He said this constantly, but I ain't about to pay him no mind.

Mark was a bank robber, and as far as I knew, he robbed all the banks by himself. But he made a mistake when he robbed a bank he had an account in. See, the banks that he was robbing, he had to have some place to put the money in. So he put it in that bank, then turned around and robbed it. One of the tellers recognized him. That's how he got busted. Mark Miller to me was a comical dude. I used to call him "Birdman" because he got two birds tattooed on his chest.

Well, Mark was a damn good mechanic, and one day he just opened up one of those Lorton trucks, crashed the gate, and got away. After he escaped, my sister was telling me about the Feds walking around with machine guns and searching everybody's home in my immediate area in S.E. They finally caught him because his wife lived in S.E., and every now and then I guess the Feds would just check her out. So one day they knocked on the door. When he answered, he knew it was the rollers, so he had his pistol in his hand. Most dudes answer the door like that. I answer like that myself. When they asked him to identify himself, he said he was his wife's brother. So they asked him to open the door, and he did—firing. He downed two of them and one of them ran down the steps. Then he jumped out of the window and got away.

Afterwards he went to this large apartment and climbed in one of the vents with the police dogs sniffing him out, and this is exactly what happened. He said police hollered, more as a joke from what he was telling me, "Mark Miller, you up there?" And Mark said, "Yeah, I'm up here." The police was evidently so surprised, he didn't know what to do. He hesitated for two or three minutes, then he said, "Throw out your guns and come on out." And Mark did that, throwed out his guns and come out, and that was how he was captured.

I think it dawned on him too late that there was only one roller. If he knew that, he could have really downed him. We used to laugh about it when he got back to the jail, and I was there too. He was on dead lock, and I was on the third or fourth floor, and I would always wait until the middle of the night when everything was real quiet, and I would say, "Mark Miller, are you in there?" And he would say, "Yeah." I would say, "Come on out with your hands up!"

He killed both of the FBI he shot—two, at a time when they have all this great training. That made it a big deal. Usually you'd be a little shaky with the FBI, and that's why it hadn't happened before. But under them circumstances he didn't really care. He was thinking about getting away. Most people know that shooting a roller, your chances of getting away are very slim, but it's still possible. Shoot at the FBI and your chances get real, real hard. People would have second thoughts. .

I admire Mark for having the heart to do it. I didn't think he had it in him. But with ninety-three years in the penitentiary, what did he have to lose? Killing evidently didn't make no difference. You might think you've got a possible chance of getting away and not having to spend ninety-some years locked up. So, what the hell? He knew also during this time that the capital punishment thing was in great debate. I guess he knew they weren't going to kill him in the chair or the gas chamber. So what could they do? They were going to give him life again, probably life for each one of them. He already had life. If you had as little as three years or something like that, then you would immediately give up, and I'm sure that he or anybody else would have, because you're not going to take the chance of getting a murder charge to get out on three years. But in Mark's circumstances, he had nothing left to lose.

Another example of a person wanting to get out so bad is JoJo the escape artist. JoJo has tried all kinds of ways to get out. The last time he got caught before he even got out. What they do is bring stuff in from outside in a truck, then they reload cartons back up on the truck, the man check them, and they back out. JoJo and another dude climbed up in there, but the other dude had his feet hanging out. After they find him they searched more thoroughly and ended up finding JoJo.

The time before that he was down at Lorton, and I understand they have a little stamp they put on visitors that glows under a certain light. Visitors would get the stamp when they come in and say who they wanted to see and show their I.D. So JoJo and his friends copied the stamp. Then they needed I.D.'s and clothes. I sent him a shirt, some slacks, a pair of shoes, and a leather jacket through the dudes that would come out on work programs. They would wear it back in, and then the dude that it's for would hide it, 'cause he not supposed to have that kind of stuff. They had the stamp all copied, but what they didn't know was that the colors of the stamp were changed every day. The day they was ready to go, they got into the visiting hall, and when they start going through the line, the first two or three got caught because the colors was changed. JoJo managed to get back to the dormitory and destroy the clothes and stuff.

When a dude escape, most of the time he don't have no money. It's always hip to try to stay in this town as less as possible; but if you don't have no money and you can't go nowhere, then what? Then you got to do something. you got to hustle. So you take a chance on getting busted again and getting another charge added to whatever you got.

Most of the time dudes go where they know they are going to get help, and that's where they come from—their neighborhood. The police know this as well. So they are just going to stake out certain places. It's a cat-and-mouse game. If I was in the institution and I escaped, I would immediately head for S.E., even though I know the police will be looking for me there. I know that's where people are going to raise money for me, where I'm going to get clothes, where I'm not going to be hungry. Eventually I may get enough money to move on to somewhere else. But you don't really want to go to a strange town where nobody knows you. You want to stay where you can do your usual things and also be matching your wits against the police. Eventually most dudes do get caught. They make some kind of mistake, or somebody rats on them. Now, that wouldn't happen in my part of town, but it would happen in N.W.

I never really tried to escape from Lorton or the jail—I knew I could jive sham my way through the joint, and that's what I did. They would give you good time—days off your sentence for doing good deeds—on a Lorton sentence, and I did a lot of plotting to get as much as I could. One of my favorite things was this. We had them giant ovens in the kitchen where I worked. I would break the thermostat on them, and the heat in them ovens would be red-hot sometimes. Then, as soon as somebody puts something in it, it would immediately catch on fire. And I'd be waiting with the fire extinguisher and backing everybody up putting out the fire. I'd get five or six good days for it.

When you finally do get out of the institution, then you got to deal with your parole officer. I never was fortunate enough to have a real good parole officer. The thing you want most in a parole officer is that he doesn't press you. Some of them you got to go see every week, and they constantly on you about a job. You be saying, "Well, man,

I'm trying to put myself into a position to get a job, but I want a job that's something that *I* like." But he want you to do anything, don't matter what.

They got a little employment place down at the courthouse just for cons or for probation people. But you go in and they never have a job in town. It's always way out in Virginia. You don't have transportation, and you have to get up, say, two hours previous to work time.

A lot of my parole officers I'd just avoid seeing. I would get up early in the morning, fill out my parole papers, go to the office, and push them under the door before they'd get there. Every now and then one of them would call or come to my house. But the thing I can't stand is parole officers who come on your job, 'cause then people tend to change their view of you. Like, when I had that job at Swiss Chalet, my parole officer come, and I believe that was the beginning of the time when the man started having me do the waitress work, the maintenance work. He no longer respected me as a cook. I was an ex-con, so he figured I needed the job. I had to do that because I was on parole and I couldn't object. But I fooled him. Sometimes you got to stand up for yourself, because very seldom will somebody else speak up for you and say, "That ain't right. You shouldn't treat that person this way." But most of the time, if you stand up to people yourself and say what's right and what's wrong for you, other people can hear you and maybe they'll stand beside you then, kind of be in your corner.

Most of the time when you go up before the Parole Board at Lorton, they be asking you all kinds of stupid questions: "Why you didn't do this? How come you get into this trouble?" You try to explain it, and then they say, "Well, the courts found you guilty and you were convicted, so we have to assume that you're guilty, and these are the merits of the case that we are going upon." Sometimes they'd think I was a smart-ass, but sometimes I'd look real sad and act real humble to get what I wanted.

10

The Star of the Show

All the time that I was at the D.C. Jail and down at Lorton
—from '67 to '69—JoJo and I was making our fight for
appeal. A lot of stuff we did ourselves, filing motions and so
forth. Now, motions not a really easy thing to do. Everybody can't do it. My specialty was bond motions. I could file
a personal recognizance motion better than anybody. Oftentimes a dude would come to me and say, "Man, file me a
personal bond motion," and I'd charge him a carton of cigarettes and write it right up.

There was a few law books that the inmates could get
at the so-called jail law library, but most of them was out-
dated, and a lot of dudes like myself couldn't really relate
to the book. So most of the learning for the motions that we
wrote came from other dudes. Say a lawyer representing me
on a case files a motion—whether it's a bond or writ of
mandamus or habeas corpus—I automatically get a copy.
Then I might tell some other guys, "My lawyer, she filed this
here for me today." They'll check it out, and if there's
something in the motion that's useful to them, they would
copy the motion so it could fit them.

I learned how to file personal bond motions from seeing
a personal bond motion filed by a public defender who had
sent me a copy of it. Immediately I transferred that onto my
own paper. When I wrote a bond motion for somebody else,
I would use just about the same basic things, but I'd make
it fit that particular person.

If JoJo and I decided to write a motion on our own, which we did a lot of times, the motion might be three or four pages long, and there had to be copies. There wasn't no machine, so we had to do all this by hand. Then you don't want to send no untogether motion to court. It's got to be neat. My job was mostly the writing part, and some of my friends would do the getting down into the law part.

We got this dude named Carter to do our appeal for us. But he was appointed, and the man had no criminal law experience whatsoever—he was a civil lawyer. He told us, "I'll do my very best, but I don't know nothing about criminal law!" We was saying, "Well, ain't nothing going to happen here." But it did, to our surprise. We didn't get a reversal, as we was hoping, but we got what you call a remand hearing. They ruled out the identification testimony of the first witness because of the suggestiveness of him seeing us in the police station. So all he could testify to was that on such and such a day, he was robbed. At the remand hearing, the District Court kind of had to correct the mistake made by the identification having been ruled admissible in the first trial, so when they sent it back, the judge finally grant us a new trial.

That's when my man Phil came in. I met him shortly after we got the news about the remand hearing. Automatically the other lawyer dropped out. Then Phil and Lyons took over. Lyons was JoJo's lawyer, Phil was mine. Right from the beginning there was something about Phil that made me trust him more than any other lawyer. He never really said, but it was a thing like understood, that *you're* my client; all I have is your best interests at heart.

He became my friend as well as my attorney. Like, if I come downtown to the bull pen, he would do things like go upstairs and get me some cigarettes, two or three packs— little things that don't seem like anything. Anybody could do them, but anybody *don't*. It made me go for the dude even more, and I just kind of let myself go, hoping that I wasn't making a mistake. But I still had that fear of getting sold out, so I used to test Phil out a lot. The last few days before trial, we really started talking to each other, getting into my past. All the time I could tell from the way that I felt around him that he was different from other lawyers I had had. I felt that he cared about *me*. And I didn't make no mistake—in the long run, it really paid off. He never let me down all these years. I couldn't ask no more of friends.

Now, our second trial was a lot different from our first because this time JoJo pleaded guilty to the indictment. He didn't take a cop to attempted robbery. What made him change his mind, I don't know, because nobody sure what he was going to do till the last minute. Then, by his suddenly pleading guilty, it threw his lawyer off a little bit. But JoJo played a master role in my second trial. Once he plead guilty to the charges, then he immediately stated on the stand that I was not with him. That was one of the strongest points in my defense. Him getting on the stand and saying, "Naw. He wasn't with me, but Peanut and somebody else was with me at the time I did this robbery. Yeah, I know I'm giving up my rights."

So when the trial started, JoJo was going to testify for me, and I had a lot of confidence that Phil was going to do the very best he could for me. But what destroyed me was, when we went into court, the D.A. says to Phil, "How you doing, Phil?" "Oh, I'm all right, Charlie." "How about so and so. . . . ?" That just crashed everything. I said, to myself, "What's happening? He faked me out!" I wouldn't say nothing to him. I wouldn't look at him. I was mad. I wanted to hit him in the mouth. This gentleman sold you out, that was my first reaction. But it really wasn't like that at all. Once the show began, I knew it. And I'm saying to myself, "Go get 'em, tiger!"

I saw that trial as a show, played act by act, but for real and for a high price, which was my freedom. Phil had brought me some clothes. I remember him telling me it was his father's shirt, a thing to play tennis or golf in, and pants that kind of went with the shirt that made me look like I really, really wouldn't do anything! "There's no way that he could be involved in anything, not looking like this." Once we got into the arena and things started off, Charlie, the D.A., he a loud talker, and at certain times he'd make his point by banging on things and screaming. He really going through a lot of changes. He yelled so much that the jury started looking away from him. I knew he had made a bad-guy move, and the jury did not like it at all. I think Phil sat there much calmer than what I was.

When it's our turn to get on the stage, he got up kind of slow, straighten himself up, and begins talking plain and average, but he getting over his points. He didn't yell once. He talked so that the jury, judge, and D.A. could hear him with no trouble, and they all understood what he said. The jury seemed more interested in what he was saying because his words seemed to roll out with great tenderness, but a greater respect.

It was time for him to do his thing, and he began by making the D.A.'s top-dog, main witness look like a damn fool and a bad guy. For two years that man was saying I had a Fu manchu mustache when I committed the robbery. The police at the first trial had a picture to this effect. In fact, that picture was a large part in getting me convicted. The dude on the stand had never changed his story. He said the same thing at the first trial and the remand hearing. Phil talk to him for about ten minutes and then said, "Are you sure he had a Fu manchu mustache or did he have long sideburns?" The dude hesitated. I knew Phil had him then, and I think Phil knew he had him, 'cause he never let him answer if it was long sideburns. Instead he said, "Did the sideburns come all the way down along the side of his face?" And the dude agreed. "Yeah, sideburns down the side of his face." Phil said, "Was it like an Abraham Lincoln beard that come down the side and around the front?" The dude thought about it and before he could answer, Phil said, "You know how Abraham Lincoln's beard was—full beard on the side, coming down . . ." The dude said, "Yeah, it was an Abraham Lincoln." And Phil out with the picture. Whop!

That just changed everybody's mind, 'cause it make this guy look like he really didn't know what he was talking about. We became the good guys, and Charlie and his boys became the bad guys. That was only one of the high points in the trial, but it was the one point that made Phil the star of the show. I knew then that we had come to fight and win, and we were wiping hell out of them. The great Charlie, D.A., did everything he could to get his stardom back, but it was too late.

Then JoJo, our ace in the hole, took the stand like a pro and testified that he had committed the robbery but with two other dudes, not with me. He said he had let off the other two and was supposed to meet them later. Then he had picked me up and somewhere in the process the police had started chasing us. The D.A. was now like a madman. He tried to make JoJo blow, but JoJo hung in there. The D.A. yelled and yelled like hell, and some of the jury seem like they were ready to boo him. Finally he sat down with his head in his hands. Phil stood again and all eyes were on him. First he looked at the judge with a look of sureness, then at the jury with even more sureness deep in his eyes and on his face. He gave the jury facts, but most of all he gave them understanding. The show was over, and he was the star.

I had never felt this about any other lawyer. I felt maybe that a lawyer had done a good job, but I didn't feel impressed. It was just his way of carrying himself, his way of talking—it got to me as well, 'cause I was all ears. I remember one of the jurors telling me after the trial that when they first went in, it was seven to five for not guilty right then. She said, "We really didn't have a hard time convincing the others that you was not guilty. Your lawyer had done such a good job convincing us."

A lot of lawyers be jiving. They'll wait till the very last minute before you going on trial before they come over to the jail. Then they really don't know about the case. They only know what they've read. They haven't checked things out. I recall that Phil or Lyons told me they had went to the area and checked out where the robbery happened. I was glad they did, because Charlie made a big deal out of us coming out of the store and the dude following us. He said, "They proceeded up Georgia Avenue and turned on Shepherd," and he got a blackboard. This is all to make the play better. It really don't mean nothing, but it's impressing the people. And Phil was able to answer him back.

Also Phil was always available to me. He wasn't too busy doing other things that he didn't have time to come see his client. I remember just before going to trial there were four or five motions that JoJo and me had in mind to bring up with Phil and Lyons. But before I could mention them, Phil said, "I'm filing this and I'm filing that"—not only the four or five that I was thinking about, but two or three extra ones.

Ordinarily you lie to your lawyer because you don't trust him any more than you trust the police or the D.A. Say a lawyer is representing me, and I got a case where I shot somebody. Maybe I was a drug user, and I go to this dealer and I say, "Man, I'm sick. Give me some drugs for now, and I will pay you double later." So the dealer get tough with me and rough with me, and I happen to have a gun. My intentions are not to shoot, but he got some drugs and I want some, and he says no. Now, maybe he and I get to scuffling, and I shoot him—bang. Okay. But maybe it really didn't go like that at all. Maybe I said, "Give me some drugs." He said, "No." And I fired. We never scuffled or nothing, I just shot him and took the drugs.

Now, the first story sounds much better, and that's ordinarily the one I would tell my lawyer. I would say I was sick, I begged this man for some drugs, he refused and tried to take my gun from me, it went off, and I shot him. My lawyer is going to represent me harder under these circumstances than he would if I told him, "Yeah, I was a drug addict, and I shot him and took the drugs." You can be guilty and have a good reason for being guilty, and the lawyer still gonna put everything into it. But if you guilty and you don't have no reason for being guilty, then the lawyer ain't gonna fight real hard.

But it all really depend on the type of relationship you have with your lawyer, how much you trust him. If Phil was representing me now, I would tell him the truth, because I honestly believe that regardless, he would have my best interests at heart. But when he was representing me, I told him the story I testified to at trial. As time went on, though, I would ask him things, putting him on the spot, asking if he thought I was guilty, and he would say, "Well, I'm your lawyer. I'm supposed to represent you no matter what I think, so it don't matter what I think." And I say, "Do you think you could really represent me thinking that I was guilty?" And he say, "I'm your lawyer. That's my job." But I never talked about being guilty straight out—until now.

One of the things you have going against you in court is the way the D.A. coaches the police and all the government witnesses. The police will say one thing and have it pretty well pat no matter what, so you got no chance there. And the witnesses going for the government come directly behind the police. The police often lie, sometimes in strong cases, most of the time in weak cases. Sometimes in strong cases they want to make it even stronger or sound more exciting or make it seem like they played a bigger part when only the officer that wrote up the report was involved. But everybody wants to get in on it.

An example is when we was picked up after we robbed that liquor store. They made a big deal out of the fact that we had a police radio in the car—that was all over the papers. It made the government's case sound real good. There go two stickup men, so well equipped and professional that they have a police radio, and every time the police set up a road block to stop them, they was aware of it by listening to that radio. Actually the thing wasn't even hooked up! They said it was in the glove compartment: a hole was bored in the back of the compartment very deeply, and the wires came out the back and hooked up to something that made it work. But that was a lie. That thing couldn't pick up nothing 'cause we didn't know how to hook it up!

But the whole trial is like a show played to an audience. They're acting, but you're acting too. Everybody play the same game. Everybody in the show together. Like the judge, he setting there like the ringmaster. He handle it all. He's the top overseer. The D.A., he immediately makes you out a bad guy, and not only you but everybody associated with you, including your lawyer. But sometimes when the game is played, the defense lawyer be sympathetic to the D.A. In a little way, without saying in court, he'll be thinking or showing the D.A., "Man, I'm sympathetic with you 'cause he *is* a bad guy." That's the impression he'll give everybody in there who'll dig it, including the jury, what's most important.

One thing I can't stand about a jury is a sleeper. I think if you picked for jury duty, and if you don't feel like you're qualified or that you going to render an honest decision, then you shouldn't accept. This is why it takes so long to pick a jury, and this is the purpose of all the questions in the beginning. What the judge should tell them is, "The trial start tomorrow, and we'd like for all of you to get a good night's rest so there won't be no sleeping tomorrow." 'Cause I have seen as many as two or three jurors sleeping at a time while I was on trial. It was a serious matter because, wow, like my life on the line and they taking a nap! It really don't make any difference to them. That just shows you how much people care. Then you'll sometimes have two or three eager beavers, and they don't miss nothing. They right there leaning and listening and hearing every word you and the lawyers say. I think that this is what everybody should be about the business of doing—being very concerned and listening real hard.

Like, this thing the judge always say: in order to find a person guilty, you have to believe that he is guilty beyond a reasonable doubt. There can't be no doubt in your mind that this man is guilty. So many times people will be persuaded by the majority. But if I believe that the man is innocent and eleven of the jurors believe that he's guilty, then I would want to constantly tell them why I believe that he's innocent. If they don't feel that my reason is good enough for them to change their verdict back from guilty to not guilty, then they shouldn't. When we go in the courtroom, that's the way it should be. But it don't happen like that. You see people be saying it's eleven to one, so they tend to go along with the eleven, even though that's a reasonable doubt. You not supposed to render any decision, but they do.

11

Hooked

First day I'm out after Phil got me acquitted on that armed robbery charge in '69, my sister Cookie invites me over to her place, saying she got two dames she wants me to meet. So that evening I change out of my jail clothes and go down to her house. We sitting around drinking and smoking a little bit of herbs—Cookie, a few other people, and me. Finally this girl Lola come in. She kind of tall and skinny, not too bad-looking. She wouldn't win no contests, but she was all right. Then Tracy comes.

My sister introduce me to both of them. Immediately I go into my bag. I get to rapping to them. I really don't want to talk to Tracy 'cause she ain't my style at all. She's real, real square—square as a pool table and twice as green. So out of the two I picked Lola. She explained to me that this dude that she go with come past her house just about every night. So I say, "Well, yeah, but I'd be happy to see you in the daytime." See, I'd been locked up a long time and what it was was this sex thing. So it didn't make no difference about the dude coming at night, as long as I get over that day. But next day the dude come early! It gets me mad, so I decide there ain't but one thing for me to do, and that's to go back and get this girl Tracy. I took her to a gambling party that night, and when I took her home, I just stayed. We got to her house, and I never left.

During the day I started going back up on Stanton Road,

hang out, run into some of the old fellows, and just mess around. While I was there, I was checking out that a lot of the dudes was involved in some kind of drugs. Some of my buddies had moved up the ladder, and they was into it. I went to a few dudes' joints, and there'd be two or three broads setting around, little jumps on. I'd be laughing, and they'd be kidding and giving me this and giving me that. The first time, I think, I snorted something and put the rest in my pocket, 'cause I really wasn't involved with that stuff.

That same week Ann came to see me, and we talked. She knew I was out, since she always stay in good contact with my family. She had gone to live with another dude, but she left the kids with my family. She was too afraid to take the kids. She knew that if she had took the kids to go live with another nigger, then I definitely would have killed her. She could go, yeah, and that would hurt me enough; but if she had took one of the crumb snatchers, then it really would have been something.

Anyhow, in a couple of days she came around and started rapping. I was trying to play it to her about her being with this other dude didn't matter to me. But it really did. It must have been love, 'cause it couldn't have been her looks —I always tell her that. And it sure wasn't her money, since she didn't have none of that.

Ann and Tracy live on the same street, so now I start staying up here some nights, down there some nights. They both knew about the other and Tracy accept it, but Ann really didn't. They used to make different comments, but they didn't want to blow me, neither of them—that's what I figured, but I was wrong.

The real thing was this. Ann, she always been a hard-working dame. Ever since she was young she had a job, always providing for the kids or for herself, never depending on nobody. But I wasn't about to work. Not at this time. All that time I been in jail, I need to relax for a while. So I sit around and sit around, and she got it in her head that I just wasn't going to do nothing. That's what she assume. She didn't know that I was making plans as to getting a large piece of narcotics and putting it on the street. If she had knowed that I would eventually be making the money that I did make, she never would have left. But assuming that I wasn't going to do anything, she left. This time when she leave, it don't upset me as much, 'cause my feelings had started to change.

So I stuck more with Tracy. I enjoyed being with her because she was half-country and didn't know anything. So my word was law to her. The onliest problem was, I had to tell her to do everything. "Tracy, it's time for dinner. Cook." "Tracy, wash the dishes." I felt like she should've had some type of initiative. She wanted to be laying around with me all the time. She was showing her affection, but I like a clean joint and good food, things of this nature. I believe what I really liked about her was, before me, she never had anything but them five kids of hers. She just scuffing around and scuffing around, barely making it. When I really started making money and I was giving her large amounts, she used to fall right on the bed crying 'cause she didn't know what to do with it. I used to wonder, This dame must be crazy or something. Then she explained to me how things used to be for her, how her husband had treated her so bad, and I began to understand.

She was a lot different from the dames I was used to. When you're in the type of life I was in, then you're automatically going to meet slick people, slick dames. Many times I been standing up on the corner looking cool, and one of them broads would slide up to me and say, "When you coming around my house? You know, I been trying to give you some for two months."

What it is, they don't have no money at that particular time to buy a spoon or half a spoon of dope, so now they offering theirself. I used to keep two or three spoons of dope in my pocket just for that purpose. I'd say, "Yeah, well, what's wrong with right now?" But them kind of relationships don't really mean nothing. It was just sex to me, narcotics to them.

During those first few weeks out of jail, I ran into an old friend of mine, Clayton. We had been in the same cell at D.C. Jail and later became very close at Lorton. At the time I met him again, I had just come to the conclusion that stickup of joints without inside help would be kind of hard. So I lay easy on it. I also dug that everybody was into the drug thing all around me.

So I called Clayton at his joint. When I got up there, he was doing a booming business. You could tell that from the quantity of stuff he had. Him and I talked and talked. He said, "Man, what you want to do?" So I say, "Well, this drug thing is kind of new to me." Of course, I knew about drugs —they had been around most of my life—but I just hadn't done it. So Clayton proceeded to teach me what he knew about handling narcotics: how to mix it, how to test it, how to taste it.

Eventually I could taste different drugs and tell how much mix in it or if there's too much mix in it or what have you. You learn what drugs can take. This means that if I sell you one spoon of pure and tell you that this can take a fifteen, you can add fifteen more spoons of mix with this. You might use quinine or lactose to mix it with. I even had mixed dope up with confectioner's sugar one time. Clayton asked me, "Man, how was the dope? Was it good?" I said, "I don't know if it's the best dope in town, but it's the sweetest!"

Clayton also taught me how to cap. During that time, cap was the big thing. A cap is a little plastic thing like you see in commercials on television where they say, "We got twenty-five million time capsules in a little cap." What you do is take a cap, tap in the dope, and put the top on. You constantly doing that, and that's the way it was sold, each cap for a dollar and a half. Most of the time people call the cap an egg: "Give me twenty eggs." Then you crack into the two parts—the large part and the small part. You learn how to fill the small part and not the large part. You learn how to blow in them to put air in so you give up less dope —get more caps out of the spoon.

After he taught me about this, Clayton gave me an amount of dope and said I could do whatever I wanted with it. He told me, "You can use all the money. But in the event that you feel like the business is good and you want to continue it, then you come back to me with this amount of money. I'll give you more dope, and you can continue to roll." He handed me something like twenty-five thousand dollars worth of drugs, and what I did with that first batch of drugs, I used all the money. I bought a lot of clothes and I done a few favors, 'cause I had the money—just like a spree, having a good time. This was all well and good as far as Clayton was concerned. He knew I had been down for a long time, and he had done something similar himself when he had come out.

So I went back to him, told him what I had done, and we started talking about business—real business—getting down to it. He gave me some more drugs, and then I began to do business like it's supposed to be done. The fun was over. Eventually I was doing something like a grand worth of heroin business a day. I went out on the streets, and through different friends of mine I would give them maybe two or three hundred dollars' worth, and they would help me turn it, twirl it. Some would even come to help me make it up—sift it out, mix it, cap it up.

Business started getting better and better and better, but once I got established, then I kind of fell into it myself. In the beginning I was handling things pretty well. I didn't go too far with the drugs, only to a certain point. But after a while you lose your zest, and it becomes a mental game that you play with your body and them drugs and your mind. Then it all turns into one big mass confusion.

I was rolling in drugs and rolling good. I'm well off. I'm dressing nice and keeping a knot in my pocket. I've got a nice ride. I've got me a stable of broads, so I'm cool. I think success and curiosity got me into the drugs. I'd be sitting around the house with a couple of dudes, three or four dames, and we funning. Taking a blow of coke, blow of heroin. It was a social thing, only instead of cocktails it was drugs. You sitting around, you take a blow. Then somebody else take a blow, and you're talking, you're high. You constantly telling yourself, It's cool; I can handle it. After what happened to my father, you couldn't have gave me all the tea in China to say that I would do this, but then it just happened.

You always tell yourself you can handle anything, and then you don't really believe it when it happens. I started off with a snorting jones. I got a habit from just sniffing the stuff. I wake up sick one day. I can't understand it. I'm telling myself I got the flu. I must have the twenty-four-hour bug or something. Nose running, bones aching. Some of my friends come and say, "Man, you better go in there and sniff two or three of them eggs." And I go in there and sniff two of them, and I'm all right. Then I knew I had a habit.

So many people fool theirself: "I'm not going overboard; I'm not going to have no habit." Eventually they skin pop. Then they mainline on the weekend. Then it come not only on the weekend but the middle of the week. The next thing you know it's every day. Then you wrapped up. It's all out of proportion—there's nothing you can do but get more heroin. And the things people do to get it is wild. You don't say, "Well, I'm going to get enough money where I can shoot dope for the next month." You just worry about the twenty or thirty dollars you're without right then.

I think that in back of everybody's mind, they be looking for that first high. You take off. It's the first time you ever felt like this in your life. So the next day you try to recapture that. But you can't. When I took heroin, I felt cool, calm. I felt that I was together. Sometimes you can get a rush—it depends on the quality and quantity of drugs. Sometimes you feel it in your stomach, you can almost feel it traveling over your body. As it be going, there's a turn from one mood to another mood. By the time it get to your head, wow! You don't be sleeping. You can hear. You know what's be happening, but you just be in such a state that you don't wanna even raise your head up to look around. Conversation is being held and you listening, you might even be involved. But your voice often changes to heavy or light. If you're taking off to get high, you in a more mellow thing. If it's an escaping thing—you got problems—then you going in a more deep or nodding or nonexistent thing.

There was a broad named Donna that I met around this time who really wasn't into drugs, and I did a lot of talking to keep her that way. I had ripped off a legal establishment one week, and that Saturday night me and twelve or thirteen of my boys went around to the Shelter Room, which was a joint we used to hang in.

Meanwhile, I run into another old friend of mine named Joanne. We call her Joey. In growing up in the projects, Joey used to hang with me sometimes 'cause she was a pretty good thief. But at this particular time she had a number of broads that was hustling. Usually when a dame playing the role as a pimp, she's a stud; but I think Joey was bisexual, because she enjoyed men as much as women. So Joey had all her broads down in the Shelter Room that night, and this broad Donna was included. I found out later that this was the first night Donna had actually been into that mob and out on the streets.

Well, Joey got to talking about what she was about the business of doing. I said, "Yeah, that's kind of hip. Do you want to have some fun?" At first she thought it was gonna be a thing where it just be me and her, but I said, "I want you to get all your girls together, and we gonna do it to death." So Joey and her girls (about eight of them) and about

twelve of my boys and me, we piled into cars and went out
to a place called Mr. Wicks, which is on the border between
Maryland and Washington, not too far out of S.E. It was like
a motel, and we got four cabins all night together.

Everybody crowded into one cabin at first, doing their
thing—smoking herb, shooting coke, shooting or snorting
heroin, and really into the sex thing. Everybody coming off
with clothes. Joey and me, we set back watching and looking, 'cause I like to catch my boys in embarrassing situations
and snap their pictures. This was a fun thing to me. Anyhow, we watched and I laughed, and then I noticed this
Donna. She tall and nice, and the dudes would talk to her
a few minutes but then kind of stray away. I also noticed
how hard she was looking at the hypodermic needles there.
When somebody'd take off, she'd watch every reaction they
went through. And I just began to watch her.

Everybody there was doing something, one way or another, with narcotics—snorting, shooting, what have you. I
asked Joey, "What's with that dame there?" She told me that
the broad didn't use stuff. One of my boys that had some
narcotics had dropped it on the table, and she was asking
him how much should she shoot before she shoot an overdose. She didn't know what was happening, but she wanted
to be part of it 'cause everybody else was doing it.

So I just sashayed up to her and said, "You don't mess
with drugs, huh?" She didn't want to admit it. She said,
"Yeah, I mess with drugs before." So I took a cooker and say,
"What's this?" She say, "It's a top." "What's it for? What do
you call it? What do you do with it?" I kept questioning her,
and she didn't know. Then I told her that she really didn't
have to be a part of this if she didn't want to. I said, "Don't
use drugs simply because everybody else uses drugs. Now,
you probably be all right tonight if you use some and get
high and have one or two of these men around here, but then
tomorrow you be sorry. Or tomorrow you'll remember
how good you felt and try it again, then the next day try

it again, and the next thing you know, you're hooked. There ain't no turning back."

I ran all the usual things down to her, come to find out her real thing was, she liked Bacardi rum. So I proceed to get in the car and go to a liquor store nearby and get some beer and wine, rum and gin. We come back and the shooters ain't gonna mess with no liquor, but some of the smokers and snorters get into it. So everybody's balling, and she jive happy being herself a little bit. It was getting pretty smoky and crowded, so I walked out and stood by the car for a while, smoking a cigarette. She came out there, and I got more deep into that drug thing, telling her it was only a way of making money and that it would destroy her eventually, and I knowed that it was gonna destroy me. I told her a lot of things that I really didn't think I believed myself. Only subconsciously I must have known it was the truth. I didn't want to realize the truth for myself, but somehow I wanted her to see it. And she did. She stayed with what I told her. I seen her when I was at D.C. General after I got shot, and she told me that using drugs was one thing she never did.

Actually, though, I never thought much about what I was doing. All I thought about was the dollar bills. I knew it was destruction for those who bought it from me and for myself when I became a user. But mainly I saw it as a means of making money, and I shut everything else out of my mind. Money do strange things to people, especially a person not really used to having a whole lot of anything. When you find yourself in a position where you able to do most of the things that you want, where you got all the things you need, then you willing to overlook a lot. The money even blinded me to all them years that I had thought about my father. It got to the point where what happened to him didn't make no difference. It happened. I'm doing all right, so what the hell? Let it keep on going like it is. It could be selfishness, or it could be just the fact that you never had nothing and you wanted something all your life so bad.

I heard it said a thousand times: "Money don't change me. I'll always have my same friends. I'll always do the same things that I done before." This same person six months later be up on a higher level and he ain't gonna speak to you. He ain't gonna give you nothing except maybe a hundred dollars to get you away from him quick.

*   *

Now, Clayton was the kind of dude who smoked herb and occasionally would take a drink or shoot some cocaine, but he never did mess with heroin. He knew the consequences. He wanted a lot of things that he knew he couldn't get if he had a habit. He often would get on me: "Man, you ain't never gonna have no money. Why don't you go and clean yourself up, man? Dry out." And I'm saying, "I can handle it. I can handle it. Give me this and give me that, and I can handle it."

The way we had it worked, he'd give me a grand of stuff a day, and I would probably sell it by that night. Out of the grand's worth of stuff, I give him six hundred dollars, and four hundred dollars was mine. That means he had to make a daily trip to my house to pick up his scratch, his money. He would constantly tell me that heroin was not where it's at. He even went so far one time as to give me some sleeping pills and brought me around to his house to make sure I wasn't shooting. He kept me there a weekend and I did it. I kicked it. I dried out, and I got myself together, and it was a whole lot better for a while. I didn't even lose time on my business by drying out, 'cause I had two good lieutenants who took care of my business.

It took me about a week altogether, but the first three days is the roughest. Every joint in your body ache. It's about a hundred times worse than the flu. You can't hold nothing in your stomach, not even water. Everything come up. And when there is nothing else to come up, you just gag,

gag, gag. To me it used to feel like a lumberjack with giant boots or a paratrooper just stomping on my stomach. Your nose constantly running, your eyes dripping, your penis dripping, your bowels break, everything.

So for three days Clayton put up with all my hollering and spitting up. Then things began getting back to the way they was at the beginning, but it was slow. By me handling so much drugs and having a habit, it was still a temptation. But I kind of forded it off. I smoked a lot of marijuana and hash instead, and I snorted a lot of coke, which is much more expensive than heroin.

Anyway, business eventually got to the point where I didn't sell any drugs direct at all. Most of the time the stuff would come to me all cut and capped, because Clayton had six broads, nonusers, that he would pay for doing the capping. Clayton did the cutting or asked somebody else to do the cutting, but the broads would do the capping. They'd work together in an air-conditioned apartment, which is a whole lot better than trying to mix drugs up in the heat. Five of them had regular jobs working for the government, but they would get a bonus from Clayton depending on how many pills they capped. Occasionally things would be in a rush. If I sold out much sooner than I expected, they wouldn't be ready, so Clayton would just bring me the uncut drugs, and I would proceed to mix them up and cap them myself.

Clayton and I did this for quite some time, and he made me a kind of success. He was steadily climbing that ladder, and if he was still alive today, he would be in a much higher position. Maybe I would too, 'cause I was his number one lieutenant and began to hire a lot of dudes myself. Now, the only thing about hiring people to sell drugs is, your help ain't regular. You might give somebody five hundred pills, and they might split on you. After all, most of the time they're only drug addicts. So you try to get the most out of people that you can.

Now, Clayton used to occasionally take a drink or shoot cocaine. I also got into the habit of shooting or snorting cocaine occasionally. We would do it together. He had it so I was probably the only one that really knew he shot cocaine. This one particular day Clayton had this large-screen color T.V., still in the box, that he gave a dude some drugs for. Him and I was about the business of setting it up. When we got the T.V. all straightened out, Clayton said, "Man, I got some good coke—if I can find it." We started laughing. I reached in my jacket pocket and said, "I got two brand-new hypes."

We proceeded to look for the coke, find it, and go into the bathroom, but we only got one tie. We use a shoestring, a necktie, a stocking, a small piece of rope—anything to make the veins stand up. He say, "I want to go first." Evidently he didn't know the real strength of the coke, because he put quite a bit in the top. If the coke is good, then you need very little of it, especially if you're mainlining. Once you draw it up in the hype and get a hit, get the blood up in the hype, then you just go real slow. You might even stop and rap for a little while, talk about how good it is with the needle still hanging there in the vein.

Clayton used to fire in his leg—he had a big vein in his calf. So he tied it up, hit himself, and pushed it all in at once. It kind of surprised me that he did it that way 'cause he knew better. My first impression was maybe the coke was not as good, remembering how much he had put in the top. But it was, the coke was dynamite. You could smell it all through the house once we mixed it up, and we had two hypes full, one for him and one for me.

Finally, after he shot it, he took the tie off and gave it to me. He kind of slumped sitting on the toilet. He said, "Man, that is some good coke!" Then he said, "Wow, I feel funny. This can't be no O.D. because if it was, whatever was going to happen would have happened by now." Meanwhile, I'm looking at him, but I'm not paying too much attention because I'm trying to get a hit myself. I'm tied up and shaking my hands, because at that time I was firing in the veins in my hands. Finally what made me notice him was he making a funny sound. I look at him and at first I can't understand what's wrong, what's happening. Then I dig it. Immediately I run to the kitchen, and get some warm water, add some salt, and start shooting it into him to try to dilute the drug. Then I put ice cubes on his neck, under his arms and private parts. Everything I knew to do I did. I was trying to walk him, but I was still weak from having kicked the heroin a short time previously, so I couldn't handle him like I thought. I only got him to the bedroom.

Finally a knock came and a key was in the door, but the chain was on. Then I heard his woman's voice calling him. I think at this point I must have panicked. I saw the second hype laying there, and for some reason I felt like I had to shoot it. So this is what I did. Probably why the same thing didn't happen to me was I was so excited, plus by having a heroin habit previous and being a larger user of drugs than Clayton ever was, my system was able to tolerate it better than his. It really didn't have a whole lot of effect on me.

Meanwhile, his woman, Cheryl was tearing at the door. I never did go down to let her in, but she finally broke the chain off the door and got in the house. I told her what happened and all that I did, that nothing was working, that I had poured half a gallon of milk down his throat and all I was getting was a little gag back from him. I said, "We got to get him to a hospital real quick."

We're on the fourth floor, no elevator, and I had to bring him down those steps. So, I put him across my shoulder. By the time I got to the first landing, the milk that I had poured down his throat came back out and all the way down my back. I fell three or four times, and the main thing I was concerned with was hitting his head. Finally I took him off my shoulder and held him up in my arms like you hold a baby. It took all the strength I had to try to go without falling, or if I fell, to fall back instead of forward so I wouldn't hurt him, 'cause he was still unconscious.

In the end I got him down the stairs and into the car, but I had some guns on me. I knew I couldn't go to the hospital like that, especially since I was going to stay there until I found out what happened. So on our way I dropped the guns off at my grandparents' house, stuffed them under a chair. When we get to the hospital, I tell his woman to make it because I don't want her to be involved. So I'm struggling to get Clayton in there myself. There was some people and some orderlies standing around and won't none of them help me. Finally I tell the people he shot an overdose of cocaine. Then they rushed him back into the emergency room and started to work on him. A few minutes later this orderly came out and said he was dead.

Then they tried to keep me around there, talking and talking. "Where all did you get the drugs?" and this and that. Clayton was dead, so I think they wanted me. I was alive and well and walking around. I probably could have told them something. That's why people like me was very often afraid to bring other people in. You know you're going to be questioned. When somebody O.D.'s, it's hard to tell if he's past the point of help. Sometimes a dude can be saved, but the person that's with him is reluctant to carry him to the hospital for fear of getting busted, so he'll leave the dude to die or just put him in an alley. So many cases they put drug addicts in the alley or on rooftops, just to get rid of them. Anyway, the hospital people are trying to stall me around, and they did until the police got there. But once I saw the police, I immediately left. They tried to catch me, but it was more my turn than theirs because I was familiar with the area, and I got away.

The hardest thing for me to do was to accept Clayton's death. It really put me in a spin, right back on drugs and much, much harder than what I was originally. Really deep into it. It was especially hard for me to face his woman. Even after his death and after I got really wound back up in drugs, she done a lot of things trying to help me.

It wasn't my fault that Clayton died, but I think you always feel like maybe there was something you could have done. I often think that there was heroin somewhere in the house, and if I could have found it, maybe I could have saved his life by shooting small doses of it into him so it slow his heart down.

After Clayton died and I got wrapped up in heroin again, for a long time I just didn't care about nothing. I was really down, doing bad, and that was when I started sticking up a lot of dealers. I did this for a little while, and then one of the really big dealers, One-armed Sam, came to see me about it. He told me he'd rather have me working for him than against him 'cause I was costing him too much money.

There's no telling how many people Sam had working for him, but I knew of about forty, and I always suspected much, much more. Sam used to mention to me, "I'm going out of town, boy, and I'm carrying a hundred grand with me." Now, when you buying a hundred grand worth of drugs, then you got mucho drugs. This will gross you maybe a million in return, if not above.

As for me, I was doing about a grand a day, but out of that grand I was only getting three hundred because I had to give him seven. But I eventually got to doing so good that it made his other dealers mad. Sam would say things like "I give you chumps a grand of stuff and it'll take you a week to sell it. Johnny, he'll be back here tomorrow for more!" See, with me, I know everybody in the projects. I know everybody in Garfield and everybody in Knox and all them guys up there work for me. They won't steal nothing from me.

I used to tell my dealers, "You play square with me, and I'm gonna play square with you." I tried to stay away from dudes that only wanted to support their habit, because they're not reliable. I wanted dudes that wanted *money*. But no matter what you do, you always have a large amount of drug users working for you. At one point I had on the street about twenty-two dudes. But all of these dudes didn't do a booming business. Some dudes, I just gave them a break. They might have small habits, so all they wanted to do was support their habits. If I give a dude fifty pills, he's selling each pill for a dollar and a half, which'd be seventy-five dollars. I get the fifty dollars, and he get the twenty-five. And this was enough to carry him day by day. My brother Nut and this dude Popcorn and this dude Scout were my main boys—they really ran things for me. They made the collection and brought it to me. I, in turn, gave them their share. Then they would pay off everybody while I went to the man.

Still, I never saw the very top of the drug business. They never came to this town any kind of way. On one or two occasions I did go to Detroit with Clayton before he died. Me and Clayton went to an apartment there that I got the impression was just an outlet, a place that you can go and pick up stuff and leave. It was a two- or three-room apartment, and the first room must have had one million locks on the door, with two dudes in the hallway all holstered up. The system was, once you say a certain thing or give off a certain move, you get in. Once we got in, it was maybe five or six dudes sitting around with shotguns and different types of rifles and pistols hanging all off of them. They had to disarm us 'cause I had two pistols on me.

I couldn't go in the room where the drugs and the money was dealt. They wouldn't let me witness the transaction. I stayed in the room where the guards were, but I saw a little of what went down. The bedroom had a steel door on it, and this one dude went up to it and must have rung some buzzers to let the dudes on the inside know it was a customer. You could hear the dude inside taking locks off for about five minutes. When the door finally opened, I could see there was only one dude in there, and at the end of the room was a table with kilos of narcotics stacked up about a foot high. At that time a kilo of narcotics cost us about forty thousand dollars, and most of the people that dealed in kilos originally paid only about seven grand for it. I was just along as one of Clayton's partners or advisors or bodyguards, so I didn't see how much Clayton bought, but he didn't do the business that Sam did. Sam would buy three or four kilos at a time.

Sam was on a pretty hip level so that if you could get away with it for a period of months or years, you could do all right. But really looking at the whole thing, it ain't that far up even at that rate of business. I remember one time Sam had a hundred sixty grand from old sales to purchase more narcotics. Now, it might be ten more dudes from different parts of the country that also put in this size purchase order from the dudes we were dealing with in Detroit. The dudes in Detroit did a multimillion-dollar business, and there was more people above them. It gets so far up that sometimes you don't want to know.

Sam and I once went to a dude in Detroit who had motel cabins rented on the outskirts of the city. He had broads there, bodyguards, watchmen, drop men. I always watching because I say if *we* bring this much money and there's twelve or fifteen of us coming to him, when he bag it all up and make his move back, I sure would like to get him. I was thinking about getting all that cash. But I never did, because you never went to the same place twice to purchase narcotics. Anyway, when you're dealing with that kind of money and that kind of narcotics, there's people around just as dangerous and desperate as you are, and their job is to protect this with their life.

Sam was a very cautious dude to work for. As long as I worked for him, he never at no time took any narcotics and put it directly in my hands. That's how cautious he was with me, and I was his right-hand man. I picked up the drugs in the woods among the rocks. He'd tell me, "Follow the path.

There's a big tree to the right. There's a rock. Look beside it."

So when we went to Detroit, he didn't tell me too much about it except we gonna make a big move. Him and me flew up there, got out to the motel, and went into one of the cabins. The dude who opened the bedroom door greeted Sam very respectfully and vice versa. Sam turned to me, and the dude scoped me out but didn't say nothing. Then Sam went in, and they closed the bedroom door. I was left outside with four or five heavily armed dudes. I wanted to see the merchandise, the stacks of kilos and the money, but I didn't get a chance to.

I realized I wasn't very high on the ladder. But it didn't really bother me, 'cause I always figure I could climb higher. The ladder was understood in everybody's mind, and you knew where your place was. I always tried for a higher step. I accomplished not half as much as what I wanted to but much more than the average dude that was doing the things I was doing.

When I was working for Sam, he and me was really pretty tight. I often believed he wished that I was his son. He had a son, that was kind of involved with the business, but he couldn't handle it like I could. I really liked Sam. I guess he was a father image in a way. But Sam was pretty known for his temper too. He would smack a nigger quicker than anybody I knew. He only had one arm, but he had different artificial arms that he used depending on what he wanted to do. When I first heard about it, I didn't believe it. I said, "Man, you all are jiving!" They say, "Listen man, watch out for him. He got an arm with a black hand on it." I said, "Cool your head, man." But one day when I was driving his car, I go in the trunk and there about six or seven arms! It really freaked me out.

Later, I seen him get mad with a broad and put on a certain arm, 'cause that was the arm that he whupped dames with, or he get mad with a dude and put on a certain arm, 'cause that was the arm he whupped dudes with. He would always ask me, "What you think I ought to do to this nigger here?" And I'd say, "I don't know, Sam. It's your money and your dope. You do what you want." Then he say, "I should let you take this dude for a *ride*." But it was more him just liking to say this rather than really ordering me to do it. He wanted the dude to believe it. He wanted to shake him up. My reputation would make the dude think, "Well, damn, he really *will* take me for a ride." Then Sam say, "No, I think I'll just kick his ass a little bit." I seen him whup on dudes, whup on broads. Me and him argued a lot of times, but it was always like we was just talking. I think he was a little scared of me 'cause he know I wouldn't take nobody bossing me around.

*   *

From '69 through most of '70, I was up and down, up and down. I'd do good for a couple of months, then I'd fall and do bad for a few months. First it was Clayton dying that left me out in the cold. Later I got in debt kind of bad with Sam and this other dude, Chuck. Sam just refused to give me any more drugs until I paid that money. Of course, that meant the word would be out, so I'd do bad. Then you say like "I'll rob a lot." But robbing people, the way we was doing it, we considered that as doing bad too, because we had to rob sometimes three or four people a day, depending on the amount of money and quality of drugs they had. See, if you can't find nobody big or get a lot of drugs or have a lot of money, you go where you know all the drug addicts hang out. There's always going to be four or five little dealers around there. We'd line them up, push them behind the bushes somewhere, and make them give it all up—right on the street. It got so I wouldn't come in certain areas in certain cars 'cause they would see my car and leave, or take the dope and hide it. I have to think of all kinds of ways to

sneak up on them—come behind them or come in a different
car and jump out real quick before they get away. Sometimes, if we took large amounts of money and drugs, then
I'd just stay in the house for a week, getting blasted all day
long.

So, you get so far, then you tumble back down. You get
yourself together, you brush yourself off, and you start to
climb back up. You get to a point where you want to be for
a while, but eventually somewhere along the line you fall
again. This happens to most people, and the biggest reason
for it is they hooked theirselves.

During the time I had a big habit, there would sometimes
be a slow night when I couldn't get anybody to set up
someone else for me or couldn't come across anybody to
rob. Then I'd begin to get sick. Now, they had a place over
D.C. General that stayed open twenty-four hours. I would
go over there and sign up for the program to get the methadone. I tell them I haven't had any narcotics all day. So they
make you pee in a cup and fill out a form. Then they give
you some meth. After that, you go out and finish looking for
somebody to stick up to get some heroin.

I never did trust meth. People not aware that methadone
is ten times stronger than heroin, and some people that's on
methadone still use heroin. The handful that actually makes
it off to meth—that's still a habit too, but it's a free habit. I
always had this thing about meth because of the little street
things that you hear about it: "Man, that stuff eat a person
up alive!" "Don't you know that if you keep taking that shit,
you be crazy?" But you don't think about that with heroin.
There was a feeling that maybe with meth, they trying to
commit mass genocide.

During the times when I was down, though, I would
mainly rob the other dealers to get the drugs or the scratch
I needed to buy my drugs. At one time in '70 when I had
fallen out of dealing but still had a hell of a habit and all my
knowledge as to where drugs and dealers would be, I

hooked up with a young dude named Cub. He and I did just about everything together. This one particular night, my woman Angela, who I had hooked up with some time before, is with me. We also had a young lady named Monica, which was Cub's young lady, and Cub's brother with us. We in the 14th Street N.W. area where there was a couple of dealers that had been dealing hard and good. These two particular dudes worked alone.

They standing on the corner right outside a little hangout that we couldn't approach, 'cause the week previous we had been in the joint and there had been some shooting. So we sitting across the street in the car, and we watching every sale they make. It's beginning to get late—eleven or twelve o'clock at night. Finally they must have both sold out. They walking partners, so they stay together. One dude was kind of red and little, small build; the other was big, dark skin, real muscular, look real tough. Now, Cub was short and a little chubby. Even though he was on drugs, he never did lose a whole lot of weight like drug users usually do.

Anyhow, the dudes walk up 14th Street and turn onto Girard Street. We're following in the car. When they get halfway down the block, Cub call the big dude by name. I jump out the car with the gun in my hand, and Cub get out the other side. We just walk right up to them. Cub grabbed the big dude in the collar and go up side his head a couple of times. Meanwhile, I searched the little dude. I say, "What you got here, Shorty?" and I take a .25 automatic out of his pocket and slip it in my own. This was a way we often got weapons—we'd take people's guns when we robbed them.

So we say, "Where the dope at?" Cub slapping the big dude around, and he say, "Cub, I ain't got no dope!" So we proceeded to search them. Shorty, he gave us his money. He had fourteen hundred dollars, so I take that. The big dude have about nine hundred, and Cub take that.

We get back in the car. I'm driving, Angela sitting up front with me, Cub and his brother sitting in the back, Monica in the middle. Instead of going back to S.E. right away, we start driving around, looking for somebody else to rob. See, we don't want to spend none of this money to buy dope—we want to take somebody else's! So we riding up and down, and suddenly Cub says, "Man, there's a Cougar following us, a red Cougar. Look like about four or five dudes in it." I say, "Man, I don't want to hear about it." I figure it's nothing, he just a little nervous. But I'm not really sure, so I get to a corner and say, "Man, I'm going to make a left. If they make a left behind us, then they're following us." As soon as I make the left, Cub say, "They're swinging in behind us."

I pick up speed. Cub wanted to know if he should start shooting back there to slow them down 'cause they really on us now. But before I can answer him, they fire—Pow! Pow! You can hear the bullets hitting the trunk, the top of the car, the sides of the car. Fortunately the back windshield don't get it, I don't know why. Everybody's ducking, and I'm slumped down and putting my foot on that gas. My intentions was to stop our car suddenly, jump out with the .40 shotgun we got in the back, blast their car, jump back in our car, and pull off.

But we never had the chance. They opened up on us too fast. Meanwhile, Cub was on one side, and his brother was on the other. Cub got two guns, he reaching out the window, firing back. Pow! Pow! So this go on for like three blocks. Then Cub shot out. His brother still firing 'cause he taking his time. Angela, she take my pistol out of my lap and turn like she's getting ready to fire. We going so fast and so close to the other car that she changed her mind and give the gun to Cub. I think he might have fired twice, and through my rear-view mirror I saw their windshield shatter. At the speed they was going, I know it got everybody in the car.

At 11th Street, I made a hard right. A police scout car parked on that corner, so I slow up. The dudes coming right behind us must have seen the scout car too 'cause they make a left. One of their tires is blown on the passenger side, and the windshield all tore up. They bump into a parked car, not hard, because they had slowed down considerably. Meanwhile, we pull on off.

I knew this kind of thing was going to happen sooner or later, so I was prepared for it. As long as you got a lot of fire power, you're all right. There was a rule with me that I always have a gun at all times, 'cause sometimes you'd be out in the street and the opportunity just present itself where you see a lot of money. Then you want to be armed.

I remember one time I took advantage of a coin-collector dude. He'd travel around to different places collecting money from machines. During this time, my hang-out was on Wheeler Road, S.E., where there was a little carry-out. (Most hustlers got a little spot where they and everybody else hang out, show off.) My partner and I, we standing there, and this coin-collector dude pulls up in his car. He got signs on it: "This car is burglarproof" and all that kind of stuff. He got a bad dame sitting there beside him. He slide on out the car, looking all hip, choked up, clean. He go in the carry-out to make his little collection, and I heard him say this was his last stop. He getting ready to go somewhere with his babe. So I say, "Uh-hum."

While he in there collecting, I just slid on in the car, told the dame to be cool, and lay down in the back seat. Then the dude come back, put the money in the trunk, get in the car. His dame was really like a mummy—looking straight forward, ain't saying nothing. He say, "What's wrong?" She say, "Hum, hum." And before he could say it again, I sprung on him. When he seen the pistol—that big, long barrel come over the back of that seat—I think his eyes about to drop out. I just told him to be cool, I wasn't going to hurt him or the dame, all I wanted was the cash. Well, he agreed with that.

I made him drive to a more secluded area. Had my partner follow in my car, a little '64 Corvair all raggly and the muffler about broken. It drawed less attention than a big car. When the police see one of them niggers laying back, big hat on, driving a Cadillac, they immediately stop them. See me in my little Corvair, they wouldn't say a thing. I might have got stopped once or twice when the man say, "When you going to get that muffler fixed?" "I'm on the way to get it fixed now, boss." And the car would be loaded with everything—drugs, guns.

Anyway, my partner pulled my car right up to the back of his car and unloaded the money into my trunk. We tied the dude and the dame up and told them not to move for about five minutes, and they agreed 'cause they was so scared. Then we just slide on away from there with almost three grand worth of change—not bad for a spur of the moment thing!

So I had the gun always on me to take advantage of opportunities and to protect myself. A gun is like a part of me. I could wake up in the morning, and before I get out of the bed to go into the bathroom, I strap my shoulder holster over my shoulder. I never would go out of the house without it. When I knew I owed a lot of money, I was extra careful. Most people, though, would have second thoughts about doing things to me for the simple reason they never know what's going to happen. In the event that they had got me, then they would have to deal with my boys, my friends.

A lot of dudes would be prepared to take one person out if they knew there wasn't going to be some repercussions, maybe start a gang war and that bring in heat, bring in the police, make things tighter, and make the money short. Rather than do that, they would just leave the person alone and try to get their money some other kind of way. Eventually I paid most of my debts anyhow.

12

Maintaining the Image

You know when people are going to rip you off. You know when somebody up to something. They give theirself away, the way they look or the way they act or the way they talk. The amount of money really don't make no difference: you just can't let people get out on you. It don't matter who you are or what you are; they'll try, and you gotta stop them. At all times you gotta stop them.

I'll never forget what I did when a dude named Baby John tried to get out on me. Baby John was strung out on drugs, but he was a good booster. He'd get up in the morning, him and a whole lot of broads, and they'd go to all them big department stores—Montgomery Ward's and Hecht's. You could tell them what you want, what size, what color —and they'd get it.

This particular morning Baby John was sick before he left. So he come to me and say, "Man, like I need some drugs now. I'm going to steal something. When I come back this afternoon, I'll pay you back and probably buy some more drugs." Solid. I gave him some drugs. But when he come back that afternoon, he buy some drugs from somebody else, sell all the goods that he done stole, and go hang out on the corner, high. He didn't say nothing to me about my money. I'm mad, even though it wasn't but ten dollars.

Now, this woman Angela was my main gal at this time, and I was around her house that day. Here come my brother

Nicey and Cub, and they got Baby John. They knock on the bedroom door. "Johnny, we got Baby John out here."

"Okay, I'll be out." I slip on my holster and my pants and go out there. I say, "Where my money at, man?" Immediately he begin to say, "Johnny, why you want to make an example out of me?" He understood, 'cause he knew the code. He living the life just as long as I have, even though he was young. "Why, man? Why me, man? Why you couldn't pick somebody else?"

"You owe me money. It don't make no difference. You are the only one that owe me money right at this particular moment."

He got to begging Angela. "Angela, please don't let him do it."

She saying, "Baby John, ain't nothing I can do. You should have paid the man his money."

So now he really acting up. He done grab hold to the bannister. "Don't let him do it! Please don't let him do it!"

I wanted to laugh real bad, but I got my gangster look on my face, and I'm telling my brother, "Pull that chump on down these steps." We called him all kinds of names, pushing him and pulling him. Finally we get him to the front door. He grab hold to the doorknob. "Angela, please talk some sense into his head!"

I guess he thought I was going to take him out, but the main thing I wanted to do was scare him. I knew it would get around what we did to him. So we get him in the car. I'm driving, Cub and Nicey sitting in the back with him. We took him up by the Catholic church over my way, where there's woods and it's real dark. I took a tree limb, stripped it down, and made him stand by the car. "Boy, you ain't never owe nobody else. You gonna pay up from now on." I proceeded to start whupping him with the tree limb. While I'm doing this, he hollering and falling out, going through that he got heart trouble and everything. Finally he faints. Most of it was acting. Then my brother and Cub, they work him over a little bit, and we push him back in the car. We take him all the way up right in front of the carry-out and kick him out on the ground so everybody can see him. He laying out there, crying, "Oh, help, please help, somebody help!" We drive off.

This broad named Toni that he used to hustle with—she dead now from an overdose of heroin—was his main partner. So when I come back up there, the first thing she say is, "You all didn't have to do that to Baby John. Especially you. I would have gave you the money." The way she said it, it was like she was trying to get out on me in front of everybody! I said, "Bitch, shut up," pulled my pistol, and shot, just to scare her. She took off down the street while I pulled my pistol back up, sat down on the corner, and finished talking.

You got to do that sort of thing. You got to maintain who you are at all times. You do it for the people watching. I remember one time in Lorton the psychiatrist asked me, "Do you sometimes grow weary portraying the image of a tough guy?" And I say, "Yeah, I really do." Because you can't ever let your guard down. Once you start one way, people expect this of you at all times. This thing where you just had to show you had the heart, you could do it.

And it was true that I could do things that wouldn't bother me like it would bother other people. Most of the people I was affiliated with could do things that really didn't bother us, where it would make somebody else scared or nervous. Still, a lot of things I consider as senseless. Let me give you a perfect example of what I think is senseless. A friend of mine, Ace, he's about twenty-seven years old and in a wheelchair like me. He was dealing drugs pretty good before he got shot. Now, he wasn't a bad dude, because he gave a lot of other guys breaks as far as being short of money. One day, though, a dude set him up to be robbed and two dudes rob him. Ace don't buck. He don't try to fight; he don't do anything. He give them all the drugs and all the money he had. He even brought it to their attention that he had a gun. He say, "Man, look, I got a gun. Take it off me." So they got everything, and then they tell him, "Turn around and walk up them steps." And when he turn around and walk halfway up the steps, one of the bastards shoot him. This is senseless. They got what they wanted, probably more than they wanted. So to me it didn't make no sense at all.

Now, there was some repercussions. Some of his boys got one of the dudes, whupped him up, broke his nose and some of his ribs, and then took him and turned him over to the police. But Ace wouldn't press charges. In order to keep his status as being the type of dude that he is, he couldn't even tell on that guy. He couldn't say, "Yeah, it was him." It's all part of the code: you can't tell, under no circumstances. You'd straighten it up yourself, but you wouldn't ever go to the police.

Now, most good hustling dudes, especially with robbing experience, they never go out to hurt people. The main thing is getting what you're going after and getting away. Occasionally somebody say, "I ain't giving up nothing." But you can change his tune easy. You ain't got to kill him. Smack him with the gun or shoot him in the foot or kneecap, he give it right up. Knock his big toe off with one of them .45's, he give it up. I think it's probably my background that it don't bother me.

But I ain't no different from somebody else when sad things happen. Then I'd be worried—like, if somebody take advantage of a kid, molest a kid sexually. Or I read in the paper one time right round in Maryland in a well-to-do neighborhood, all good-doing whites, they was putting LSD on candy and razor blades in apples. Sick! Little kids knocking on the door, trick-or-treating, and they give them apples with razor blades or candy with LSD. The kids could die. These people are sick. But yet them same people is set on the jury or be a judge or be the D.A., and they call *me* a dirty common criminal 'cause I'm trying to make some money! I ain't trying to hurt nobody; I'm just trying to get money the way I know how.

I tell you what really get people. I surprise a lot of people because knowing the way I live, the things I done, they don't believe I pray. They don't believe that I enjoy walking in the rain. Little things like that. A lot of times I'll be setting out at nighttime, just dusk dark and the sky will be real pretty, and I groove, I really groove. They don't believe that I pay attention to things like this, but I do.

One of my friends, a dude named Bones, he been in jail most of his life. He older than me, and he been to quite a few other joints than me. He done had the experience of killing two or three people in jail. Now, somebody had left a baby on a doorstep in the middle of winter. Bones was in Lorton and read about it in the paper. Immediately he writes the paper and offers his help. At that time, he was a yardman down at Lorton making about five dollars a month. He said he would contribute that money every month and also try to get the other inmates to start some kind of fund for this baby. But Bones is a very uptight, real tough dude. I seen him just smack other dudes right out of their shoes. He won't take nothing off nobody. Taking a life with him was nothing. It's easy. It just come naturally.

I couldn't never explain the difference. Maybe it's because the majority of the people that we be doing things to are into drugs or some kind of hustling. They know that all this is a part of their lifestyle as well as ours. They know that they going to be faced with these things sooner or later. We always faced with it day by day. But we are sensitive about children. Still, we're called animals and convicts—I don't know what all they have labeled us. So it really surprised me that it was publicized, what Bones had said, what he had done. See, most of us do feel that way, even though we do a lot of cruel things.

I *know* that I done a lot of cruel things, but it was something that I had to do at that particular moment for one reason or another. I have never did something unnecessary, especially when it comes to violence. But sometimes, in order to get what you want, or prove a point, or because some robbing drug dealers was trying to move in on you, you had to be tough. If you didn't, you would lose everything you had. They would step on you, take yours, get you out of the way. Then they would make the money, and you just be out in the cold. So you had to be tough. So many people expected so many things of me 'cause my reputation most of the time had preceded me. I had to act accordingly.

Besides having to keep my reputation, I tried to follow a lot of other rules when I was conducting business. For example, sometimes some job come up and you don't have the kind of dudes you'd like to have with you. The thing about a good stickup crew is that no matter what you're doing, everybody got to have their own function, know what they going to do, and be good at what they're doing. My main thing was containing people. I'd get everybody and put them in one place and keep them there, maybe even tie them up. If it was a lot of people, then I contained a lot of people. If it was only a little bit, then I'd also do other jobs. Most of the time, though, I used to give my mob an assignment before we robbed a joint: "You do this, you do that, and I'll contain the people."

Now this is important, 'cause during this time, around the spring of '70, I was sticking up legal joints as well as drug dealers. Most of the time I had my regular mob with me. I remember this little bar where a lot of sissies used to go— a lot of homosexuals. Sophisticated sissies I call them. Suit-wearing tie kind. They had big government jobs. Only reason a young dude would be in there is for the purpose of somebody picking him up and giving him fifty dollars.

The guy that owned the joint was a pretty die-hard dude. A week or two previous to our going in there, he had actually shot two people that tried to rob him. So I'm telling Cub, "Man, when we get in this joint, you and I going to have to get him." My brother Nut's job was to get the cash; and Leo, Cub's brother, was to stand in the middle of the place with a shotgun and make all the sissies get on the floor and put all their hides, all their wallets, in one pile.

When we went in, we got a booth and sat down to look the joint over. There was a dude at the bar drinking a beer, and I immediately saw that he had a shoulder holster. I looked at him close, especially at his shoes, and I said, "This a roller." Evidently the guy that owned the place had hired a special police that didn't wear a uniform to keep an eye on the joint.

So we order some beer, 'cause we gotta rearrange our plans. When the lady come with the beer, just out of hospitality Leo say, "Do you want me to leave you a tip? Or would you like to have a beer now?" And the lady say, "Don't be trying to get smart with me. I got children your age ..." and so on and so on. Leo say, "All I did was offer you some beer. I'm not trying to get fresh with you." She going on, "Little young niggers come in here and think they can take over the place." She running her mouth for about ten minutes. I'm telling Leo, "Man, don't say nothing to that broad."

So we just sitting there, and finally we come up with the idea that the dude that owned the place a pretty tough dude, so I got to get him. Okay. Cub got to get the police. Nut's job is still to get the cash, and Leo's job the same—get all the hides piled up, pick them up, stand around with that shotgun, and watch everything. The signal was, I get up and go play a number on the jukebox. So I go over and drop a quarter in, punch the number three times so it play over and over. I turn around, and the owner of the joint is sitting at a little special table with a broad. She can see me, but his back is to me.

I turn away from the jukebox, pop my fingers a couple of minutes, then move closer to him. I come out with my gun, and the broad panic. She say, "Don't play with that thing around here." The owner went to turn, but when he did, I put that gun against the back of his head and said, "I know you got a gun. Put it on the table."

"Punk. You better get the motherfuck out of my place."

"Yeah?" I stepped on back and shot him in the leg. He fall on the floor. I say, "You want some more?"

"No, no! You got it! You got it!"

After I shoot him, the same broad that gave us all the static about the beer, she just about turned blue. She looking all funny, just wanting to please everybody now. She scared to death; and Leo, the one that she'd been arguing with, standing there with that big shotgun. Now, Cub immediately stepped up to the police, politely put his pistol right up on his neck, took his gun, and told him to be cool. The man just kept on drinking his beer. Another dude was on the telephone. I made him get off. There were two waitresses in the joint—the one that had got in an argument with us and another one, a little young one. Both of them was nice-looking dames.

We got everybody laying on the floor. Nut goes to the cash registers and takes out the cash. All the faggots were trying to sound like women, but they was piling their hides up on the floor, and we had them crawling around. Nut was on the other side of the bar—a big, tall bar—I guess it was real expensive. At one point, he was walking along on the top of it, and then he jumped down behind it. He was back there a long time without coming up or saying anything. Finally I said, "Are you all right, Jack?"

And he come up smiling. "Yeah, I'm all right."

"You get all that dust [money]?"

"Yes."

"Well, let's roll."

So we get the wallets and things on the floor, and we take the keys to the joint and go on out to my old raggly car. The money man always leave first. If anybody gets busted, get away with the money. Just before Leo steps out, he takes the shotgun and smashes all the glasses and bowls on the table that we had been using, and turns the table over. Then he come out, and I just pull the door, lock it, and go to the car. On the way home I ask Nut, "What was you doing behind that bar so long?" He say, "Man, did you see that dame with that green dress on?" Immediately I step on the brakes, stop the car, take my pistol out, grab him in the collar, and shake it in his face. I say, "Boy, I done told you over and over. This is business. We got plenty of money. You can have any dame you want, dames better than that dame. What you want to do? Get an armed robbery charge and a rape charge at the same time?"

"No, it wasn't like that."

"Man, please don't ever do that no more." I'm really angry, really upset.

"No, man, I ain't going to do that no more." I think he was really sorry because he knew how I felt.

A little after that, when the weather was warmer, we robbed another legal joint—a big drugstore. But most of the things I done was low-level-type crime. I didn't do some of the bigger crimes I would like to have done because I had no real way to obtain the information I needed to carry them out successfully. Or I didn't have the necessary equipment. There was one or two small bank jobs that I have been involved in, but they really didn't produce the money I felt you should get for doing a bank—the chance that you take, the time you got to serve in the event you're caught and convicted. I've been in a bank and took six thousand dollars. I've been in a Giant Food Store and took eight thousand dollars. Evidently something wasn't done right somewhere. You get a teller or two, and you've got to get out of there —quick, fast, in a hurry. No time for bullshit. Unless it's well planned and well executed, it's get what you can and get out quick. The robbing that I was accustomed to, that was all it was—getting in, getting what you could, and getting out fast.

My friend Duke and I broke into a bank very late one night and waited for the people to come in that morning.

When the people started coming in, we started gathering them up. Then one man tell us about the time lock. This where all the money at, in the safe, and he can't get into it because of the time lock. Well, what did we know about the time lock? We couldn't do nothing.

You think of a lot of things to do to get over. You might even think that you've got a pretty good idea, and then you find that it takes investing money, money that you don't have. When we was down at the Youth Center, Duke and I often talked about watching a bank, finding out who the president of the bank was, some of his habits: where he lived, who he lived with, a little family background. The whole idea was to snatch him, take him to the bank, make him open up his safe, take all the cash, and get rid of him. Then he would be the one that they'd be looking for because he would be the one who disappeared with all the money. But we never had the opportunity to do this. There was always something else going, and we'd say, "Well, we'll get around to this bank thing later." But for one reason or another we never did.

I know about robbing on my own scale, but going out for a bank or a Brinks truck, people would think that out of my league. If I robbed a Brinks truck, the police probably wouldn't look for me, because they would figure this is out of my league. But I felt all I needed was having the right people together at the right time with the right equipment.

We made an attempt once on a Dunbar truck, which is an armored car. There was only two dudes on the truck. One stands fast with either a pistol or a shotgun, and the other makes the move with the money. Duke and myself and this dame pulls it. The dame have a baby carriage with her iron in it, and she pushing it right up to the back of the truck. As soon as she done that, we're supposed to make our move. But when she gets there and she getting ready to reach into the baby carriage for the sawed-off rifle, a scout car pulls in one end of the parking lot and another scout car pulls in the other end. They came 'cause some teenagers raising hell in a sandwich place within the shopping center. That squashed it. Once the dame saw it, she came right on back to the car. We never even got out, and we never tried it again. Bad breaks. I catch a lot of that.

But I can honestly say that I got away with much more than what I ever got caught and convicted for, so in the long run that made it worthwhile. When I got shot, I wasn't at my peak. I know I could have went much farther. I always felt that way. Once I become a heavy user of drugs, though, the thing I mostly cared about was getting enough for my shot. You don't put out like you ordinarily would, and whatever you do, it don't usually exceed what you want for that day.

At the time I got shot, I saw that particular night as being a turning point if we had succeeded in getting away. The people we went after was big fish, and it would have been big money. It would have been the start of my march back up the ladder. I had been to a certain spot on the ladder, and then I had came down. If we succeeded that night, the money would have been so plentiful that I wouldn't have had to worry about the everyday hustle and bustle of trying to get drugs. I could have used what I had to get more money and drugs, and build up my business.

But to be truthful, you can't really run a business too good when you're on drugs. Some people say they can, but it's too easy to get wrapped up in being a user, like I did. I guess there's no getting around the fact that by my being a drug user, there was a big dent in the success I had. Jumping out of the frying pan and into the fire, that's what happened. There is also been times when I made big comebacks, laying in the house, kicking it with sleeping pills. But truthfully, when it boiled down, it always came back on me. I ended up getting involved heavier and heavier each time. What was success ended up being failure.

13

On the Loose

One night about this time, six of us was just riding around in a car. A dude named Ty Ty, a young boy named Jason, another young boy named Cheese, a dude named Raymond, and a dude named Lee. Raymond was the last one to join in the ride. I didn't really know him. All these dudes I named, except for Ty Ty, are younger than myself. So now Lee, he wanted to rob a gas station. Robbing a gas station is not my idea of a good robbery. There's no real money in it, and it's too complicated. People get hurt unnecessarily.

Lee talked Cheese into robbing the place with him, who in turn tried to talk Jason and Raymond into robbing the place with them. Ty Ty and myself just listened. Out of the four of them, Jason is the closest to me. So I tell him, "I don't approve of what you're getting ready to do. I really don't want you to be a part of it." Jason says, "Well, I'm not going to participate, but I am going to walk down the street and watch." The only reason we don't take off, Ty Ty and I, is because we don't want to leave Jason in no bad position, even though Lee and Cheese doing something that we don't approve of.

Cheese and Lee go in the gas station. The man immediately bucks. He got a .45, and both of them carrying a .38. Cheese never got a shot off. The man killed him right there. Lee in turn shot and killed the man. There's another gas station across the street, and the man from there runs over with a gun. He shoot Lee in the head. Don't kill him but shoot him in the head. Jason and Raymond witness all this. Ty Ty and I are standing outside the car. When we hear the shooting, we get in the car and start it up. Jason run back to the car and begin to tell us what happened. I drive the car straight out of there. By this time, police are coming, and there are people everywhere. I know that Raymond got away, Cheese is dead, and Lee is shot. The one man is dead, and the other man is looking for anybody he can shoot. He even got the gun pointed at the crowd of people. Okay. We leave, 'cause there ain't nothing we can do.

Later, somehow Raymond gets busted, and he immediately involves me, Ty Ty, and Jason. He told them the whole thing, but he didn't tell it like it was. He told it in a way to save himself and make everybody else be deeply involved. So they pick us all up. I'm the last one. Upon picking me up, the way I seen it was like this. Cheese was dead. Lee was shot and caught in the act. Lee had killed a man. There were witnesses to this effect. I felt Lee, being in the position that he was, should have took all the weight. There was no defense, no nothing, so why should I go to jail, or Ty Ty or Jason? And Raymond, he's snitching. He saying whatever the government wanted him to say.

I think Raymond told less when he came to me for fear of me, 'cause they pick me up, hold me for two days, and let me go. They're not releasing nobody else. They picked me up a total of three times. They don't really have anything on me, but it being a murder/robbery, automatically I'm involved. I was in the general vicinity, and I had talked to the people that had participated directly in the crime.

The first two times they picked me up, I said nothing but "Call my lawyer." The third time, getting a little tired, I was also very annoyed with the Homicide Squad because they was getting a big kick out of Raymond constantly changing his story to more of what they wanted. They wanted him to tell it in a way to get everybody involved. So the third time that they locked me up, I made a statement, and I tell them, "Yeah, Cheese and Lee did go and rob the place. I made Jason stay in the car. Raymond was standing outside the car. We heard the shots. On hearing the shots, we pulled off." Even though Raymond's snitching and I know it by now, I'm still trying to protect this sucker 'cause I can't put myself in that snitching bag under no circumstances.

For some strange reason they let me go again. But they held everyone else. By Ty Ty being the oldest, they was really after him, even though he never even got out of the car. Ty Ty had a hearing, and I told his wife I would come to court and testify in his defense, which I did. I said that Cheese and Lee was directly involved. They was the ones that did it. Well, there wasn't no out for them, so what I said didn't hurt them none. After I said all this, the D.A. was constantly trying to mix me up. "Well, wasn't all of you out hustling? Wasn't all of you doing this?" I'm saying, "No, it wasn't like that at all."

The hearing recessed, and a detective from Homicide Squad and the D.A. handling the hearing came up to me, threatening me. "What the hell is wrong with you? You're supposed to have said so and so." They said the things that Raymond had told them. They said, "You're supposed to tell about the part of trying to steal a car." Well, it happened. But we borrowed that car, we didn't steal it. Anyway, no one steals a car to go rob this particular type of place. But they had changed it around like it was a planned thing for us to steal the car to go there and rob the place. They was angry with me and even threatened to charge me again.

Raymond made it easy for them to believe. He and the D.A. had made a deal. Now, when it all boiled down, Raymond didn't go to jail, but Ty Ty, Jason, and Lee did. And, of course, Cheese went to the graveyard. Raymond made a statement to the D.A.'s advantage, and they wanted me to condone it. They were trying to make me tell Raymond's story; but if they thought I was telling a lie, they would have locked me back up and kept me involved. On the other hand, I never would have showed up if I thought they had anything they could get me on. I would have fell completely out of sight.

I think they coaxed Raymond something like this: say something happen and somebody come to question you about a friend of yours. They say, "What did he do?" And you might say, "He didn't do anything. He was sitting here talking to me." But they know you real scared and they know that you semi-involved, so they say, "You sure he ain't do nothing?" And you say, "No, he ain't do nothing." They say, "You going to jail 'cause you telling a lie. I know he did so and so, 'cause so and so say he did." Which is lies, 'cause so and so never said anything. Then they'll give it to you right on a platter. "Didn't he tell you that he would watch for you?" "Yeah, I think he did say he would watch." That's how the police do, and that's how the D.A. do, and I know.

*   *

I was busy doing all kinds of things until the police raided my house in March of '70, supposedly for a sale I made to an informer in February. Earlier that week, I had gotten a nice piece of money, so I had promised Tracy's children that I was going to take them out for a day. We went to the zoo and stayed all day long. When we first come home, we're on the step of the apartment building, and there's a whole lot of young boys standing outside. I see a police car, and I dig the apartment light is fuller than it normally be. What I started to do was go straight down the steps to my sister's house, 'cause my sister lived in the basement of the same building. But Tracy, she runs up to the apartment door. She call and she say, "Johnny, there's somebody done broke into our house!" Roller open up the door, and she still standing there. I turn, 'cause I'm getting ready to split. But when I turn, one come off the steps in the hallway and another one, which I thought was just one of the young dudes, was a roller too. So they get me and carry me in the house.

They search everything and don't find nothing. I ain't got nothing really on me, just a syringe. I ain't even got a pistol, and that's really unusual. They bring me in and proceed to search me. Some big old nasty redneck push me down to the floor, put his knee in the back of my neck, and handcuff me. I'm just laying on the floor, he's putting his knee in my back, and I don't say nothing.

Evidently some old dude told them that I was doing a real big business. So they came prepared to bust somebody who's doing a big business. They have what they call a field kit that police and narcotics squads use. You can take about the amount of heroin that you would get in a capsule, put it in the kit, and if it will turn a certain color, then it's heroin. If it turn another color, then it's not. When they found the mix in the plastic bag, they say, "We got you now, Jack." So they take it over to the table and make their little tests on it. It ain't heroin. The man get really mad. I'm still laying on the floor handcuffed, looking all around. Everything is in shambles. They been tearing up everything, using sledge hammers, about ten or twelve rollers just walking all around, walking all through.

That one nasty dude, he wanted to take all the kids. Tracy had five kids from her husband, and I had my three kids with me—they always with me. That made eight children there. All of these children crying and screaming and running all over the place. And the dame, she acting crazy. Then the phone rang. What happened, they raided about twenty places in Southeast, other associates and so forth. So now everybody trying to warn everybody else: "Get yourself away, go home, clean up." But the police was so swift, nobody had time to do anything. Everybody thought it was a one-crew raid, but it was about ten separate crews. We found that out later when we was in the cell block. Everybody and their mommas and sisters was locked up. They had all of Southeast down there. They locked people up that didn't even matter. This old police who raided our place had made up his mind that he was going to lock up Tracy. There was an FBI man there as overseer, though, and he said, "The man ain't charged with nothing but a misdemeanor. I don't see no reason why we should lock the lady up. We could leave the lady here with the kids. Then we don't have to go through the trouble of having somebody pick the kids up." The old police didn't want to go for that, but the FBI man must have had more authority than him. So they didn't take nobody but me, and they charged me with P.I.C.—possession of implements of crime—for all the hypodermics and pistols they found.

Now, what I always did was give my sister or somebody close to me enough money so I can have bond money. I knew by the time I spent the night down there with the habit that I had, the next day I was going to be some kind of sick. So as they carry me to the detective car, I said to my sister's husband, George, "Look, just get me out tomorrow." Sure enough, all my people was down there the next day, and they got me right out. My brother had drove my car by, so I jumped right in, and I must have left all of them around the courthouse, 'cause I was gone to get over.

I'm glad I wasn't home when the police came that other night, 'cause during that time they was going wild over that "no-knock" theory, and there wouldn't have been no warning. The first thing I would have thought was somebody's attempting to rob me or do bodily harm to me or my family. I had plenty of guns and ammunition in the house, but there was a rule with me that I didn't keep no whole lot of narcotics there, only personal use, because of the kids. And I made it known to people that I didn't have it around, 'cause I didn't want nobody coming, threatening them, hurting my kids. Still, if I had been there that night, I'm more than sure that I would have grabbed a gun. Then I probably would have been dead or up for murder, and two or three of my kids might have been hurt.

Anyway, I go to court in May on this, and the govern-

ment not ready till the end of June. Finally they get a
conviction on P.I.C., and I got one year on that plus ten days
and a three-hundred-dollar fine for each of the weapons.
Once in a stickup, I got nine years for one weapon, and now
that I got a whole lot of weapons, I get ten days for each!
After the conviction, I go over to the jail and stay there a
couple of days. I'm supposed to be going down to Lorton,
but somehow they send me to Occoquan instead. Occoquan
is a minimum-security misdemeanor joint. Not my type of
joint at all. They don't have no fences. Also, the judge had
cut my sentence to two hundred and twenty days, and gave
me mandatory work release.

They picked five of us to leave Occoquan every day and
finish fixing up a halfway house that we was supposed to
move into. There was a little painting to be done, setting up
the beds, getting the mattresses in shape. Meanwhile, I'd
been going through a lot of wild changes because I hadn't
completely dried out behind drugs. Some dudes would go
out on the bus in the morning and come back at night, and
one day one of these dudes asked me what was wrong with
me, why was I sick. He said, "Man, I left this morning and
you was laying in that bed. What's the matter?" At first I
told him it wasn't none of his damn business, but eventually
it got around about the dope. So he tell me that he had
fifteen pills and some works. This was all I wanted to hear.
I said, "Solid. What's your thing?" He said, "I shoot three
eggs tonight, then three in the morning before I leave." That
left nine, and he said I could have them. I said, "Man, like
my thing is twenty-four eggs. That nine probably only take
the sickness out of me, if the smack good." But I took the
nine and fired it.

We get to gambling in the dormitory the next few days,
and fortunately I had about eighty dollars on me. The day
that the judge sentenced me, Cub and Tracy was at the
court, and at a certain point I knew I wasn't coming back
out. Tracy had her little boy Anthony with her. They sit-

ting on the bench behind me, and Tracy passed Anthony over to me. I'm talking to Anthony, and I go in Anthony's pocket, and there was a quarter of dope in there plus eighty dollars. So I had some money, and I was able to win about a hundred dollars in the gambling, so I tell the dude that gave me the pills before to go to a certain place and see certain people and tell them he knew me and that I was at Occoquan, and they would take care of it. I gave him forty dollars, and sure enough, nine o'clock that night he came back and gave me the dope. So I was all right for a while.

Meanwhile, my partner Cub had also got busted, on a stickup that we had been planning and planning. When he went to do it with somebody else by me being locked up, he hung in the wrong place too long and got picked up. But not for the robbery. They didn't rob nothing 'cause they didn't have time. They had some narcotics in the car, and the Narcotics Squad busted him. So during the day, when I was supposed to be working at the halfway house, I went to a friend of mine that had this connection with the bondsman, which is a very important thing. You always got to have a good connection with a good bondsman. It's necessary for there to be a guy who can pull you out right away. I go to him and tell him that I want Cub on the street. He say, "Okay, I dig it." So the next day when I come out from Occoquan, Cub out. Me and Cub get together and do our thing, get all high.

That evening, just before I go back, this dude named Moore tells me about a little stickup. He say, "It ain't gonna pay no whole lot of money, but it's better than nothing." I say, "Solid. That'd be hip." The next morning when I came in from Occoquan, we get this dude going to open up a liquor store on payday morning. We take about eighteen hundred dollars from him, nine hundred apiece. I go downtown and buy me a couple of outfits. Then I go home to get ready to go back to Occoquan. I'm getting my little sex thing over with and my little drug thing over with, I take my bath, put me on an outfit, and go get in the car. I'm driving a friend's car, a red Cadillac with a drop top. When I get up in front of Number One, the bus still there. During this time of day, about fifteen, twenty minutes before the bus leave, there's a lot of cars parked in front of Number One. Dudes going back, and other dudes running from car to car saying, "Hey, man, you got any coke to sell? You got any heroin?" Right in front of Number One! Finally the man on the bus got it loaded on up, and I'm not in it. I'm setting there, feeling good, looking at this little dame I got beside me, one of them minis all up around her waist, got some money in my pocket, nice outfit, driving a Cadillac. That bus driver gun the motor up, and when he pulled off, then I pulled on off. I was just tired of all the waiting around.

I went back home to Southeast and set around until late at night. Then me and Cub went on by the carry-out. One-armed Sam was there. As soon as he see me, he say, "Man, what the hell you trying to do? With just the little bit of time you got, you should go on back there." Sam and Cub, they're encouraging me to go back, 'cause they figured that I couldn't run my narcotics business and be on escape at the same time. I would be a danger to everybody's business. The rollers would be looking for me and maybe end up busting something else.

Finally, around eleven o'clock, I decided I was gonna go back. So we go to this joint right around the corner from the court where there's a counselor that I know pretty well. He used to be a hack, got in some trouble, and end up in jail himself. Then he went into this counseling thing. So he said, "Well, man, I can call them up, talk to your counselor, and see what's happening. I can tell him that you been here, that you really was undecided; but after talking, you realized that you wanted to come back." I say, "Solid." So he calls down Occoquan, and he tell my counselor, "John Allen here, man. He been here for about four hours. He just missed the bus, and he was a little afraid. Now, he would like very much to come back, but he don't have a ride to get down there tonight. Would it be all right to catch the bus tomorrow?"

They said, "Who? John Allen? Oh, he already been marked 'escaped' at nine thirty." Usually they give you a couple of hours—he hadn't given me not one hour! He say, "Tell Allen to go to the District jail and turn himself in there. Tell them what happened." When I heard this, I said, "Yeah? Okay. Solid." I went on out, and there's no way that I'm going to the District jail and tell them people to lock me up 'cause I'm supposed to be at Occoquan. No. It don't go like that.

So I catch a cab over to Ann's house—she lived uptown at the time. I know they going to be searching Southeast, 'cause Southeast is my area. I know that eventually they going to get to Ann, 'cause they know that she the mother of my kids and that I mess with her off and on. But we didn't have no whole lot of dealings with each other when I was into the drug thing. We'd just see each other occasionally.

Anyway, I went on up there, told her what was happening, told her I was gonna stay for a couple of days. She was a little leery 'cause at the time she was living with another dude, but fortunately the dude was out of town. I asked her did anybody in her building sell drugs, 'cause I didn't want to go out on the street. She had never really been involved with drugs—the only way she knew of it come from me—but she knew there was some people around that sold drugs. I gave her some money, and she bought me about fifty pills. That helped me over for that particular day. Next day I bought fifty more pills, and then the day after that I just went on back to Southeast, simple as that. Started doing things like I had been released, and ain't nobody hardly paid it no mind. I was just back out.

For some reason, during this time I was always able to avoid the rollers, who were supposed to be looking for me. But I remember one time when it was pretty close. I was in the carry-out in my number one spot—leaning against the jukebox all the way in the back with my back against the wall. I don't know who they was looking for or whether it was just a show of force, but all of a sudden there were rollers coming from everywhere. I could see them outside, gathering up a crowd, police running over here and running over there. A few people break out running, and someone would run after them. So what I did, I just climbed across the counter and went in the back, put on an apron, some rubber gloves, and got deep down in one of them big sinks with one of them pots. Had my pistol down in front of my apron, took my shoulder holster off and put it in the trash can, put my dope in the trash can, and started washing pots.

They was asking everybody for identification, dames as well as dudes. When the rollers do things like that you automatically assume that they're looking for you. Everybody thinks that. They lined people up and asked for I.D.'s. Of course, people didn't like it, and they was hollering and cussing. One detective was trying to keep things in order, saying, "Mr. or Miss, all we want is some identification. Something serious has happened, and we are trying to locate a party." Don't nobody believe that, though. I know I didn't, 'cause you couldn't tell me they wasn't looking for me. The day before, Cub and I had shot some dudes in the legs right up there in the alley, and we thought one of them had spilled their guts.

This kind of thing tend to upset the whole neighborhood and can make big things happen. This time of year, the summer months, as the temperature rise, people's tempers get very short, and it don't take much to set off an explosion. If it wasn't for this one particular detective that tried to do things in an orderly fashion, I don't know what would've happened. I think the police was scared and the people they dealing with was scared, and when you got two scared factors dealing with one another, there's no telling what might go down. Fortunately nothing did.

The place belongs to Sam, so they really couldn't come

all through the man's establishment, but I made the mistake
of wanting to know what was happening. So I take a pan
of garbage—I still got on my apron—and I go outside. I'm
dumping it, and I'm looking all around, real cagey-like, hoping that don't nobody recognize me and say, "That's the
one." Something I don't usually do is have a blind side. Very
seldom you can walk right up on me without my knowledge, 'cause I'm always looking over my shoulder. But this
police did it. When I turned, I'm looking him right in the
face, and he says, "Sir, may I have some identification?" And
I'm looking dumb. I say, "What?" And he say, "Identification." So I say, "I work in here. What you talking about? I'm
working!" He says, "I didn't say you wasn't working. I want
some I.D." "What? What's that? All these police . . ." I'm just
mumbling and babbling like I was a damn fool, and I got
right out on it.

I've had so many narrow escapes I couldn't count them.
One time my sister was having a party, and the police was
looking for myself and my brother. The police knows about
the party and figured we might drop in, and we're so bold
we goes to it anyway. They come in. My sister tells them
they could search. And both of us are underneath my sister's
bed! But we ain't worried too much about getting found,
'cause it ain't but three police, and it ain't no way they're
gonna get us out that house with thirty or forty niggers
there. So we just trying to keep it smooth. They get to
searching but not to no great extent like they would on a
drug raid. All the time they searching, my sister's raising
hell. So when they get to the bedroom, the man just glanced
in. He say, "Let's go," and we right under the bed, laughing.
So I never got caught all the time I was on escape from
Occoquan until after my friend Duke showed up.

Now Duke was a loner that growed up with me in
Southeast. He was one of the best hustlers Southeast ever
produced. For a young dude, he had done a lot of things and
made a lot of money in his time. He had a beef in Virginia,

so they had to send him to a Virginia joint with something like fifteen to life down there. In the summer of '70, he escaped and eventually showed up at my house. Evidently he had done something, 'cause he had some money and clothes, and he was driving a car that wasn't hot. He was staying in Georgia, coming back up every now and then, doing a little something, going back to Georgia. We got to rapping, and I told him I was on escape myself.

One night he came and get me. Him and his dame was together, and she had a joint to rip. It was a legal joint that closed at eleven o'clock, and it was only about three doors down from Number 11. We setting there in the car, Duke and I, and the broad's standing there on the corner. It's getting close to eleven. We're giving them about an hour to clean the joint up and come on out. Suddenly a police car pulled up behind us. We got a good tag on the back 'cause the car wasn't no hot car, but we got a stolen tag on the front. So we got two different tags on. They sat there about five minutes, I assume they checking out the license plate. I was saying to Duke, "I sure hope these suckers don't look at the front plate." Fortunately they didn't.

A few minutes after they left, the broad came back to the car and said, "Hey, they coming out, they coming out." It was two security guards, about six employees, assistant manager, manager. Some got in cars, but the manager for some reason didn't have a car, nor did he ride with any of the rest of them. He walked to the bus stop, while everybody else went their own way. Immediately we follows the bus. Somewhere along 4th and Mystic Avenue, he gets off. Duke jump out of the car. There's been an accident on the corner, and it's two or three police standing around, but Duke go after the dude anyhow. I'm driving around real slow. Finally I hear someone whistling. I stop the car real quick and look over in this alley. Duke's got the dude. He took his sweater off and wrapped it all around the dude's face and he holding a gun to his head. We take the dude, put him in the back seat of the car, and drive around fifteen or twenty minutes just to throw him off. We ask him how much money's in the joint, and he immediately tells us how much down to the penny and what safe it's in and that he knows the combination and doesn't want to get hurt. He'll cooperate. Solid.

For some reason Duke had to take his sweater back, but we still needed something to cover the dude's face up. So the broad takes off her panty hose, and we wrap the dude up with that. We drive around a few more minutes, park behind Number 11, and walk through this little alley. Duke push the dude up to the door. He stick the key in the door, go in, stay something like two or three minutes, and come right on out. Then we go back behind Number 11. Scout car's parked there. We laid the dude down, told him don't make a sound in the next five or ten minutes or we gonna kill him, get back in the car, and pull off. We took something like eleven hundred dollars for that particular night's work. The broad don't get no shares 'cause Duke her man. Whatever he want her to have, he give it to her. I had nothing to do with that, so she couldn't get none of my money. Now, this became a regular thing with Duke and me, doing little jobs, 'cause Duke didn't like other people to be involved. Which was why it was just him and me the night I got shot and he got killed.

14

The End of the Line

It was November of '70—Thanksgiving night—and Duke and me were at my house, just rapping, talking about something to do. The phone rings and I answer it. It's a dude from uptown telling me about a big drug dealer that I had people watching. So I told Duke, "Damn, man, we ain't got no transportation. If we could get uptown, we might get over pretty nice." Duke said, "I got a short." So I say, "Solid." But what Duke failed to tell me was that the car was hot, three days stolen. Now, if I had known that that night, I never would've used that car.

The car was taken from Maryland, and Maryland don't have no inspection stickers on the window. My car do, but my car not running. I'm thinking we'll put my tags on this other car, peel off my sticker, and put it on too. That'll make everything solid. Couldn't nobody report stolen tags or nothing. Suddenly the phone rang again. The dude say, "Man, you better hurry up, 'cause I don't think this dude is gonna be where he's at very much longer." So we neglected to make the changes, which was poor thinking on my part. Instead we take Duke's car—a 1970 Dodge Charger—I'll never forget it.

We finally get uptown and catch the dude coming out of somebody else's house—it was a little gambling joint. We unload him, take the stuff all out of his car, and his pistols off him. The dude have plenty of narcotics as well as a large piece of money. After we take it, I left the man in a pretty embarrassing position 'cause we took off his clothes and tied him up. Now, what I should have done was be smart enough to just head on back to Southeast. We would have come out a whole lot better. Instead I decide I want some cocaine, and we go 'cross town looking for one particular dude that I want to buy from. I'm riding around 14th and T. Now, I know that the police stops almost anything and everything up there, no matter what, and we got all this stuff in the car. Plus we had picked up two whores while we was riding around. I circled this particular block two times, going around from 14th Street all the way around to 13th, up to U, and then come back. But on the third time, instead of going all the way up to U, I cut through Waller Place, and I see the scout car setting there in front of me, double parked on the side. I was going around it, very nonchalant, when the light and siren come on. So I stopped. Duke and I never said what we would do or what we wouldn't do, if the police stopped us in one of these kinds of positions.

The police got out of the car. One walked up on the passenger side, one walked up on the driver's side. The one on my side said, "Can I see your license?" Now, I had a man I used to pay for a phony gun license, car license, anything I needed. So I had a phony driver's license and registration, the whole works. He looks at it and give it back to me. Then he said, "Why ain't there no sticker on this car's windshield?" I said, "This is my sister's car. She had it parked in the parking lot, and some kids broke her windshield playing ball. We just got the windshield installed this evening, and I'll get the sticker first thing in the morning." I said, "I took the chance driving the car without the sticker to carry some of my friends home 'cause we had like a family reunion." He was saying, "Yeah, but you know that's against the law" and this and that, and I said, "Yeah, I understand what you saying." Meanwhile, I took a twenty-dollar bill and a five-dollar bill and rolled it up. I said, "Man, you could let me go this time," and I'm handing the money out of the car. By now, the chump on the other side, he's at the back of the car checking the license plates. Just as the chump on my side take my cash and was about to say, "Go ahead on," this other chump break out from behind the car, pull out his pistol, and say, "The tag's stolen, the tag's stolen!" When he say this and run upside the car, the other dude who almost gave me consent to leave, he just standing there kind of bewildered.

The next few minutes went fast, fast, fast. Next thing I remember thinking was, Well, I'm on escape, but I'll get maybe two or three more years for it. Duke, he got fifteen to life, he gonna get five more for his escape plus what he already got. So I decided I was going to take the weight. I tried to tell the man, "Well, you got me—take me." I was ready to go with them, but meanwhile I took my gun out of my shoulder holster and put it on my lap, so when I get out I could drop the gun on the floor and they wouldn't find it on me. That would be another charge. I would've took a U.U.V. [unauthorized use of a vehicle] as long as Duke got away. I would've told them that Duke didn't know the car was stolen, plus Duke had all kinds of identification in somebody else's name, so they probably wouldn't have found him out.

The roller make Duke step out his side of the car and then the two whores get out. Soon as both of their feet hit the concrete, they break out running. The police on Duke's side turn around and shoot at them about three or four shots. But they just keep on going. Meanwhile, this policeman on my side, he took his gun out of his holster and he just standing there pointing it at me. By the time the other roller finished shooting at the whores and turn back around, Duke got his own gun out. They start tussling, evidently trying to shoot each other. I'm still sitting behind the wheel, kind of dumb.

Now, I think that sometimes you can tell from the expression on people's faces exactly what they feeling or

thinking at a particular time. The look that this police holding me in the car with his gun had, you couldn't tell me that
this man wasn't gonna shoot me. I just felt it. Then all of a
sudden a sly grin came on his face. Many times this same
type of grin had come across *my* face when I was about to
do something. So I recognized it in him immediately. I reach
in my lap and I pull my gun out. The gun surprised him. He
jumped back like he was ready to give up and threw his gun
hand up. So I shot him. Bam! He hollered like a broad and
fall all in the street. I just shot him in the shoulder so he
couldn't use his gun, but there he was rolling around in the
street.

I couldn't get over the fact that so many police got there
in so little time! I chalked this up as behind the 14th Street
area being a high crime rate area, which means automatically more and more police there. Now, here's the police on
a motor scooter show up all of a sudden. I get out of the car
and run around it, and somebody tell me to halt. I turned and
just started to fire. Meanwhile, I think Duke rassling with
one police and suddenly there's about three of them there.
I don't know where from, since I never seen them come. I
remember wanting to help Duke get away, and I remember
being afraid to shoot for fear of hitting him. By this time,
my gun that I had in my holster I had fired several times, and
it was empty. I had another little .32 revolver in my pocket,
and I pulled that out. I'm standing there, and it seemed like
all the police in the world are shooting at me and I'm shooting, shooting, and finally this ain't got no more bullets in it.
I even changed the clip in it, and I'm ducking and shooting,
and Duke and them still in front of me. I don't know
whether to run over to him or what to do.

What eventually happened, I see them get Duke's gun
and twist it out of his hand. Just before they twist it away,
though, Duke shot it, and it grazed one of the police's head.
He rolled over and that must've thrown Duke off balance,
'cause they got the gun right away after that. Then another

police held Duke down and they shot him, shot him while he was on the ground after they had got his gun. Just shot him. And I heard Duke say, "Oh, man! I'm dead!"

So now I threw one pistol down 'cause it's empty. I got the other one in my hand, and they still shooting at me, but I don't know which way to run. I want to run now 'cause there ain't no reason for me to stay there. I can't get to the car to get the money or to drive it away. I can't help Duke 'cause he done said he dead! And I assumed that he was. Do you ever wanna run so *bad* that you just trip all over yourself? I wanted to get away that bad, so I just tripped over myself and I fell. And when I fell, I stuck both hands out automatically to catch myself. My gun flew out my hand ten or twelve feet in front of me. When I first hit the ground, I looked up to see where my gun had fell so I can try to scramble to get to it, and just in them few seconds I heard someone say, "Get that bastard right there!" And the next thing I remember I got that feeling of bullets in my head, going through my head, tearing through my body. Just in that second, I heard Pow! Pow! Pow! and I remember feeling like somebody had picked my legs up. But it really wasn't so. I was just laying half on the concrete and half on a little grassy area. I remember not being able to move. And I heard another officer say, "Man, don't shoot him no more, don't shoot him no more. He not armed! He not armed!" Then there was a lot of footsteps running around. And I remember thinking, Duke dead. Damn. Then I thought, I'm gonna die.

I wasn't in no pain. I didn't have any pain at all. But I just couldn't move. I couldn't move. And I couldn't understand why I couldn't move. I knew that I had been shot, but that's all. I'm laying there and I'm saying, "Duke dead, and now I'm gonna die." And I kept telling myself, "No, I can't die like this. No, no." Then I remember trying to feel where I was shot. I must of got my hand as far as my side, to feel the side of my shirt, and I felt blood, warm blood. I was thinking, Damn, I must gonna die, life running out of me, running all over the concrete. I got to stop it. And then I said, "God, don't let me die. Please don't let me die, Lord." I kept saying over and over, "I can't die like this. I can't die like this. God, don't let me die like this."

Finally I must have passed out, because the next time I look up, there's crowds of people around. Somebody's calling my name, saying, "Johnny! Johnny!" But every time I look at the crowd to try to see who it is, it's real blurry. All I can make out is the police keep pushing everybody back, and some dude was arguing and hollering, saying "Y'all done shot all through my house! I could of got killed!" And people pushing and pushing. And when I turn and look on the other side, two of them big-assed German shepherds was standing up on top of me. One of them kept slobbering, and it kept falling in my face, and I remember being scared to move my hand to wipe my face for fear the dog might attack. It was just *confused.* Everything was all jammed up. Then I heard the ambulance. I heard the sirens. You can tell the difference between an ambulance siren, a fire engine siren, and a scout car siren. So I knew it was the ambulance. And I say, "They coming to get me, I'm not gonna die. I'm not gonna die on the sidewalk. They gonna get me to a hospital."

But when they came, they didn't get me at all. They got the police—the one I had shot—and they left. Then another one came. And got the one Duke had shot. And they left. Then I must have passed out again, because I woke up just in time to see them putting Duke's body in the ambulance, and I'm still laying there on the ground. Must have been almost an hour. The dogs kept slobbering in my face, and I keep on trying to figure out some way to stop the blood. I say to myself, "If I don't breathe hard, maybe if I could hold my breath, the blood'll stop." This is my life running out. It's running all along the sidewalk, and I'm trying to look, and I just can't hardly see! But I seen them putting Duke in the ambulance, and I knew he dead. I could feel that he's dead.

Finally an ambulance come to get me, but I never heard it when they came. I wake up just as they putting me in. I'm laying on my back. There's two police in the ambulance with me. And I hear one of them say, "I betcha he's a goddamn junkie. They shot Bill and Mack. Dirty sonofabitch." He grabbed my arm and pushed my sleeve back up and told the other police, "What'd I tell you? What'd I tell you?" Then he took my hand 'cause my arm was limp, I wasn't moving, and he slammed it back down.

I must of went all the way out then, 'cause I don't remember nothing till we get to the hospital. When they taking me out the ambulance, they pulling me around, and my hand was dragging on the ground. I don't know if the attendant saw it or not, but I know the police purposely stepped all over my fingers. It was just a sick move he made. I guess he was angry 'cause I shot his partner or shot a member of the police force.

I get in the hospital, and there was doctors all around me, saying, "This right here probably hurt. This probably hurt." By this time, I'm just out of my head, and I recall grabbing a nurse by the wrist and saying, "I want some dope, I need some dope. I use dope. I want some dope." And the nurse saying, "Get your hands off me, get your hands off me!" The police ran in there, hit me on my arm. That make me let her go. When I release her, somebody else say, "You sure this man not a police undercover man or something?" because I had a police holster on. Plus I had some I.D. cards, like from Narcotics Squad and Homicide Squad, which I used to use to make other people believe I was the police and to get them in a position where I could stick them up. But one of the rollers who was white said, "He ain't no goddamn police. I hope the fucker die." Then they made him get out. I don't remember very much after that except that all this evidently took place in an emergency room, 'cause it was real light and there seemed to be people running everywhere.

The next time I wake up, I'm in a bed. I look around, and

there's an old man laying next to me. I'm immediately trying to get up. But when I try, I can't move. I'm wondering, What's going on? What the hell's happening to me? And then I remember my back. I stick my hand back there, and I say, "Now, I'm not gonna die, 'cause somebody done patched up my back."

I remember my mother coming in and the doctor telling her I wasn't going to make it. She say to me, "You know Duke is dead." But by then my mind had changed things all around, and Duke wasn't dead to me. We had got away, and I was at my house, and Duke was leaning up against the wall —he always had his back against the wall at all times— saying, "Damn, Jack, we just did make it from that one." And I was saying, "Yeah, one of them suckers shot me in my back." I was laying on the bed, and the girl Angela that I messed with was setting there. And I said, "Angela, go get me some dope," and she say, "Okay," but she wanted to hear what me and Duke was talking about. He was saying, "Yeah, man, one of them shot me in the chest. But we gave them the natural blues, didn't we?" I said, "We damn sure did. How many of them did we shoot?" Duke say, "I shot one." I say, "I think I shot two of them."

Then I wake up again, and I tell my mother, "Duke ain't dead, Duke got away." My mother said, "No, Duke dead. And the doctor told me you not gonna live until morning." I'm saying, "No, no," and I remember my mother finding my hand and me squeezing her finger and she was squeezing mine, and I said, "I'm not gonna die. No." A lot of people come in the room, relatives I think, but I can't picture none of those faces but my mother's.

One time I hear my brother's voice, Nicey. Immediately my mind clicked because I know he also on escape. I'm trying to tell my mother to warn him not to come, 'cause I know I'm being watched. But I can't get it all out. They told me later that when Nicey get ready to go in, the police don't recognize him. I remember saying to him, "Man, bring me some dope. I know you got to go, but bring me some dope."

From then I don't remember nothing else till I was in this other hospital, D.C. General, and didn't know how I got there. They said I was tearing up the blood transfusion stuff and breaking the I.V. bottles, but I don't remember any of that. For some reason, I thought that they was trying to kill me, that they knew I wasn't gonna die, so they wanted to kill me. I would look out the window at D.C. General, and there was a little bridge with cars going back and forth, but to *me* it was an airport with planes landing. I said, "What they want to do is take me out on that airfield and let the plane run over me." I'm really gone at this point, out of my mind. When finally I start coming around little by little, I find that my arms are strapped down. This made me have even more fear of what was happening. I would wake up, see my mother, go back out, wake up, see one of my sisters, go back out. I thought these were just a short time apart, but it was more like days and days.

It must have been about two weeks before I got my thing in place about where I was and what was going on. But once I started to get together, I started remembering what had happened. Remembered Duke being dead. That really got to me. When I first realized that Duke was dead and that I was alive, I cried. It was the first time I had cried in a long time. I cried and cried, saying, "Man, why'd he have to die?" I couldn't shake the feeling of Duke being dead. I could still close my eyes, go out, picture Duke, and talk to him. Finally, little by little, I got over it—if you ever do get over something like that.

Of all the things that ever happened in my life, I think that was one of the worst as far as losing somebody real real close to me. I had the same feeling when Clayton died of an overdose. I remember thinking to myself, All of these dudes, real good dudes and real good friends of mine, and all of them dying one way or the other; and I keep doing the same things, but I keep living. Why, why, why am I still living? Why I'm not dead?

All of this time with my arms being strapped down, I couldn't move, and I just assumed that my legs was strapped down too. I never suspected that I couldn't walk. One day this doctor I had, a little Chinese or Japanese guy, came into my room. I say, "Doc, I don't feel real bad today. Why don't you give me permission to get up?" And he said, "You can't walk." Just like that.

"What?"

"You can't walk."

"You gotta be crazy, 'cause I know that I can walk!" That's when I first started trying to move my legs, and couldn't. I struggled so hard to get up, to prove that doctor wrong, 'cause I knowed he was wrong. I kept saying, "I can walk. I know I can walk. You crazy! Something's wrong with you!" But I couldn't, you know.

After that I relied on the pain medicine a lot. I'm pretty sure they was giving me something for withdrawal from my drug habit. I just took myself out of it. That went on for a while, and then I started to *hate* everything and everybody. I didn't get along at all. I cursed everybody out. I constantly trying to spit on people. I did everything. Nobody liked me, nobody wanted to be near me. Nurses had jobs they had to do, like come in in the morning and wash me up. I would talk so nasty and bad to them that I made at least two nurses run out of my room, tears in their eyes. I started throwing things at people—water pitchers and stuff like that. I did that for quite some time, and everybody hated me. I didn't care, 'cause I hated everybody. My family, as much as they came, I ain't want them to see me like I was. I was constantly thinking about what I was going to do. How was I ever gonna make it like this?

It was at that time that I first tried to commit suicide. I had a lot of thin string. I looped it and looped it so it would be thick. I had an "L" frame on my bed that you can lift yourself in and out of bed with. I tied the string to the "L" frame and pulled myself up so my back was against the front of the bed. I had three or four pillows, and I put the pillows under me one at a time till I was setting all the way up on them. I made sure the rope was good and tight around my neck. See, I was going to slide off the pillows and just hang there, but I said to myself, "I'm gonna smoke one last cigarette, and then I'm gonna hang it up." I reach over to my stand to get a cigarette, and just as I reach for the pack, I slide off the *side* of the pillows instead of down the front like I planned. And the rope immediately tighten up on my neck! That's when I realized that I did not want to die. I was choking. My tongue was all out, and I know I did change color, and I'm trying to get this rope off my neck! I knowed that sooner or later I'm gonna pass out, then it's gonna be too late. I'm scuffling but it seemed like the way I'm pulling, I was choking myself more. Finally I pull on it so hard that I just pulled the whole frame down on me. I guess it was the strength within me to *live*. I had convinced myself that I wanted to die, but I was wrong. Within me, I really wanted to live, no matter what condition I was in. When I got my fingers up underneath that string and snatched it loose on my neck, I remember laying in the bed and thinking, Whew! Now that really was close! And what in hell is wrong with me? I don't want to die. I had a scar around my neck for a long time.

Finding out that I wanted to live changed a lot of things for me. I knew that I couldn't get along the way I'd been doing, hating everybody and not caring how they thought or felt. So I started being more friendly with people, and in return people started being more friendly with me. I had the feeling to commit suicide maybe two or three more times, but I always overcame it without telling anybody about it. I always said, "Damn. If I do kill myself, I let down a lot of people, not only myself." 'Cause too many people were saying, "You can make it, Big Al! Because you *are* Big Al! You got the guts to do it. You tough enough to do it!" They constantly telling me and telling me, and it was what I needed. It pulled me through. It made me start thinking, Well, wait. If they have all this faith in me and I don't have no faith in myself, then I'm letting them down. And these are my friends.

I went through so many changes, though, at D.C. General, knowing that I been on my own ever since I was a kid. I did everything for myself all my life. Now, all of a sudden, there was just so many things I couldn't do. That was the hardest thing of all for me to accept. I don't know if I would've got through it without my friends and my family —without the help of people close to me.

I realized that I wasn't in a position any more where I could just hit someone in his mouth if there was any trouble. Some people took advantage of that; some people didn't. There was one particular police who had made me mad over at the jail in '66, and I had threatened him. He come to work in the locked ward after I got shot. There used to be three officers who worked in there—one stayed back in the dorm, one sat at the main desk, and one sat at a desk outside the door. One day I'm just setting there, talking to a couple of my friends, and this particular officer said, "Hey, tough guy," so I look at him. I'm still very weak and tired, and I don't say anything. I just turn back and finish talking. Then he says, "Yeah, you don't look so tough now in that wheelchair! They tell me you're going to be in that wheelchair the rest of your life. Ha! Tough guy in a wheelchair."

This blowed my mind. I'm so angry that I want to do something to him, but I'm just too weak. When I turned toward him, I couldn't think of but one thing to do, and that was to spit. And this is what I did. I tried to spit in his face, but I hit his clothes. He drew his hand back, and two or three dudes jumped up. Ain't nothing gonna happen like that. Then the nurse come in. I'm so upset and so mad 'cause I know that this is a cold-blooded punk, and if I was on my two feet, I would smack him unconscious. But I'm in such bad shape that the nurse got to go drug me up and put me in bed. It took me a long time to get over that.

One of the other things that happened on the locked ward that really got to me was, one day there was a white dude and a black dude playing cards on the table right in front of the T.V., and I wanted to see the T.V. So I asked them very nice, "Since you playing cards and I want to see T.V., why don't you all move behind me?" The dude say, "After this hand, man." So I say, "Okay, I don't mind." But after that hand, they deal another hand. Then I got kind of angry. The white dude say, "Wait a minute, man. Don't be pressing nobody about no damn T.V. Ain't nobody want to see no television." So I say, "But I want to see the television." "Well, you just gonna have to wait," he say.

Immediately this spark up everything about me. I turned the table over that they playing cards on, and I'm rolling toward the dude in my wheelchair. He backing up, 'cause he surprised! "Where this dude get the strength from, the way he be laying around?" He made one mistake. He let me get close enough to get my hands on him. I held myself in the wheelchair with one hand, and I got him in the collar and pulled him down to me. I like to choke him to death. The nurses stopped me, but they didn't do anything to me.

A couple of days later some of my friends came to the hospital from the jail, and they had heard that some dude had tried to jump on me, which wasn't the case. My friends, they mad, so they immediately jumps on the dude, which was . . . well, that's the way it go.

During this time at D.C. General, and later when they moved me to the jail hospital, I met a couple people that I really admired. Dr. Myers was a plastic surgeon at D.C. General. So I told him, "I can arrange for you to have a lot of business, if that's what you want." He says, "No, no, don't do that." I think Dr. Myers operated on me about three times. He never abandoned me the whole time I was at the jail. He moved from one hospital to another, but he still come to see me regular. He checked me out, and if something was wrong, then he would straighten it up.

Dr. Chase at the District jail was another guy I really admired. Both of these guys was the best in their profession. They knew it, and they carried theirself as such. I'd be sitting around talking my gangster talk, and Dr. Chase would say, "You ain't no real gangster, chump. From now on you're going to take your medicine like you're supposed to." It wasn't like I was scared of him, but I respected him. I dug him, so I did what he say to.

He wasn't no chump either, because I remember one time when a big dude at the jail grabbed his jacket and tried to hit him. When he used to make rounds, I'd be riding around behind him, and I'd have all the charts on my lap. The officer opens up the door, and I say, "All right, all you niggers stand at attention and say your names." This is a joke, and they laugh. This one particular dude didn't like it, though. But he wouldn't get it out on me, so he tried to take it out on the doc. Bad mistake. He grabbed the doc, tried to get the doc to move out of the way, and the doc laid him out unconscious.

I really admired him for that, 'cause ain't nobody supposed to be stepped on. I don't care who it is. Not you, not me, not the lowest dude in the world, not the highest dude in the world. Now, in life somebody's got to be stepped on. That sounds kind of funny, but I'm going to try to explain the best I can. Sometimes, in order to achieve a certain thing that you have to do, you have to hurt somebody or step on them in some form or fashion. But the person that is being stepped on, the harder he or she fights to keep from being stepped on, the more he or she is respected and admired by the person doing the stepping. Then the next time, you try to get around having to fight them or shoot them to get what you want.

Altogether I was at D.C. General from November of '70 to January of '72. Then they transferred me to the jail hospital from January '72 to September '73. At the jail in the daytime, everything was just fine; but once evening came, things became difficult, because a couple of times I was in a room with nuts. I mean real nuts, people who should have been in St. E's, people who was chained to their beds. Okay. I didn't need any chains, but I was automatically chained to mine, and I had to go through a lot of trouble to get a room with some halfway-safe people.

I never felt safe in this condition at the jail at no time, or hardly even now on the streets. I always think about my past and what somebody might attempt to do for something I done several years before. A lot of wrong things happened to me at that jail until I got myself established. But once I did get things going and got to talking to people, it become like my home away from home. I had quite a few privileges that no one else had. I had a T.V. and a radio in my room, and my door stayed open quite a bit.

I had a lot of charges on me from the night of the shooting, so I got six or seven two-to-six-year sentences running concurrently. I made parole on those charges in '73 and ended up at Glenn Dale Hospital as part of my parole plan.

Meanwhile, Ann and I had stayed in touch. At this time Ann was having another relationship. Still, on the day I was admitted to Glenn Dale, she went with me, and I didn't end up getting there till three or four in the morning. We started talking about old times, the good as well as the bad. Her and I just came to the conclusion that we still loved each other, and we wanted to be together with our kids. Before you knew it, we was married. I think that's what she wanted most of her life. I know it's just about what I wanted all my life—to be married to Ann, be with my children, and try to live a happy life.

The rules at Glenn Dale was pretty strict. You could only go home every other weekend. You could go home either for Christmas or New Year's, but you couldn't go home for both. And they had rules about drinking. You

couldn't even drink beer or wine, which is all I drank anyway. I saw Glenn Dale at its worst. I saw it as being another
penitentiary. So I formed a group called Action on Wheels
that I was chairman of, and we put a lot of proposals to the
Glenn Dale staff. One was that every medically able man or
woman should be allowed to go home on weekends and
holidays and any time they had business to take care of.

I did learn some good things at Glenn Dale, and I made
some friends there, but I was very glad when I got out in
early '75 and went home to live with my family.

15

Changes

Since being in the wheelchair, I find that most things haven't changed as far as my position in the neighborhood go. If I was to go down Stanton Road now, it would take me an hour to get half a block to my grandmother's house, because so many people would be stopping and talking. I don't care if you up, down, or whatever, there's always somebody gonna say, "I don't care nothing about that nigger." But all the old timers, they still got the same respect for me as they always had, treat me the same. We talk about the same things. I still be pretty much in the know as far as what's happening. I might go out two, three times a week—I call that checking my traps. I hang out a little bit in this spot and a little bit in that spot. Since I don't go out much, I always have a lot of company. People with troubles, they still call me to talk about it or try to get it solved. So I do pretty much the same things as I used to do, aside from sticking up and hard drugs.

Quite a few of the old crew are in institutions across the country, quite a few still out on the street. Most of the people I know that really was into things with me doing about the same things now. Of my old personal crew, a few of them dead for different reasons, different ways, or in institutions. About three or four of my old good buddies that really used to be into things, I'm sorry to say they drunks now. They be hanging around, asking for a quarter, fifty cents, trying to get some wine. I don't dig that, but what can you do? You can't run nobody's life for them.

I've had a lot of opportunities to get into illegal things again. I been approached about a contract to down somebody. But I backs off them all in kind of a smooth way, so that if I felt it absolutely necessary for me to be into those things again, then I can go all out and do it. But I'm not ready for that. I'm not even sure how I feel about it—the constant pace. I guess by doing so many things, the zip gone out of it. I'm thirty-four now, and I know that got a lot to do with it. To be honest, maybe I'm just tired.

I still like the notoriety, the excitement, the danger—that's cool. But I guess I don't feel for myself that I could really function like I want to. If I felt I could, then it would be an altogether different thing. I would automatically just fit right back in, like a hand in a glove. But because of my condition and the different way things have to be worked in the streets now, it would be a problem for me. Take drugs, for instance. They take a closer watch on them now. You have to put more time and energy into it than you used to seven or eight years ago. And I'm not ready for that at all. Then the way the busts have been jumping off, there's evidently been a lot of so-called thorough dudes that haven't been abiding by the code. They've been giving people up, snitching. I can't put myself in a position where I might be doing something and then have somebody tell on me. I couldn't handle that; I would go completely berserk.

I been really close to the edge where I actually been involved in a couple of things and then backed off. But that was only because I was real pressed, financially or mentally. Sometimes I get tremendously bored. Sometimes I stay in the house two, three weeks, doing nothing but looking out the window. But that sort of mental pressure don't happen very often. The financial thing do happen quite often, though. The onliest thing about that is I hate asking people for things, especially money, 'cause money's tight. Inflation. The little that people got, they don't want to give it up.

A lot of changes have happened to me personally, but no more than what's happened to the neighborhood generally. Once the whole neighborhood—men, women, and children —stuck together at all times, regardless of what the crisis was or what the obstacle was in front of them. As long as they was facing the outside world, that is. Of course, sometimes families would get into a feud and start fighting with each other; but if something happened in the neighborhood where the police would be involved, all the fighting between the families would immediately stop, and everybody would come to where the police was to try to see what was happening. Upon getting that all straightened out, they'd go back to the battle. When it came to the outside, and especially the police, it was dealt with with an iron glove. There was real unity in the neighborhood.

But now both the family feuds and the unity look like they're gone. The younger dudes don't stick together like they used to. I have had walking partners, and the same two or three dudes will be my walking partners for years and years. Now dudes change day to day. We didn't do that. It kind of got me when I first came home, because I wasn't aware of the change. My brother Nut kept saying, "Things ain't like they used to be, Johnny. Things ain't like the old days." I kept saying, "How come so and so ain't doing this or that?" Eventually, by being around, I saw that what he was saying was really the truth.

At one time, everybody in the project knew my grandfather, my grandmother. All of us in the family come out of their house regardless of where we are now. But there is very few of the old families left. They either moved away or died off. The young ones got married and moved to different areas. Things changed, and the neighborhood changed. One time, unless you were an outsider, nobody bother you. Now they would break into my house if they can get away with it as quick as they break into somebody else's house in another area! Some dudes even tried to stick my grandfather up! Say, a few years ago, nobody would have even thought about it. You got to be crazy. This was out of the question in my younger days.

There is a lot of petty things that go around that I personally don't like or approve of, like breaking into somebody's house or stealing somebody's welfare check—different little things that make the neighborhood have no unity. This makes things really bad for me. I might go to the enemy for help, not knowing that this person *is* the enemy. I'm still going on the old code. I'm changing kind of fast, but I still don't go for that dog-eat-dog thing in the neighborhood, and I often try to change things around.

People don't stick together like they used to when it comes to dealing with the police either. If somebody get busted, then they might try to come up with the bond, but they be a little slow about it. Certain dudes still try to help one another, but it's not as widespread or tight as it used to be.

I honestly believe, though, that if I was on the street twenty-four hours a day like I used to be, I would have things back the way they should be. I wouldn't necessarily have to go back into hard drugs; but if I could get a substantial reefer business going, then I could pull them all together, 'cause they know I always kept plenty of money in everybody's pocket. I think I could make it go with a lot of changes in the neighborhood. I surprised myself with the power I still had in the neighborhood even after I was injured. I tested it a couple of times to see just what would happen. I would be down on Stanton Road and send word to different people, say, "Tell Slippergates to send me a hundred dollars and two ounces of herb." But I'll never have the power I used to have. Then I ruled with an iron glove, but now I have to rule with the golden words.

I'm pretty good at that, which is probably why a lot of younger dudes have been coming to rap with me when I'm home. There'll be a sixteen-year-old comparing himself with another sixteen-year-old that's a pretty good thief and is always flashy. This dude that comes to me, maybe he plays in little basketball games, so I say, "Man, think of the advantage you got over him. You might play basketball, and all he might do is be slick. You continue to go to school and play basketball. One day you'll be making two or three hundred thousand dollars a year, and he'll be in jail, reading about you and wishing that he was in your shoes. Man, you got to crawl before you walk." I'm trying to tell them to stay straight.

Maybe my way wasn't the best way. Some of the things I look back on really wasn't too hip. Ever since I've been talking, I've been telling about myself—my life and how exciting it was, that I'm not sorry for nothing that happened or something I did. But in reality, and to be actually truthful as well as fearless, I believe I am kind of sorry about some of the things that happened. I know if I think about it too often, I get emotionally upset. I often look at my brother and just get the urge to grab him and hold him close to me. I think about Duke and JoJo and Clayton and Cub—these guys were more than brothers to me, these were dudes that I actually loved in a way. They was like a part of me. When Nut shot an overdose and I thought he was dead, then a part of me was dead. When Clayton shot the overdose and died, then a part of me died. When the police killed Duke, then they killed a part of me too. All these guys was just part of me, and I cared a lot about them. You never forget.

Maybe I'm hoping for something different for my kids and my younger brothers and sisters. When I was their age, there wasn't a thing where you go to school and then at the summer vacation you report to the counselor if you want a summer job. Now, whether you work out on it, that's up to you. These kids want to be flashy, they want to have their little things for the summer, go on trips to beaches. By their having money and it's not coming from their parents, they able to do this. They don't have to press their parents.

They've got a little more of a chance. They don't have to steal.

When I was young, I used to work on a horse and wagon in the summertime. It was the horse and wagon with the fruit on it getting pulled. Work all day and steal as much as you can, 'cause the man you work for ain't paying you more than a dollar and a half. I remember one day I worked from nine in the morning till nine at night, and the chump gave me fifty cents. I was real proud of that fifty cents, but my grandmother say, "That's all he gave you was fifty cents?" As kids, we also used to do this thing we called junking. There was this dude named Fat Harry who was the numbers backer in the neighborhood, an all-around hustler. Mr. Harry. He had a truck, and we used to go to what we called good neighborhoods, rich neighborhoods, and go rambling through their trash to get different things to sell to the junk shops and to keep for ourselves. I used to save glass. Find bottles, break them up, and get fifteen cents a bushel for broke-up white glass, ten cents a bushel for broke-up brown glass.

Now they have all kinds of programs for the little people. For instance, I couldn't tell you how many times I went to school without eating in the morning. Like they say, "Breakfast's the most important meal! Always eat a hearty breakfast!" I'd open up the icebox, and there won't be nothing there but the water jug and the grease can. But now kids can go to school and get a free breakfast, and they don't have to go all the way back home at lunchtime either. They just stay and get some lunch. When I was going to school, you paid two or three cents a day, and they gave you a carton of milk and a cookie! But that ain't no grub! That's why things are much better now. Whoever the group of people that thought of this, I would like to shake each one of them's hands, because these meals do prevent a lot of things. Otherwise, all these kids would be in the street. Hot as hell out there, nothing to do, nothing to look forward to, nothing.

I very much want my kids to be square, and I'm pretty sure they will be. For one thing, Ann worked all of her life. Ever since she stopped school, there's never been a period of her life where she didn't work. My kids know that if they need things, their mother provides it for them. Their mother works in order to get it for them. Their father, he's a hustler. He stays away a lot. He gets what they want, and it might be more than what they wants at times, but it's not a regular thing. Mom is constantly working, and it might not be all of what they want, but they're getting there, because it's steady. And Mom don't drop out of sight for two or three years every once in a while like Pop do.

They know I was on drugs. They know I sold drugs. In fact, they know some things about me that I didn't think they knew. I think that makes them very interested in school. They try a little harder, and they understand things that grown people don't think they understand. So I've really got my fingers crossed for them.

16

Ambitions

Looking back on my life, there were several things I wanted to do that I never did. I wanted to own some big dump trucks, because I knew there was money in that. If you can get some good drivers to drive your trucks from eight to twelve hours a day, you can make a nice piece of money. I wanted a restaurant. At one time, I started to buy into a go-go joint. I was in a position to do it, but what stopped me was the clientele was changing. The people were starting to turn into steamheads, so the drug business got slower. They were drinking alcohol, not using drugs or smoking herb.

I used to drink at one time; and when I drank, I wanted to fight. I wanted to cuss people out. I wanted to beat people up. I wanted to do something crazy, break things up. I'd be happy too, but you couldn't say too much to me—I'd get mad. But smoking herb and drinking wine, I want to be cool. I want to dig some music. I want to crack a few jokes, laugh, and see funny things. Trip out. The same thing with heroin. You want to be as cool as you can be, but you don't want nothing to blow your high. Everything I've done, I've done to extremes, from drinking to drugs. But I was glad to stop both the drinking and the drugs.

Everybody knows that there's the possibility that through hustling—with drugs or otherwise—you are going to jail. In fact, anybody with anything on the ball knows that regardless of what you're doing, eventually you're going. I've done a lot of things, and I've made quite a bit of money illegally. Way far more than I ever made legally. But still, if you look at it, it's all been on a real low level. It's still not up there with the big boys, where I always wanted to be—sign my name and get a million. I recognize this, and I think most people recognize this, no matter how good their hustling thing is. They can hustle day and night, live comfortable, and do the things they want to, but they are still doing it on what other people would see as a small scale.

Out of all the things I've done, which have been quite a few, I've never been in the big time. I'm not saying that I don't want to be. But people like me know they're not big time, so maybe they open a laundromat on the corner or a little carry-out. It's their heaven, plus it's their means of saying, "That's how come I can drive this Cadillac—I own a restaurant." It's a little greasy-spoon joint, not as big as this room, crowded with people all the time, and on the side the man got two or three people standing out there dealing dope. That's where the money is coming from, not the restaurant. But he can say, "I gross x amount of money from my restaurant." As for myself, I always wanted to own a restaurant or a shirt shop so I could say, "That's why I am able to drive this Cadillac."

There's so many things you can't do without that kind of show. Say I was fortunate enough to be in a position to take a large amount of money from somewhere, one of my goals is a home I always wanted to buy. Now if *I* had the money, I just couldn't buy a home. There would be too many questions asked: "Where did you get the money? Where did it come from?" Even a car, I might get questioned on. "You don't work nowhere." Or, "You work where they only pay sixty or a hundred dollars a week." But say you got a little shop. They don't know what's happening. The shop might not make a dime; you might not sell even a shirt collar. But you can put it down in your books that you did; and even though you have to pay taxes on some of that illegal money, that put you in a position to buy a home or a car or

whatever you want. That's why it's important to have something like that, especially if you continue to hustle. You can
have large amounts of money, and they'll say, "Oh, that
nigger doing good. That nigger got two or three shirt
shops." They think it's the business that's turning over the
money. Especially when you still doing something illegal,
your place is always crowded. Chumps may be buying nothing but a soda, but still it's crowded, so can't nobody be
saying, "He didn't make that money."

If I had been in a position, I probably would have gone
into two or three things rather than just one. There would
always be more money, more things to do. Say I was successful through the dump trucks—I've got all this money to
hustle. Maybe I'd have my eye on a little barber shop. As
well as a great talker, I'm a great listener, and I could listen
to people there for hundreds of hours and get hundreds of
ideas. I could get some people working for me, and at the
same time, I would be helping people in the neighborhood.

I really think there's a lot of similarity between the people who live out in the middle-class neighborhoods and the
people I know. What do most people want out of life? Fun,
to be successful, whether it is legal or illegal. Everybody
wants to live comfortably and be all right. Lots of dudes are
flashy. Why, I know a lot of square dudes who are flashy.
You would think they are hustling when they really aren't.
They are working. Everybody wants to have their own
joint, own their own home, and have two cars. It's just that
we are going about it in a different way. I think keeping up
with the Joneses is important everywhere.

If Clayton hadn't died and I had followed him up the
ladder, really being up there for me would have been own-
ing maybe five to seven little businesses, like shirt shops,
laundromats, cleaners. I wanted to have a big house somewhere away from where I did my everyday thing so I could
just go lay easy and close my eyes without having to keep
one open. At one point, I was selling ten to twelve thousand
dollars' worth of narcotics every three or four days, and I

had people working for me. As you go along, you're constantly changing and getting bigger. The higher you get on
the ladder, the more opportunity you get to stay out of the
limelight and get the money at the same time.

I always thought of myself as being a hustler. I come
from a hustling family. My grandfather told me, when you
hustle, what you're really hustling for is so that you won't
have to hustle later. If you can hustle and make it, get three
or four stores, don't be overcome by your success, and be
satisfied to stay at that level. That would be really cool. I
ain't never want to be real, real rich, but I want to live
instead of just survive.

That's where your goals come in. Your goal while you're
doing all your hustling is to get things together enough to
do something legal. You might go all the way to the top
doing illegal things, like being a really big drug dealer. Or
you might go up maybe midway on that ladder and then
jump off into legal things. Which way you go depends on
the structure you plan and what you're satisfied with. I
could strive to be really high on the illegal structure, but at
the same time I would be satisfied in the middle.

It seems to me that everyone should be able to do what
he or she wants to do as long as they don't hurt anybody in
the process. But see, sometimes in my lifestyle, the way I live,
people got to be hurt, so you accept that as part of your
business, part of your life.

I want to be free inside. Like, many times I went to my
mama and said, "Mama, I need some shoes." And Mama said,
"I know, but I'm not able to get you shoes because this is rent
week. There is nothing." "Hi, Mom, I'm going to graduate
from elementary school. Sure be hip to have a suit." "There's
nothing I'd like better than buying you a suit. But we've got
to pay the grocery bill." So I stole, and I got my shoes and
my suit. I looked as good as everybody else. Probably 60
percent of the people in my class stole their suits.

If my children came to me, "Hey, Jack, I need a hundred

dollars to buy this outfit I seen," I want to be able to go in my pocket and give it to them without having to say, "I need this money to go toward the rent. I've got to pay this bill or that bill." Then my son comes to me and says, "I want a bicycle," I can say, "Go get a bicycle"; or my daughter saying, "Prom coming up and I need a gown." Some people struggle to get this through legal means or kind of skip the rent and put the kids first. I know my mother did. I know my wife does. She will neglect herself in order that the kids be satisfied. I guess I do that a lot myself. I might have two or three dollars, and if one of them ask me for it, I would give it to them.

I want them to be able, when they leave the prom or the football game, to have a place where they can come and be comfortable and bring their friends and sit around listening to some music. Not lying around the walls, or scared to sit in chairs because they are going to fall apart or on the couch that keeps going to the floor. These are the things that I am talking about.

As important as all these things were, though, I never really went into the things I wanted to get into. I just kept spending everything as soon as I got it, especially when I took the money and it was somebody else's. I didn't like flashy clothes, but I liked expensive clothes. I'd go downtown to buy shoes in both the black and white sections of town. The only problem with that was when a robbery jump off, the police would be going around town to stake out some of the stores and see who's coming in buying a lot of clothes.

There was one store, D. J. Kaufman, near the Capitol, that I used to go to. Whites went there too, but it was mainly a black store. It was white-owned, though. Hip white people know what black people like and what the hustler types like, what they can afford. The stores cater to that and make money off it. A lot of my money also went into cars. There was a white businessman in Virginia who catered to the hustling type, and he knew what type cars to get. He was strictly a cash man. If he had a car for five grand and you had four grand in cash, then you could give it to him and go with the car.

I spent most of my money on clothes, cars, and motels, where we'd be partying. I wouldn't go out and spend a whole lot of money on liquor, but I did a little gambling. I lost some pretty big pots, and the debt money always circulates and circulates. I think in the areas I knew, the gambling money is the main money that circulates from this apartment to that apartment and stays in the neighborhood. When it all boiled down, most of the other money left the neighborhood. If it stayed in the neighborhood, then the neighborhood wouldn't have been the neighborhood that it was. If it had the kind of money in it that was made in it every day, the neighborhood would have been much different.

I never thought about that back when I had money. There's so many things you don't think about when you rooking and running. What the hell do you care? Long as you have some money, you can go downtown or wherever you want. We didn't care about the neighborhood other than the fact that you want to make sure your neighborhood cool, that you're all right with everybody. As far as trying to start some businesses, there's a few people that did it and made it, and some that did it and didn't make it. But over all, it just went out of the neighborhood, and that's why the neighborhood always stayed like it was.

What made me aware of this was some of the better business people, the legit people, started pulling people's coats to it. "Keep your money in the neighborhood, that way you can bring the neighborhood up." By being so few legit people, it took a long time for the message to get around, and everybody still don't say, "Yeah, solid, that's what we gonna do."

Any way you looked at it, there wasn't a whole lot of successful businesses near where I lived. If I wanted to buy some really hip clothes, there wasn't any place around there where I could go. And there wasn't a lot of people who stayed straight who made it either. I know one or two dudes that did things with me when I was a teenager that ended up being cops. But I can't think of a soul who did anything like become a doctor or lawyer. There was one dude that come up pretty rough with me who become a dentist. But other than him, there was nobody I ever knew who did anything professional. My grandmother and my mother told me that doctors or dentists were a good thing to be, but I didn't know a soul who was one, so I really couldn't see being one either.

My mother has some property in the country in South Carolina somewhere, and she signed the property over to me. I think you have to pay taxes on it every year, but I ain't paid nothing. At an early age I thought if I ever got me fifteen grand, I was going down there and look at the property. I thought that by things being cheaper in that part of the country, I'd build me a house or remodel the one down there, and just have a spot I can come to, grow stuff, maybe let somebody live there.

Well, I had the money. Maybe five times over I had the money, but I never got around to doing it. Some people make their goals; some people don't. Some people are able and still don't. I was able, and I didn't. Like, when you have the money, then you think of so many things to do, more immediate things, right at hand. Then, when you broke again, you say, "Damn. I should have took two or three grand and put it into that." Then, wham! Next week you got two or three grand again, and it's gone. Some people are born to reach their goals. I guess I just wasn't.

*   *

About a month before I got out of Glenn Dale, I was tired of sitting around the hospital, so I put on my hat and coat, and decided to go outside. I'm sitting outside, enjoying the fresh but brisk air and the sunshine. This time of year there's very little leaves on the trees, and I saw a bird's nest—just an ordinary bird's nest in a tree between two branches—and it was fascinating to me. I wanted to hold it, or if not hold it, to be able to look inside it.

Usually I don't like to feel sorry for myself. I don't want nobody else feeling sorry for me either. But maybe this was a day when I did feel sorry for myself, and I said, "Look at all the beautiful things. Look at that bird's nest." And seeing the bird's nest, my very next thought was: Life, there's probably life in that bird's nest. There's probably an egg or two in there, and that's still unborn life. Eventually the egg would be hatched, and there would be a bird, and it would be flying, and it would be free. Really free. I got a kick out of that. Even a couple of days afterwards I went out just to look at that nest. I couldn't talk to anybody else about that because, of course, I always got to maintain my image of being "Big Al, the tough guy." People just don't understand when I see things like this and how I feel about them—things that so many people take for granted.

There's a dog in our Southeast neighborhood—she don't have an owner, and the neighborhood is the ghetto. The people aren't what you'd call doing well, but each one of these people in the neighborhood always contribute something to this dog, some bones or scraps or leftovers. Well, the dog was pregnant and had her puppies in the hallway of one of the apartments. Those hallways are very cold, so some of the people would bring the puppies inside. They was only a few days old when I encountered them. My youngest brother, Mo, had brought them in one night in a box 'cause it was pretty cold. Of course, the dog followed. I said, "Where'd you get the dog?" He said, "She not my dog. She's everybody's dog, and different people take care of her."

The dog come in, and she laid down on the rug. My brother took the six puppies out of the box and put them close to their mother, 'cause they was still nursing from her. I felt good for two reasons. I felt good that my little brother had in him this compassion for this animal, and I felt good 'cause I, too, felt what he felt. Even a dude like myself—I think about these things too. Not often and not a whole lot in the past, but now. Now and in the future. I often tell myself, "Boy, you must be getting soft." But it's not really that. It shows that as much as I have done wrong and probably continue to do wrong one way or another, I still will have some good in me—even if it's only not so much for the human race but for the animal race. I don't have a whole lot of compassion for the human race because people can be cruel.

I never thought I'd see the day when a gangster be talking about birds and puppies. But that's life. Right? No, not right. *Solid.*

17

Surviving

In February of '75, when I came home from Glenn Dale, I moved in with Ann and the kids in a place up in Northwest. For a while, things was going well for us. We didn't have a whole lot of financial difficulties because she was working at Marvel Cleaners full time.

I didn't really do anything. I stayed home. She left for work in the morning. The kids left for school in the morning, came home lunchtime supposedly for lunch but mainly to check on me, to make sure I was all right. That was my first few months home. They found out that I could function pretty good. But things got turning about when I developed a guilt complex in my mind that I held in for quite a few months before I said anything about it. I had a guilt complex about how the children felt about me and me being confined to a wheelchair—what they felt when they was around me, what they felt when their friends was around. So one night the three kids and myself, we started talking about it. Basically what I found out is that they were glad I was home, glad that their mother and I were together, and still very much proud of their father. They ignore the wheelchair, they ignore me being a paraplegic. If something was said or done to them, they come to me with it. So this took care of that little complex.

But then I developed another complex involving Ann and me. I didn't feel that I provided substantial enough. It seemed like Ann was doing everything. She was taking care of the kids, me; she was working; and she was getting a little jive supplemental payment from the government. I was getting a little payment from Social Security, but I really didn't feel that I was doing enough.

I wanted a job. One day my counselor from Glenn Dale called me, and she told me, "I got a great opportunity here for you. They hiring at the Labor Department, and they want handicapped people. They willing to train you. It's close to what you wanted 'cause it's kind of in the counseling line." I really went for that. She set up the appointment, and I filled out the government form. I thought it best when I took the form down there to also take a copy of my record, because on the form I stated I did have a record.

So I went in to see the dude at Labor, and he looked over my application. He says, "Your record really don't mean much. It can't be held against you." I say, "That's cool, but I thought I'd bring a copy just so you all would be aware of it." He say, "Well, having a record still won't interfere with your job." That's what he said up until the point he seen the record. After he got to looking over the copies, he say, "All this the record?" I say, "Yeah, that's it." He say, "Okay. We'll call you." And that was all. He never did.

Then I was interested in microfilming for a while, but the program went bankrupt. My parole officer and myself got together, and he checked out a couple of places like Goodwill that I really wasn't interested in but to satisfy my own curiosity and to try to make an extra buck or two, I would have tried them out. There just wasn't nothing. Finally he came up with one good thing, and that was being a law clerk. You go to school for eighteen months and then just do research. I supposed to get in touch with the lady to find out more about it but couldn't never catch her in. She was on vacation, then she got sick, and so I got tired. At Glenn Dale they gave me some tests and came to the conclusion I would be better filing stuff and things of that nature. I didn't dig that at all!

Since then, there really haven't been a whole lot of offers. A friend of mine had a little store, and he offered to give me a job; but that wouldn't have been my bag because there was a lot going on in that store, and I know eventually I'd have been involved. So I backed off of that. I'm glad I did, since about six months later the store was closed, and he was down at Lorton. There's another dude I know got a record shop down Stanton Road, and I was telling him that I could use a job. He said, "Well, like you could come and there's a few things that I could find for you to do." But I saw it as being mainly a guy trying to be nice to a crippled dude. I told him it was cool, but I would rather not.

The result was that after being home for almost a year, I felt as though I was completely dependent upon Ann. I didn't do much of anything. I'd sleep, read a book, write a letter, talk on the phone, watch T.V., never get out of bed till five, six, seven o'clock in the evening. I felt that the money I was contributing to the household really wasn't nothing. I had thought several times to get back into some drugs. I knew there was still big money in heroin, but then I had to take into consideration where the family lived and the hazards of it, because I know of many homes that I walked in to rob somebody, and the kids and wife was there. I didn't want that happening to me, so I backed off that idea.

Finally Ann and I talked. It had got to the point where she was working two jobs. It was taking too much out of her. She was still working at the cleaners, and then she go to Georgetown University to clean offices at night. It done something to her social life too. It never was a thing that because I stayed home Friday or Saturday night, then she had to stay home. We both went our own ways. I hung out and she hung out. But she got so tired she couldn't do much of that. She was just down, and I felt as though I was causing most of this by being home. So I decided to leave. She didn't want me to, but I told her that I thought it would be best. So I split and found a place in Southeast in the same general area where I came up. I feel as though I made the best decision, because health-wise she doing much better. She only working one job now. She began to get hold of herself a little better as far as going out and letting her hair down. Right now we've got a beautiful understanding, because she comes over here when she wants, any time day or night, and I go up there any time.

But there ain't no doubt I was very upset for a long time about us splitting up. I don't think that Ann and me would ever get a divorce. I think that we might even get back together again, but not now, not with things as they are, because I'm still not capable of providing.

I've dealt with this wheelchair thing on a daily basis as it come. I roll with the punches. But I hate it. I hate it. I hate being dependent upon anybody for anything, because at a very young age, I depended only on myself. I had people depending on *me*. It was hard to accept the switch. I manage to conceal a lot of things within myself because I feel as though it's something that just got to be done.

It's also tough to keep my reputation up. I can't let nobody take advantage of me, and people try to do it more now that I'm in the chair. Last July I'm setting outside with a few friends—drinking some beer, some cold wine, smoking a couple of joints. Wank came from around the corner, blind mad. He run to me, he can hardly talk. Immediately I know somebody done something to him. When he finally do get it out, what had happened was this. A dude named Gray, who's eighteen or nineteen, is around this store, and he got all the little boys, ten, twelve years old, lined up. He taking their quarters or whatever money they had. Smacking them up side the head, kicking them in the butt, doing this and that to them. He come to Wank. Wank got a dollar. Gray tried to take the dollar, and Wank said, "You ain't taking nothing from me. You or nobody else. You not my father." Wank actually tussled with Gray, but he's no match for the dude.

Wank tell Gray, "I'm going to get my father." And Gray says to him, "Go get your crippled motherfucker father or anybody else in your family that you want to get. I got something for them." And he pulled up his shirt and showed Wank a gun. When Wank first tell me about it, he just told me that Gray said, "Go get your crippled motherfucker father," and when Wank said that, immediately everything in me went back. I thought the way I was thinking six or seven years ago—what I would have done: to act immediately, that's how I thought that day.

I was angry to the point that I couldn't stop. I felt as though if I was on my feet, Gray wouldn't open his mouth to my son! I was going to show him that I was more of a man than him. When Wank said Gray showed him a gun, that just blow up the old Johnny Allen—along with the fact that I couldn't actually trot around the store but had to say to one of my friends, "Hey, man, push me around the store." Still, I was determined that I was going to get Gray. It seems to me if a man can't look after himself, his family, his own, then he is less than a man. And I always felt that if you don't have nothing to die for, then you don't have nothing to live for either. It's as simple as that. And I was ready to die.

I got my black briefcase out of the closet, which had my shotgun in it. I had all my material right there, so I just put it on my lap, and a friend of mine pushed me around to the store. Gray was still there, and I called him, said, "Man, why you keep pressing my son? What seem to be the problem?" He got real loud, and he got to calling me names. Me being in the state I was, I returned some of the remarks. But I still got on my mind what Wank said about he had pulled his shirt up. He had on a button-up shirt that hanged out. He had fastened a button at the top and unloosened a button at the bottom. He put his hand underneath his shirt and once he did that, then it became a thing where I knew it was down to the line, because I didn't know if he was gonna up with the pistol or what.

So I up with the shotgun first. He sees the shotgun, completely panics. The state that he was in when he see the shotgun made me feel so good, I wouldn't have missed it for the world. He forgot about his gun. He forgot about everything. He remembered only one thing, and that was the old Johnny Allen. His face was a mass of confusion. He was scared to death. And I was satisfied.

If he had pulled the gun out, I would have blown him away. I hesitated about two minutes. He didn't know what to do. Run, hide, where to go. First he ran into the apartment wall, and before he could get his bearings together, he broke around the corner, and that right there gave me all the satisfaction in the world. This chump was taking advantage of my family simply because I was down. In the event that I wanted to kill him or to hurt him bad, I had all the opportunity in the world. I had him cold, but I got complete contentment from his reaction.

When I got back to my place, I was really pleased with myself. I figured it was all over. I figured he was man enough to do what he done, so he should be man enough to be able to take it. I told my daughters and my sister what had happened. I wasn't angry any more. I was sitting at the table when there was a knock on the door and somebody outside said, "Open up. Police." My little four-year-old nephew opened the door and closed it back. "It *is* the police." Then Wank went and opened the door, and the police pushed it on in. They were standing there, and I was sitting right in front of them. All of them had their guns cocked on me, saying, "Don't move, don't move." So I didn't move.

The police that was doing the talking, I believe, was a little bit scared, because when he went to Stanton Road to talk to Gray before he came to my place, Gray said I had robbed him with a sawed-off shotgun. The general attitude of the police upset my oldest daughter and my sister, so they jumped in front of me, thinking that the police is going to shoot me. That's when everything began to happen. More police came and started to search. We said they didn't have any right to search. We got to arguing about a warrant: where was the warrant? Some little smart police lady picked up a bag of reefer off of the table and said, "This I want right here." I said something to her, and my oldest daughter, Sugar, her and the police lady almost got to fighting. By that time someone had called down the hill to my mother's house, so here come my mother and three of my sisters. The police sergeant said they can't come in. "This is my brother's house. Why can't we come in?" So they come in. There's mass confusion. The police don't know what to do. They trying to get me out. I'm trying to calm my daughter down because she really goes to pieces.

Before they took me out, the police looked in the closet. The first time they didn't find the shotgun, but then the sergeant came back, searched the closet again, and found it hanging by the strap. I don't believe they would have looked as hard as they did if there hadn't been two shotgun shells on the table. A man say he got robbed with a shotgun. They see two shotgun shells. They say, "Well, there got to be a shotgun."

Meantime, the police, not knowing how to handle a wheelchair, are being pretty rough. So Wank say, "Wait a minute. Wait a minute. I'll take him out." Wank take me down the stairs, and all the rollers come out to the scout car. They ended up putting me in the back of the wagon 'cause they couldn't fit my chair into the car. That was a rough ride. They were rushing downtown, and me in a wheelchair. I'm going sideways, trying to hold on to the sides, banging against the sides, tilting back.

The police took me to Robbery Squad and questioned me down there. They said, "You know you don't have to talk." I said, "Ain't no doubt about that, but I ain't rob nobody, so I don't mind talking." So he said, "Well, what happened?" I told him what happened. Then they go back and confront Gray where they had him in another room, and he changed his story. First he told them I took two hundred dollars from him, then he told them it was a hundred and ten, then twenty. Finally he said he must have dropped it when he was running. So they don't charge me with robbery, but they take me down to Central Cell Block in Robbery Squad. I stay overnight in the hallway and get ready for court in the morning.

The next day I went to court, and they let me out on personal bond. A few days later at a hearing, they found probable cause on possession of the shotgun charge. We had a suppression hearing a little later, but that motion was denied too, and I ended up pleading guilty at a stipulation hearing. When the judge heard the whole story, I got probation. I think he realized it's hard to be without a gun where I live because he tried to get me to move. But I can't do that.

One problem with having this come up when it did was that I was supposed to start working in July. There was a place that wanted to train paraplegics to do computer work. The dude that ran the business was a quadraplegic. He had tried to get a job himself for a long time and couldn't get one, so he ended up starting this business. I went for an interview twice, and they was supposed to call me to let me know, but they never did. It was like so many things that didn't work out.

I'd probably have a greater chance of success if I got involved in something illegal again, but I'm still a little reluctant about that. A lot of the things that people come to me with, I mainly listen. Sometimes I recommend somebody else. Age got a lot to do with it. My family got a lot to do with it too. I be reluctant because of my kids and their age and stage now. I feel that they maybe need me more now, and I want to be around if they do.

There was an incident that made this clear to me. One night in January of '76, one of my daughters tried to kill herself with sleeping pills. She was sixteen then. We had always been real close and talked a lot. At this time I could tell she was all upset, but she was kind of holding back on me. This particular day, she had been in a bad mood and was keeping to herself. About eight o'clock, we were all sitting around the living room when she suddenly appeared, stumbled, and fell. I thought she had just tripped until we rolled her over and looked.

Immediately we lifted her into a chair. "What's wrong? What's wrong?" I kept asking her. She kept saying, "I want to die, I want to die, I want to die." Hearing her say that, I panicked. I felt as though most of the struggle that I had put out to live, the things I lived through, was for them, my children, and here's one of them telling me she wants to die!

This really upsets me. So I go in the bedroom to look for some medicines, and I see that empty sleeping pill bottle. Now *that* really upsets me, so I tell them to get her up, keep trying to make her walk. I'm making her drink milk. At one point, I got real, real angry and said something to the effect that "If you don't try to walk and drink this milk, I'm gonna kill you." I was so angry and hurt. I couldn't figure exactly what would make her even think of taking those pills, since I always felt I had a good relationship with my kids, and I know that their mother has. So it had to be something other than that, but then wasn't the time to question her. Fortunately the ambulance came really quick, and finally she got it together.

Now she's a different young lady, and I'm glad because that incident was a hurting thing. I just couldn't get over her saying, "I want to die, I want to die." It remind me so much of the night I got shot and how easily Duke gave up on life, saying something to the effect that "Man, I'm dead." All the while, I'm laying on that concrete for two hours, saying to myself, "I'm not going to die." I felt that I related the two experiences. When he said that, he died, and then she saying it! I couldn't have took it, nothing happening to one of my kids.

That was a very bad experience for me. I feel as though it's something I couldn't have handled. If she had died, I probably wouldn't have cared no more about anything. I often think about that. I wonder and I pray that nothing happens to those kids, any of them. Most of the things that I do now and why I'm so cautious about the things I do, it's because of them. My kids mean everything to me. Maybe now that's what I'm really living for.

EPILOGUE

On March 15, 1977, John Allen, along with three co-defend-
ants, was charged with armed robbery in connection with
the holdup of a cab driver in Washington, D.C. A prelimi-
nary hearing was held, and John's case was bound over for
grand jury action. During the intervening three months,
John was a resident in the prison ward of D. C. General
Hospital. The charges against him have since been dropped,
and he is now living at home in Southeast.

ABOUT THE EDITORS

Philip B. Heymann is a graduate of Yale University and the Harvard Law School. As an attorney, he has worked in the office of the Solicitor General and as a public defender in Washington, D.C. He has also held a variety of positions in the Department of State, and was an associate special prosecutor and consultant to the Watergate Special Prosecution Force. Since 1969, he has been a professor of law at the Harvard Law School. He is the co-author of *The Murder Trial of Wilbur Jackson: A Homicide in the Family.*

Dianne Hall Kelly is a graduate of Cornell University and the Harvard Law School. She is currently an Assistant United States Attorney in Washington, D.C.

Hylan Lewis is presently a professor of sociology at Brooklyn College and the Graduate Center of the City University of New York. He was also vice-president of the Metropolitan Applied Research Center, and is the author of *Blackways of Kent.*